SHORTLISTED

Shortlisted

Women in the Shadows of the Supreme Court

Renee Knake Jefferson and Hannah Brenner Johnson

NEW YORK UNIVERSITY PRESS

New York

NEW YORK UNIVERSITY PRESS
New York
www.nyupress.org

References to Internet websites (URLs) were accurate at the time of writing. Neither the authors nor New York University Press is responsible for URLs that may have expired or changed since the manuscript was prepared.

Library of Congress Cataloging-in-Publication Data
Names: Jefferson, Renee Knake, author. | Johnson, Hannah Brenner, author.
Title: Shortlisted : women in the shadows of the Supreme Court / Renee Knake Jefferson, Hannah Brenner Johnson.
Description: New York : New York University Press, 2020. | Includes bibliographical references and index.
Identifiers: LCCN 2019039538 | ISBN 9781479895915 (cloth) | ISBN 9781479816095 (ebook) | ISBN 9781479816019 (ebook)
Subjects: LCSH: Women judges—United States—Selection and appointment. | Women judges—United States—Biography. | Judges—United States—Biography. | United States. Supreme Court—Biography.
Classification: LCC KF8744 .J44 2020 | DDC 347.73/263409252—dc23
LC record available at https://lccn.loc.gov/2019039538

New York University Press books are printed on acid-free paper, and their binding materials are chosen for strength and durability. We strive to use environmentally responsible suppliers and materials to the greatest extent possible in publishing our books.

Manufactured in the United States of America

10 9 8 7 6 5 4 3 2 1

Also available as an ebook

To kindred spirits.

CONTENTS

LIST OF TABLES AND FIGURES

This book finds its origins in the nominations of Sonia Sotomayor (2009) and Elena Kagan (2010) to serve on the United States Supreme Court. Both were exceptionally well-qualified candidates, with educational pedigrees and legal experience rivaling if not exceeding any male justice ever to serve. Rather than heralding these qualifications, however, the media focused on other attributes after President Barack Obama dared to nominate not only one but two single females. Examples of articles appearing at the time include "Then Comes the Marriage Question,"[1] appearing in the *New York Times*, and "The Supreme Court Needs More Mothers,"[2] featured by the *Washington Post*. The blog *AbovetheLaw.com* ran a story, "Elena Kagan v. Sonia Sotomayor: Who Wore it Better?,"[3] critiquing the nominees' appearance in similar blue blazers during their respective confirmation hearings. *TheDailyBeast.com* demanded, "Put a Mom on the Court"[4] in response to their shared childless status and also cautioned that a "Fat Judge Need Not Apply."[5] Reading these and similar headlines, we struggled to recall any mention of body weight, clothing choice, or parental status when President George W. Bush nominated John Roberts and Samuel Alito just five years earlier. Both of us—unbeknownst to the other—clipped these articles from the newspaper much in the same way as Sandra Day O'Connor did in the early 1970s when the press speculated about the possibility of a woman nominee to the Court.

As relatively new colleagues, we exchanged these articles as well as blog posts and other online discussions. We typed lengthy emails to one another, reacting to what we read in the media and watched on the television. The gendered nature of the headlines and related photographs, even the particular location of an article on the newspaper page or the photo selected, led us to ask each other a number of questions. What are the similarities and differences in subject matter of news coverage for nominees? What sort of introduction do they receive in the early articles that appear after their nomination is announced? Does coverage differ between male and female nominees? We wondered whether the bias and stereotyping we saw in news stories reflected perceptions and practices in the workplace that keep women from attaining the highest ranks in numbers equal to their entry into the profession. Ultimately, we speculated that a more systematic analysis of these media depictions would help advance the conversation about persistent gender inequality in the legal profession and beyond.

The importance and complexity of these questions warranted more analysis than what anecdotal clipping of articles and exchanging of emails could possibly reveal. So, we embarked upon an empirical study of the media's depiction of Supreme Court nominees with an inter-disciplinary focus, situating our work at the under-explored intersection of gender, law, media studies, political science, and sociology. To conduct the study, we compiled, read, and coded thousands of articles from the *New York Times* and the *Washington Post* about every Supreme Court nominee from William Rehnquist and Lewis Powell, who were both nominated and confirmed in late 1971 and sworn in during the first weeks of 1972, through Sotomayor and Kagan. We selected the early 1970s as a starting point, mindful of the feminist movement's influence at the time. Our empirical research revealed that women are, in fact, portrayed in explicitly gendered and often unfavorable ways, specifically in the context of appearance, marital status, motherhood, and sexuality. The media frequently commented on the female nominees' attire, childlessness, dating life, and sexual preferences, among other topics completely unrelated to their competency for judicial office, in stark contrast to coverage of their male counterparts. We concluded that the gendered media coverage of nominees serves as a proxy for how women fare in the legal profession and all workplaces.[6]

Our study was the first to undertake such a comprehensive empirical evaluation of the gendered portrayal of Supreme Court nominees.

This is surprising because vacancies on the Court generate a significant amount of public scrutiny and attention. Less surprising, perhaps, were the study's results. After embarking on this project, we soon learned that others were engaging in similar conversations about the media's portrayal of nominees. We posted an abstract of our media study article on the Social Science Research Network and quickly received an email from Linda Greenhouse, a professor at Yale Law School and *New York Times* op-ed contributor and former Supreme Court reporter. She relayed that her students were also concerned about these very same issues.

One article in particular stood out as we read through thousands for the media study. That article contained a rather colorful description of the physical appearance of a female judge from California who appeared on President Richard Nixon's shortlist for the Supreme Court in 1971. We were stunned to be learning of her story for the first time in this way. Why hadn't we read about this accomplished female jurist in our high school history classes, or even our law school classes on feminist history? How many other women were shortlisted before Sandra Day O'Connor became the first to join the U.S. Supreme Court? Who was the first president to include a woman on the shortlist? How might the Court be different had women been selected before O'Connor? Might this have avoided the continued disparities for women, especially minority women, in positions of leadership and power in law and other professions?

To answer these questions, we first researched presidential archives. (You can read more about this process at the end of the book.) We uncovered not only the story of the female California judge, but also those of eight additional women formally shortlisted by presidents before Sandra Day O'Connor, going all the way back to the 1930s. We wanted to learn more about these women, so we visited libraries and museums across the nation to review collections of their personal papers. We looked to the research of historians and other scholars. We read autobiographies, biographies, news articles, and oral histories. We even attended the memorial service of one of the women. (Since many of the women are no longer living, we intentionally decided not to conduct personal interviews in order to maintain a consistent approach for all.) As we immersed ourselves in the lives of these women, we observed commonalities and themes that are relevant today for addressing unequal gender representation in positions of leadership and power. We also saw in them images of ourselves both personally and professionally.

This is how *Shortlisted: Women in the Shadows of the Supreme Court* began. Our commitment to this project persevered through several professional moves over the course of a decade that took us to opposite ends of the country. We hope the stories of these women inspire you as much as they have inspired us.

Introduction

shortlisted, *adj.* qualified for a position but not selected from
a list that creates the appearance of diversity but preserves
the status quo

As the *New York Times* reported in 1971, Mildred Lillie *fortunately* had
no children. The article marveled at how she maintained "a bathing
beauty figure" in her fifties.[1] Lillie was not, however, featured in the
news as a swimsuit model.

Instead, she was shortlisted. President Richard Nixon had included
her among six potential nominees on his list for the United States Supreme Court. At the time, Lillie had served as a judge on California
courts for more than twenty years. Her resume was as competitive if not
more so than others on Nixon's list. Lillie could have been the nation's
first female justice, but she was not chosen. Instead, Nixon claimed to
care about diversity but preserved an all-male Court.

This book exposes the potential harms of being shortlisted and offers inspiration for women to chart a path from shortlisted to selected
in any career. Stories of women shortlisted for the Supreme Court illuminate how this can be accomplished—their early successes in a world
hostile to women offer excellent guidance for navigating the inequalities
that endure in the #MeToo world. We share their stories and their collective strategies for moving from shortlisted to selected in the pages
that follow.

But first, back to the "bathing beauty," the Honorable Mildred Lillie.
The *Times* article provoked outrage on the opinion page even in that
era. As one reader observed:

To the Editor:

Your description of the "qualifications" of Judge Mildred Loree Lillie (biographical sketches of Supreme Court nominees Oct. 14) illustrates perfectly the absurd sexist prejudices to which all women are persistently subjected. Why did you choose to objectify this woman and diminish her accomplishments by including such a totally irrelevant and subjective item? You implied that Judge Lillie's body was just as significant as any single professional attribute she possesses. There was no discussion of the health—much less the physique—of any of the other possible nominees. Perhaps you could rectify this inequality by printing a discussion of the extent to which Senator Byrd has retained his schoolboy figure or the manner in which Herschel Friday fills his swimsuit.[2]

—Barbara B. Martin, "Sketch of Judge Lillie," *New York Times*, October 23, 1971

The image of Lillie in swimwear reflects the sexism of that era and resonates even today as consistent with society's ongoing obsession about the female body. The prevailing sentiment during Lillie's time placed men at work and women at home, with minority women often cooking and cleaning for others. Women were largely excluded from the professional class. As articulated by Justice Bradley, concurring in the Supreme Court's decision to deny Myra Bradwell admittance to the Illinois Bar in 1873: "[T]he civil law, as well as nature herself, has always recognized a wide difference in the respective spheres and destinies of man and woman. Man is, or should be, woman's protector and defender. The natural and proper timidity and delicacy which belongs to the female sex evidently unfits it for many of the occupations of civil life. The constitution of the family organization, which is founded in the divine ordinance, as well as in the nature of things, indicates the domestic sphere as that which properly belongs to the domain and functions of womanhood."[3] Even as the United States neared its bicentennial, a woman certainly had never occupied a position on the Supreme Court. In fact, women were not supposed to pursue the law at all.

The simple fact that President Nixon shortlisted Lillie for the Court pushed back against gender norms that dominated the era and still persist. His shortlisting of Lillie is an early example of the very idea this book explores—being sufficiently qualified but not ultimately selected from a list that creates the appearance of valuing diversity but preserves the status quo. Nixon faced immense political pressure to place a woman on the Court but personally believed women belonged only in the home—he did not think women should even be allowed to vote![4] Shortlisting a woman allowed Nixon to pacify those demanding equal representation on the Court while simultaneously maintaining it as a man's world. But Nixon was not the first president to shortlist a woman and would not be the last.

Before Sandra Day O'Connor secured her legacy as the first woman nominated and confirmed to the Court in 1981, a handful of presidents formally shortlisted at least nine others for that role. *Shortlisted* is a project of first impression. We are the first to identify and explore the stories of these women in light of their shared experience of being shortlisted. Until now, their individual and collective stories have largely gone untold.

* * *

In early 2020, three women sat on the United States Supreme Court. Justice O'Connor retired in 2006. Only four of the 114 justices have been women, a mere 0.035 percent. No president has nominated a woman to the position of chief justice. This glaring lack of gender parity on the Court is reflective of leadership positions across all sectors of the legal profession and the workplace as a whole. Women enter law school and most entry-level legal positions in numbers roughly equal to men. For nearly two decades, around fifty percent of all law graduates have been women, and that number increases every year. Yet they do not advance into the upper echelons of the profession in similar numbers.[5]

Numerous studies document the lack of women lawyers in positions of power and the results have remained relatively static over the years.

The data cited here captures the state of women in the legal profession in the years ranging from 2018 to 2019. According to the National Association of Women Lawyers annual survey, twenty-two percent of managing partners and twenty percent of equity partners in the nation's largest law firms are women.[6] Only three percent of equity partners are women of color.[7] Women represent less than twenty-six percent of female general counsels in the Fortune 500,[8] make up almost thirty-two percent of law school deans,[9] and account for thirty-two percent of tenured law school professors.[10] Only thirty-eight percent of law review editors-in-chief at the top fifty U.S. law schools are women.[11] In 2019, women held just over twenty-three percent of statewide elective executive offices,[12] down from a peak during 1999–2001.[13] Nationally, as of 2018, the percentage of women in Congress was twenty-three percent in the Senate and twenty percent in the House.[14] In the same time frame, only thirty-six percent of the judges serving on state supreme courts or their equivalent were women.[15] Just a handful of states have a *majority* of women on their highest court, and many have only one.[16] Only twenty-three percent of lawyers who argue cases before the Supreme Court are women.[17] The situation deteriorates even more when factoring in race, ethnicity, and sexual orientation.[18]

Contemporary discourse on gender and the Supreme Court in disciplines like gender studies, law, media, and political science (including our own previous research, described in the preface) has mostly focused on the stories of the women who are selected, not shortlisted.[19] Reporters, commentators, and scholars frequently retell Justice O'Connor's story as the first woman to serve on the Court, followed by a discussion of the three successful female nominees who followed in the wake of her legacy. The year 1981 is remembered as a pivotal and celebrated year as President Ronald Reagan made history by nominating the first woman to the Court. Over the course of the next thirty years, four more women would be nominated, three successfully confirmed. Ruth Bader Ginsburg was nominated and appointed to the Court in 1993, followed by Sonia Sotomayor in 2009 and Elena Kagan in 2010. Harriet Miers was nominated but withdrew from consideration in 2005.

Coverage of the women nominated and confirmed to the Court is important, but here we expand the narrative to include the untold stories stumbled upon in our media study, the stories of those shortlisted. It is valuable, as a preliminary matter, to tell their stories as part of the larger historical record of women's entry into the legal profession. But beyond that, their stories also expose barriers that endure whenever a candidate is shortlisted but not selected. Their collective history offers insights for transcending modern shortlists. Our work builds upon earlier scholarly efforts that developed the theory of the "leaking pipeline,"[20] in other words, the idea that women enter the profession in numbers equal to men but do not advance into leadership positions at the same rate, if at all. One way the pipeline "leaks" is via shortlisting, with qualified women considered in the mix of candidates but not selected.

Shortlists help to identify and explain latent discrimination and bias both within and outside of the judiciary. Many attempts to achieve diversity are effectively nothing more than window-dressing intended to create the appearance that diversity is valued. Take the so-called "Rooney Rule," named for former president and owner of the Pittsburg Steelers Dan Rooney, which is a policy adopted by the National Football League requiring that at least one ethnic minority be interviewed when hiring for head coaching and senior leadership positions. Some herald the rule as a success because it has increased the number of minorities who interview for these positions, arguing that even if a minority candidate is not selected, there is benefit in at least considering them. Aspirational policies like these, however, have done little to change the demographics of who is actually hired.

Some companies have experimented with similar policies. In 2017, the Diversity Lab launched the Mansfield Rule for law firms and corporate legal departments, named after Arabella Mansfield, the first woman admitted to practice law in the United States when she received a law license from the Iowa Bar in 1869.[21] The Mansfield Rule requires that employers consider diverse candidates for thirty percent of open positions in leadership or governance; thus, for ten potential hires, three must be women or minorities.²² With a significant cohort of prestigious firms and corporations committed to the effort, this new policy seems promising, but it is too soon to assess the impact. In 2010, the Securities and Exchange Commission began requiring companies to disclose efforts to address diversity when choosing board directors in their proxy statements; however, this effort has not increased the number of women on Fortune 500 boards.²³ The data reveals a dismal picture where, even after implementation of the SEC rule, the number of women named to boards actually decreased by two percent, down from approximately twelve percent to ten percent.²⁴ We do not mean to diminish the importance of policies like these, but we are more concerned with who is actually selected, not just who appears on the shortlist.

This book not only recounts the history of women shortlisted for the Supreme Court, but it develops their stories as a framework to identify the harms of shortlisting and strategize solutions for women to be selected, not just shortlisted. The individual life of each woman profiled here could easily be the subject of an entire book of her own. (For two women, this is actually the case.²⁵) However, the stories of women shortlisted before and immediately after O'Connor's confirmation have not yet been told in any meaningful way and have certainly not been studied in relation to one another as they are here. We believe there is power in a collective narrative of their lives, especially as we strive to better understand and ultimately ameliorate the dynamics that perpetually keep women on the shortlist. Each woman profiled here repeatedly went from shortlisted to selected as she ascended to the judiciary, the dean's office, or the president's cabinet, even if not selected from the ultimate shortlist for the Supreme Court. Their stories offer lessons to inform and remedy the pervasive, enduring gender inequality in positions of leadership and power.

It is time for more women to move from shortlisted to selected.

PART I

The Shortlisted Sisters

An Untold "Her"story of the Supreme Court

[T]he Court which has said to woman "You cannot enter
here," must now open its doors at her approach when she
comes armed with the proper documents.[1]
—Myra Bradwell, *Chicago Legal News*, 1879

The dominant narrative surrounding the United States Supreme Court
focuses on the individuals who are nominated and confirmed. Academics and authors devote entire careers to telling and re-telling mainstream
stories about the Court and its justices. The four women who have made
it onto the Court, in particular, are subjects of extraordinary attention.
Justices O'Connor, Ginsburg, Sotomayor, and Kagan have become popular culture icons, appearing on book covers, t-shirts, stickers, coffee
mugs, tote bags, tattoos, action figures, and, in the case of "Notorious
RBG," even closet air fresheners and breath mints. These are compelling
stories, to be sure. But what of those women shortlisted before O'Connor
became the first woman to serve on the nation's highest court?

Part one of the book tells a new Supreme Court history—*her story*—to
include these important, and overlooked, narratives. It is a history of
bathing beauties, lesbians, mistresses, and more who repeatedly went
from shortlisted to selected for positions of power as lawyers before
being considered to fill the ultimate role of Supreme Court justice. This
book not only fills a glaring omission in the Court's history, but it also
advances a critical aspect in the evolution of feminism and women's
rights. Stories of the shortlisted sisters began as first wave feminism was
just taking hold during the suffrage movement and continued through

the rise of the second wave in the 1960s and '70s. Their legacy offers many lessons for feminism and the future of women's rights movements.

To best understand the significance of the shortlisted sisters' stories, it is worth briefly revisiting the history of women's rights in America to provide some context for their coming of age. Women were not among those whose rights were secured by the United States Constitution in 1789. More than five decades later, women gathered in Seneca Falls to hold the first Women's Rights Convention in 1848. The gathering featured a document, the Declaration of Sentiments, which outlined a list of grievances authored by middle- and upper-class white women.[2] Modeled on the Declaration of Independence, it contained a list of complaints surrounding women's inequality including education, employment, moral expectations, property rights, and voting. Many of the demands have since been resolved, evidencing progress. After all, women today no longer face total disenfranchisement or a complete ban on formal education. But a number of the grievances listed in the Declaration of Sentiments remain relevant, such as the critique of male dominance in employment and a lack of pay equity: "He has monopolized nearly all the profitable employments, and from those she is permitted to follow, she receives but a scanty remuneration."[3] The Seneca Falls convention was a successful endeavor in many ways, but notably less so for minority women, especially black women. This error is one that feminists have repeated time and time again.[4]

It was not until 1869 that a woman was admitted to the practice of law: Arabella Mansfield shattered that glass ceiling with her admission to the Iowa Bar. The same year, Washington University in St. Louis became the first law school to admit women. Three years later, in 1872, Charlotte Ray became the first African American female lawyer, admitted to the District of Columbia Bar after graduating from Howard University.

It would be a full decade following Mansfield's achievement in Iowa before a woman would be admitted to the Supreme Court Bar. Belva Lockwood holds that distinction. The Court initially denied her application, so she turned to Congress and boldly convinced the male legislators to pass a statute entitled "An Act to Relieve Certain Legal Disabilities of Women." President Rutherford B. Hayes approved the legislation in 1879 and Lockwood was admitted that same year. Just a few years earlier, the Court had rejected Myra Bradwell's appeal from the denial of admission to the Illinois Bar—as noted in the introduction, it was here that Justice Bradley extolled the virtues of keeping women in the home.[5]

One year after Lockwood's admission, she became the first woman in the United States to argue a case before the Supreme Court, representing a female client with an unpaid debt.[6] Though Lockwood lost the case, she appeared again in 1906, this time winning a case on behalf of the Cherokee Nation seeking payment from the federal government for land ceded to the government.[7] She went on to be nominated as a presidential candidate in 1884 by the Women's National Equal Rights Party, campaigning on promises to give women equal rights in marriage and to place a woman on the Supreme Court. Grover Cleveland won that year, and when Lockwood ran again four years later, Benjamin Harrison was elected president. (The litany of men running for and winning the presidency continues into the present day.) More than a century passed—102 years—from Lockwood's admission to the Supreme Court Bar before a female justice sat on that bench.

Feminism's first wave focused on securing the right to vote, one of the main issues noted by the women at Seneca Falls. The suffrage movement, led by well-known activists like Susan B. Anthony, Elizabeth Cady Stanton, and Alice Paul, was marked by different perspectives on not only the best way to achieve the desired end, but also how to address race. For example, "[w]hen Paul staged the famous women's rights parade of 1913 in Washington, she ordered black suffragists to march at the back of the line in order to spare the feelings of Southern sympathizers. Ida B. Wells-Barnett, who had been leading a group of black women from Chicago, vanished into the crowd along the sidewalk, then stepped back into the street as the Illinois delegation marched by, joining her white friends and integrating the demonstration."[8] This same sort of racial tension endured even fifty years later, when "Paul ignored pleas that she decline to accept support for the ERA [Equal Rights Amendment] from the segregationist presidential candidate George Wallace."[9] Racial divisiveness and struggles to accomplish social change continue to this day.

After securing the right to vote with the passage of the Nineteenth Amendment in 1920, many of the same women began to lobby for broader rights. The Equal Rights Amendment was introduced by Paul in 1923. It was not until 1972 that it finally passed in Congress and was sent to the states for ratification—where it still sits. Again, some minority women felt excluded from these efforts, which accounted for at least part of the reason why states like Illinois failed to ratify it in the 1970s. When Illinois finally voted for its passage in 2018, Representative Mary E. Flowers, a black legislator, critiqued the law as being designed to advance the rights of white women but not all women, similar to the fight for suffrage.[10] On the House floor, she explained, "There were some laws on the books, but they did not apply to me."[11] Instead, "I've never had my rights given to me. I always had to fight for what was mine."[12] With Illinois becoming the thirty-seventh state to ratify, just one more is needed before the constitutionally-required three-quarters vote by all states occurs. Should a thirty-eighth state do so, however, it remains unclear whether the ERA will be deemed ratified within the appropriate time-frame.[13]

Even without a constitutional amendment to document equal rights for women, many believed that the dearth of female leaders would not be permanent. More women entered the pipeline once undergraduate and professional schools increasingly opened their doors and federal lawmakers passed formal measures like Title VII of the Civil Rights Act of 1964 (banning employment discrimination based on race, color, religion, sex, and national origin) and Title IX of the Education Amendments of 1972 (protecting access to education in federally funded institutions of education). This belief, while reasonable, has not borne out. No matter the field or profession, the percentage of women in leadership roles comes nowhere close to their percentage of the population.

One hundred twenty-nine years after Seneca Falls, in the midst of feminism's second wave (which focused on issues like labor, pay equity, sexuality, reproduction, and dissatisfaction with domesticity[14]), women marched the streets of Houston in 1977 at the first—and only—National Women's Conference, with delegates representing every state. Participants hoped that the endeavor would galvanize final support to pass the ERA, but it did not.[15] Instead, women struggled to put their professional training to work, and often found themselves rejected for positions because they might "distract" their male counterparts, become pregnant, or simply take a position held for a "more-deserving" man. Women who managed to secure positions in the workplace found themselves forced to endure sexual harassment and were paid less than men with the same qualifications and responsibilities.

Landmark sexual harassment and discrimination cases, like *Meritor Savings Bank v. Vinson*[16] in 1986, made remedies available to some women but did little to change misogynistic culture. Nowhere was this more evident than when Anita Hill disclosed her experiences of sexual harassment perpetrated by Supreme Court nominee Clarence Thomas in 1991. Hill testified for eight hours in front of the Senate Judiciary Committee about the sexual harassment she endured while working for Thomas when he was director of the Equal Employment Opportunity Commission (EEOC) and a supervisor at the U.S. Department of Education. Her testimony included revelations that Thomas shared graphic descriptions of pornography and made references to pubic hair. Although Hill's role was to provide testimony in the context of hearings about Thomas's suitability as a justice, it appeared that Hill herself was on trial or under investigation. A similar phenomenon bizarrely repeated itself nearly thirty years later when Republicans on the Senate Judiciary Committee hired a "female prosecutor" (distinctly noting her gender) to question Dr. Christine Blasey Ford, who alleged that Supreme Court nominee Brett Kavanaugh had sexually assaulted her as a teenager. We return to this parallel phenomenon at the end of the book. Despite Anita Hill's highly credible testimony, Thomas was confirmed 52–48. The ordeal caused bitter disagreement within the African American and feminist communities. Nonetheless, Hill's testimony would forever change the landscape of sexual harassment, making the term a household word and dramatically increasing the number of complaints lodged with the EEOC.

Outraged and inspired by Hill's experience, a record number of women ran for—and won—congressional offices in 1992, making it what *Time* magazine dubbed "The Year of the Woman."[17] Keep in mind, however, that this number of wins was only twenty-seven, which emphasizes how grossly underrepresented women have been in Congress. The magazine cover story championed the "flurry of fresh female faces" as a response to second-wave feminism: "If the women's movement of the 1970s was the lightning flash of female empowerment, then the long-awaited roll of thunder began to resound in this year's election results. From coast to coast, women candidates, thrust forward by Anita Hill–inspired outrage and helped along by anti-incumbency sentiment, were in contention as never before."[18] Hill's testimony and the election results that followed marked the start of feminism's third wave.

Twenty-five years later, the nation watched one of the most objectively qualified persons in history run for the presidency—a Yale-trained lawyer, law firm partner, New York senator, and U.S. secretary of state who had also spent eight years working in one of the most prestigious areas of the White House as first lady. Hillary Clinton was the first woman to ever be nominated for the office by a major political party. Polls predicted widely that she would win, but instead the nation chose Donald J. Trump, a man who exposed the reality of American misogyny in unprecedented ways. He shamed Republican opponent Carly Fiorina's appearance ("Look at that face! Would anyone vote for that?"[19]) and stalked—literally—Clinton on stage during a presidential debate.[20] His bragging comment to "grab 'em by the pussy"[21] played over and over during the campaign, foreshadowing what would follow. As president, Trump ridiculed Fox News anchor Megyn Kelly as having "blood coming out of her eyes, blood coming out of her wherever"[22] and told ABC reporter Cecilia Vega, "I know you're not thinking, you never do"[23] after she thanked him for calling on her at a press conference. He also targeted black female journalists with persistent name calling.[24] These disparaging, denigrating comments about women are so common[25] that it was newsworthy when Trump *did not* make them.

In response to Trump's election, women across the country marched, yet again. This time, instead of donning suffragist white or burning bras, they gathered by the millions in hot pink pussy hats to protest the commander in chief. The day after his inauguration, the Women's March in Washington, D.C., became what has been called the largest protest in U.S. history,[26] and even more marched in cities throughout the United States and around the globe. Almost simultaneously, the #MeToo movement emerged in full force. First created by Tarana Burke, an African American woman, in 2006 (Burke, incidentally, rarely gets attribution for her significant contributions), the effort went mainstream over a decade later when celebrity actress Alyssa Milano tweeted about her own experience with sexual assault/harassment on October 15, 2017, prompting millions of other women to do so as well.[27] The #TimesUp movement launched in January 2018 to support women in sexual harassment cases, raising a legal defense fund of more than $20 million. Many women (including the authors of this book) revealed publicly for the first time sexual assaults and harassment that they had kept hidden their entire lives. Some published detailed descriptions of the trauma, such as the op-ed penned by journalist Connie Chung in the *Washington Post*[28] and the profiles by actresses Ashley Judd and Gwyneth Paltrow featured in the *New York Times* along with eighteen other survivors.[29] Not only did the effort bring women together to share their experiences, but it brought prominent men down from their positions of power.

One year after the #MeToo movement went viral, the *New York Times* inventoried the number of "high-profile men and women in the United States who permanently lost their jobs or significant roles, professional ties or projects (e.g., concert tours, book deals) within the past year after publicly reported accusations of sexual misconduct."[30] The list featured

201 men and three women, including comedian Louis C.K., news anchor Matt Lauer, journalist Charlie Rose, actor Kevin Spacey, media mogul Harvey Weinstein, and numerous state politicians. While nearly half of their replacements were women, this hardly made a dent in the gender disparities in leadership and power, especially for the legal profession, which has yet to experience its own #MeToo reckoning. Only two men on the list were practicing lawyers or judges—Eric Schneiderman, the former attorney general of New York, and Alex Kozinski, the former chief judge of the United States Court of Appeals for the Ninth Circuit (more on him in chapter five). The relative absence of the legal profession from the list does not mean women in that industry are not experiencing sexual harassment and assault. A study of nearly 7,000 lawyers from 135 countries published by the International Bar Association in 2019 found that thirty-seven percent of women and seven percent of men reported experiencing sexual harassment in the workplace.

With the failures and shortcomings of the first, second, and third waves of feminism exposed yet again, many women, especially minority women, rejected feminism entirely, though arguably the fourth wave of feminism began in 2012 with the advent of social media. Despite these powerful surges in the name of feminism, many are left feeling lost in the undertow. Some argue that whatever wave of feminism we are in, it amounts to nothing more than another version of white supremacy.[31] Others acknowledge the flawed past of feminism while simultaneously pushing toward meaningful equality that embraces the complexities and struggles of intersectionality, including ability, class, education, race, religion, sexuality, and other underrepresented statuses. As Chimamanda Ngozi Adichie explains in *We Should All Be Feminists*, "My own definition of a feminist is a man or a woman who says, 'Yes, there's a problem with gender as it is today and we must fix it, we must do better.'"[32] We choose this as our definition as well, and we see this book as providing one pathway for all of us to do better.

Though the initial #MeToo reaction led to some men in power being replaced by women, we are concerned about the inevitable backlash.

Some men have responded by avoiding women in the workplace entirely. As one news article explained in late 2018:

No more dinners with female colleagues. Don't sit next to them on flights. Book hotel rooms on different floors. Avoid one-on-one meetings. In fact, as a wealth adviser put it, just hiring a woman these days is "an unknown risk." What if she took something he said the wrong way? Across Wall Street, men are adopting controversial strategies for the #MeToo era and, in the process, making life even harder for women. Call it the Pence Effect, after U.S. Vice President Mike Pence, who has said he avoids dining alone with any woman other than his wife. In finance, the overarching impact can be, in essence, gender segregation.[33]

This contemporary gender segregation looks and sounds much like the world the women profiled in this book had to navigate as they advanced through their careers, regularly excluded from spaces where "business" was conducted by men. While that news article suggests this is limited to the world of finance, we fear that it may become the status quo across all sectors and signal a return to an era we thought long behind us.

This #MeToo backlash makes the stories of the shortlisted sisters all the more relevant today. Each of them endured—and thrived—in worlds where men regularly excluded women and yet they repeatedly ascended into prestigious positions of power previously held only by men. The first two chapters of part one introduce these incredible women and place their lives and accomplishments in historical context. Chapters three and four explore their stories in connection with those who followed, including the women who made it onto the Court and those who did not. Part two then turns to the consequences and harms of shortlisting and outlines ideas about how more women can move from shortlisted to selected.

1

The First Shortlisted Woman

FLORENCE ALLEN

As we consider national and international situations we realize that the woman lawyer is needed by America and by the
world as never before. She is needed by the country, for her
training enables her to join with men in teaching citizens
and particularly the youth coming on, the meaning of the
Constitution of the United States.[1]
—Florence Allen in her memoir, *To Do Justly*, 1965

Florence Allen was a woman before her time as the first female judge
in Ohio, the first female to sit on a state court of last resort, and the
first female appointed to an Article III federal appellate court, the
United States Court of Appeals for the Sixth Circuit. She was also the
first woman whose name appeared repeatedly on official lists of possible candidates for appointment to the United States Supreme Court.[2]
We initially uncovered Allen's name listed as one of forty individuals
in an undated and unsigned letter suggesting names for the Supreme
Court preserved among Herbert Hoover's presidential papers. The letter, addressed to White House Press Secretary Ted Joslin, was likely
written in 1932, as it references filling the vacancy created by Justice
Holmes, who stepped down from the Court that year.[3] In the same
archive, we discovered a one-page typed "Application for Appointment"
for "Associate Justice of the Supreme Court of the U.S." that was filled
out with Florence Allen's biographical information and professional
accomplishments.[4] According to one historian, Hoover's attorney general, William Mitchell, considered Allen for a seat on the Court.[5] He
was reportedly amenable to a woman filling that role, and when Hoover

wrote to Mitchell inquiring about this possibility, Mitchell responded that he would be happy to appoint a woman "if he could find one."[6] Apparently he was not trying very hard, since Allen was quite well-known throughout the White House, the state of Ohio, and the entire nation. In a 1930 editorial, the *Christian Science Monitor* noted a "missing element" in all newspapers that published lists of possible nominees: no one "mentioned the name of a woman."[7] The piece endorsed Allen and Mabel Walker Willebrandt, whose name also appeared in the Joslin letter. (She served as an assitant attorney general under Presidents Harding and Coolidge.)

The reference to Allen as a possible nominee during the Hoover administration would prove to be just the beginning. We found evidence that she was also officially listed as a contender for the high court in 1937 during the Franklin Delano Roosevelt administration, and public support for her candidacy was quite strong. Harry S. Truman later considered Allen for the Court, and women also lobbied Dwight D. Eisenhower to this effect. While Allen was not ultimately nominated, her legacy as an exceedingly accomplished lawyer and jurist who achieved a multitude of firsts set the stage for a new era of diversity on the Supreme Court and in the workplace as a whole. One cannot help but wonder, however, what the impact of Allen's appointment to the Court as early as the 1930s would have been on both judicial decision-making and the path for women in professional and leadership roles. We reflect further on this in chapter seven.

There is historical evidence to suggest that Allen was *recommended* for a seat on the Court at least as early as 1924, during President Calvin Coolidge's time in office. A letter sent by E. L. Kenyon of Elkhart, Indiana, to Coolidge when Justice Joseph McKenna planned to resign from the Court urged, "If there is a woman in the United States who represents the legal profession, and who is qualified to fill the position of a justice of the Supreme Court, I believe Miss Allen is that woman."[8] Kenyon conceded it would be unusual for two sitting justices to hail from the same state of Ohio (Chief Justice William Howard Taft's home state), but he nonetheless opined, "It has always seemed queer to me

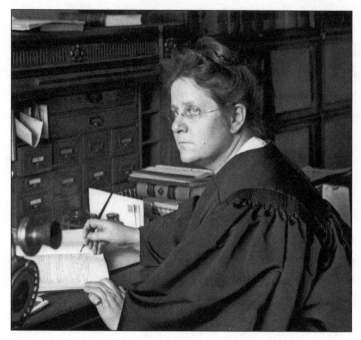

FIGURE 1.1. Florence Allen (Credit: Courtesy of the Ohio History Commission, AL00128)

that women did not enter the legal profession ages ago, and I believe that in another century you will see if you can look back from the great beyond that women are the justices of this world. For is it not a fact that JUSTICE is depicted by a woman holding up the scales. I cannot recall of seeing Justice represented by a man, either in statuary or pictures. Can you?"[9]

Similar early advocacy for a woman on the Court appeared in a news article from *The Day Book*, published in Chicago on February 12, 1913: "Women Candidates for Harlan's Seat on the Supreme Bench."[10] The front-page article featured photos of two women, Emma M. Gillett and Ellen Spencer Mussey, with the author suggesting that "[m]any people will agree that President Taft might—and probably will—do a whole lot worse than to appoint a woman as a justice of the supreme court, in the late Justice Harlan's place."[11] But proposals like these were rare, until Allen.

Beginning early in her career, Florence Allen gained notoriety for her achievement of many extraordinary successes never before attained by a woman that continued throughout her lifetime. She was an author, common pleas judge, federal appellate judge, legal aid attorney, prosecutor, public speaker, state supreme court justice, and suffragist. Kenyon sent that letter to President Coolidge even before Allen's arguably most significant accomplishment: her appointment to the United States Court of Appeals for the Sixth Circuit. While her life has been studied to some extent by historians, she is not a household name in the same way as Sandra Day O'Connor or Ruth Bader Ginsburg. She barely even graces a history book with the exception of her own autobiography, *To Do Justly*, and a biography, *First Lady of the Law*, published in 1984.[12] Her consideration by multiple presidents as a possible justice on the Supreme Court, paving the way for the other women shortlisted (and eventually selected), has largely escaped significant exploration.

Allen was born in Salt Lake City, Utah, on March 23, 1884, just fifteen years after Arabella Mansfield became the first woman admitted to practice law in the U.S. Allen's father, Clarence Emir, was a state legislator and successful mine developer in Utah; he was eventually elected to serve in the U.S. Congress. Unlike many women of that era, Allen was not the first in her family to attend college. Allen's older sister, Esther, would become the dean of women at Ohio State University. Her mother, Corinne, was the first woman admitted to Smith College. Allen described her mother as incredibly devoted, with a strong interest in her children's lives. Her mother would frequently implore them to "Make your point and sit down,"[13] advice that would serve Allen well in her career.

Education played an important role in Allen's upbringing. She attended Western Reserve University in Ohio, graduating in 1904, and then spent two years in Berlin studying music.[14] When she returned to Ohio, Allen completed her master's degree in political science in 1908 at Western Reserve. She then enrolled in the University of Chicago Law School in 1909, the lone woman out of about one hundred students.[15]

She took criminal law with Roscoe Pound, the renowned legal scholar who went on to serve for twenty years as the dean of Harvard Law School. Male students in Allen's class expressed their admiration of her; they complimented her by saying that she had a "masculine mind."[16] This reference highlights stereotypes and biases that female attorneys have faced throughout their careers both historically and in the present day. The archetype of a lawyer is male, and it is against this backdrop that women are compared. Allen, however, had a mind of her own.

After her first year at the University of Chicago, Allen transferred to New York University School of Law in the hope of finding a more supportive environment where she would not be the only female student. There, she encountered a dean who was encouraging of her academic pursuits, and a law school culture where she and other women enjoyed the opportunity to participate fully in campus life. Allen recollected, "There was this wonderful woman, a symbol of the inevitable march of progress, of the inevitable granting of political liberty to women. She needed no defense, and neither did we. There we were in the Law School on equal terms with men, and we said to ourselves, if we pass our examinations and are admitted to the bar, no one can prevent us from practicing. This was the spirit given us by New York University Law School."[17] The atmosphere at NYU differed markedly, in a positive way, from institutions like Columbia Law School, where Allen would have liked to transfer but for the fact that the school did not admit women as full-time students. Columbia did not change its policy until 1927; this may seem shocking until one considers that Washington and Lee—the last law school to admit women—barred them until 1972.

Allen graduated second in her class from NYU in 1913 and after graduation she returned to Ohio. Whatever ambitions she had to practice in New York were quashed when prestigious law firms in that city did not extend offers to her.[18] In fact, firms back in her home state were hesitant to hire women lawyers as well, so Allen opened her own law firm and volunteered with the Cleveland Legal Aid Society.[19] Her "first case was that of an Italian woman who was suing her husband for divorce because he had deserted her and their children. The woman's brother paid Allen $15. In her first year she made $875."[20] (Years later as a judge, she refused to take over the divorce docket from her male colleagues because she disdained the notion that this was somehow uniquely women's work, even if it was where she got her start.) She soon combined her office with the Legal Aid Society, and was later appointed as an assistant prosecutor in Cuyahoga County. Although she earned less money in this new position than she had in legal aid, she valued the experience it provided her over the salary.

Between 1910 and 1920, Allen devoted a good deal of time and attention to the suffrage movement. Her interest in this cause was inspired by a woman she heard speak in college, who would later become a significant role model, influence, and mentor: Maude Wood Park. Park visited Western Reserve University to encourage the female students to create a women's suffrage club. Allen credited Park with teaching her the importance of organizing women to bring about change—a lesson that would become vital later in Allen's career.[21] During her time working as part of the suffrage movement, Allen also learned the value of taking every opportunity to use her voice and speak about the causes, regardless of location or circumstance.[22] As she campaigned for the reelection of President Woodrow Wilson in 1916, Allen learned of an important case on women's suffrage in municipal elections granted through the East Cleveland Charter Commission that would be heard before the Supreme Court of Ohio. Allen ended up litigating the case before the state's high court and won, but women soon lost their newfound right to vote granted by the high court as a result of a popular referendum.[23]

The referendum was only a temporary defeat. Allen continued to persevere alongside other suffragists. Those efforts culminated in victory when women finally won the right to vote with the Nineteenth Amendment's passage in August 1920. Allen expressed the importance of this work in the following way: "This battle for the rights of full citizenship is a matter of such ancient history that we are inclined to accept the privilege of the vote as if we had always had it, forgetting what we owe to the hard-working and courageous women who devoted their lives to this cause."[24]

Women voters had a direct effect on Allen's subsequent political and judicial career: "I was the beneficiary of the entire women's movement."[25] Her entrance into the judiciary was made possible in large part by the campaigning she did for the suffrage movement. Allen reflected, "So I had friends everywhere. Moreover, they were not merely well-wishers; they were capable workers. They had made house-to-house canvasses before they got the vote, and now with the consciousness of political power they went forward joyously to make a house-to-house canvass for me."[26] She launched her campaign for the common pleas court in Ohio just days following the ratification of the amendment and was elected in 1920, beating nine male opponents.[27] While on that court, she instituted a number of reforms and worked diligently to alleviate the court's backlog of cases. To this end, she presided over almost 900 cases. Allen was also the first female judge to sentence a man to death.

Two years later, Allen continued on her trajectory of firsts when elected by the voters as the first woman justice on the Supreme Court of Ohio in 1922. As part of her campaign, Allen was required to secure 21,000 signatures from eighty-eight counties on a petition for her name to appear on the ballot. She received a large outpouring of support from the women she worked with in the suffrage movement. Allen remembered, "The women put the petitions into practically every one of the eighty-eight counties, and the local women in the counties obtained over forty-two thousand signatures,"[28] twice as many as was required. Her name appeared on the ballot without any affiliation; she faced opponents from both political parties and was bitterly opposed by the Republican Party. Nevertheless, she won, and credited her victory to the women who worked tirelessly for her throughout the state, and the press who reported favorably on her campaign. The *Washington Post* noted, "Newspaper woman, teacher, investigator of immigration conditions, lawyer, assistant county prosecutor and judge of common pleas court are the steps which have led Florence E. Allen to an associate judgeship on the Ohio supreme court, as far as records show, the only woman in the world who will hold such a position."[29]

In 1928, Allen easily won her reelection campaign to the same court by 350,000 votes; again, she credited her friendships with the women of Ohio.[30] There is perhaps no better illustration of the power to change laws and policies by going directly to the people and asking for their vote. This highlights how important voting rights are in the struggle for equality, not only in *obtaining* the right to vote, but also in reforming limitations related to gerrymandering, poll locations, and voter identification.

Allen was revered and respected as a jurist. Her gender did not seem to impact public perception of her competence or qualification. As one commentator observed at the time, "Miss Florence E. Allen, elected justice of the Supreme Court of Ohio last fall, is establishing the fact that she is entitled to prominence not simply because she is the first woman to be elected to the supreme court of any State, but rather because of her unusually clear and up-to-date thinking. There is no jurist in Ohio today who is manifesting a deeper consciousness of present-day ideals than she."[31]

In 1934, after a career filled with professional accomplishments, Allen was nominated by President Roosevelt to the United States Sixth Circuit Court of Appeals. The nomination to this federal appellate court was strongly supported by Eleanor Roosevelt, who was one of many first ladies[32] to support female judicial appointees and who would continue to be a champion for Allen in the years that followed. In an article written for *Home Magazine* in 1932, she praised Allen's work and speculated that increased visibility of women like her might eventually lead to the perception that "sex should not enter into the question of fitness for office."[33]

The Senate unanimously confirmed Allen for the Court of Appeals, making her the first woman in the United States to receive a lifetime federal appellate judicial appointment. While her confirmation was unanimous, members of the appeals court themselves were not thrilled at the prospect of being joined by a woman: "None of the judges of the Sixth Circuit favored her appointment and one of the men was reported to be so upset he took to his bed for two days."[34] The courthouse facilities were also unprepared for the presence of a woman. Allen "had to make a long trek to the public areas of the building to use the restroom, and it was weeks before permission could be acquired from Washington to appropriate one of them and equip it with a lock and key to give her some privacy."[35] Even when her presence on the bench lost its novelty, the male judges continued to exclude her from their lunches.[36] Judge Allen would be the only woman appointed to a federal appellate court for thirty-two more years.

Allen's professional accomplishments are remarkable by any standards, and our research also uncovered that she was determined to be fully self-sufficient and financially independent in her adult life. She never married, but historians have pieced together the details of two long-term romantic relationships. Allen shared a home with Susan Rebhan, a YWCA organizer, for many years before Rebhan died unexpectedly in 1935. Rebhan orchestrated all of Allen's campaigns for office. After Rebhan's death, Allen shared her life with Mary Pierce, a school director, who also supported Allen in her work.[37] Allen and Pierce were buried next to each other upon their deaths. These relationships were not likely viewed as traditional romances, in part because of the time in which they existed, and we examine them in greater detail in chapter six. For now, we delve further into Allen's consideration for the Supreme Court.

Room in Roosevelt's Court Packing Plan for Allen?

In the 1930s, the appointment of a woman to the role of a Supreme Court justice was novel in ways that a contemporary audience might not appreciate. Recognizing the historical context at the time in which Allen's name surfaced in presidential circles is crucial to fully understanding the significance. Like modern women who experience success in their professional pursuits but encounter painful resistance along the way, Allen too plateaued. Though she achieved an extremely high level of leadership and power, the Supreme Court proved off limits.

Women's organizations like the American Association of University Women, American Legion Auxiliary, Business and Professional Women, General Federation of Women's Clubs, New York Women's Trade Union League, Women's Bar Association of D.C., and Women Lawyers of New York City actively supported Allen's potential nomination to the Court. Their members spoke publicly about the importance of appointing a woman like Allen, and they directly appealed to presidents and members of the Court with their message.[38] These efforts, while not ultimately resulting in their desired end, did establish an important foundation for the women who later followed.

Allen was one of the first women to try and crack the glass ceiling well before it was even known by such a name. One historian aptly described the context in which qualified, exceptional women like Allen found themselves: "Except for her sex, Florence Allen met the basic political, professional, and representational standards for Supreme Court selection."[39] During her time on the Sixth Circuit, Allen served for several years on the Committee on Cultural Relations with Mexico, wrote a book on the U.S. Constitution, and was chair of the International Bar Section on Human Rights.[40] Meanwhile, she continued to author important judicial opinions.[41]

It is, in some respects, almost unbelievable the extent of Allen's accomplishments given their entirely unprecedented nature. Although never making it to the Supreme Court, the public attention paid to her nonetheless carved out a path where there previously had not been one, showing other presidents at least the possibility of a female Supreme Court appointee, and also modeling to other women the potential for their own professional achievements. Allen was a force in her own right even before her name appeared on the list of potential Court candidates. She illustrates the reality that women often not only need to be qualified, but must be exceedingly so, in order to be taken seriously, especially when they are a first. Allen herself possessed a certain self-awareness, writing that "her work must be as nearly letter-perfect as possible because people are ten times more critical of a woman in an unprecedented position than of a man in the same position."[42] Justice O'Connor later reflected a similar sentiment when she contemplated accepting the nomination herself; we explore this more fully in chapter six, evaluating the potential downfalls of being the first, or a token.

President Roosevelt's tenure in the executive branch was characterized by his efforts toward innovation, but he encountered resistance to his ideas along the way. Faced with the challenge of helping the country recover after the Great Depression, Roosevelt created a series of government reforms famously known as the New Deal. He introduced left-leaning programs like the National Labor Relations Act, the Social Security Administration, the Wealth Tax, and the Works Progress Administration. Initially, the federal courts were rather obstructionist to Roosevelt's goals. At the Supreme Court level, starting in January 1935 and spanning nearly seventeen months, the Court found eight of ten cases involving his New Deal legislation unconstitutional, effectively thwarting Roosevelt and his administration's efforts to move the country out of the Great Depression.

In large part due to his dissatisfaction with the Court's decision-making and overall conservative dynamic, Roosevelt sought to radically restructure the Court through his now infamous court packing plan. It was during one of his "fireside chats" that Roosevelt first shared his ideas for judicial reorganization, proposing the Judicial Procedures Reform Bill of 1937. Appealing to Congress, he asked for an increase to the total number of seats on the Court. Roosevelt proposed that for each sitting justice who attained the age of seventy but refused to retire, a president could appoint a new member to the Court. That same year, a memo was prepared for Roosevelt with a list of possible nominees. Dated August 3, 1937, with a handwritten note that it belonged in the Supreme Court Appointments file, the memorandum included, among an otherwise unremarkable three-page list of men, the name of a woman. The entry read, "Judge Florence E. Allen, of Ohio, located in the Sixth Circuit."[43]

Had Roosevelt's Congress approved this new appointment scheme, the Court would have increased in size from nine to fifteen justices, and Allen might have been selected. Roosevelt believed that a larger Court would benefit from an infusion of new ideas, and that one's increased age stifled such possibility. Could a woman be part of this world? Ultimately, Roosevelt's plan did not gain traction with Congress and never became law. Even so, he had many opportunities to appoint Allen, or another woman, and never seized them.

Although Roosevelt's appeals to Congress for judicial expansion were unsuccessful, he faced an unprecedented eight vacancies and one lateral appointment of a chief justice during his time in office. These vacancies gave him the ability to reshape the Court, though not exactly in the way he initially contemplated.

Roosevelt confronted the first high court vacancy four years into his presidency, when Justice Willis Van Devanter announced his intention to retire. Van Devanter was a vocal opponent of New Deal legislation and his retirement ignited whisperings about the president's plan to transform the Court to create his ambitious programs. In addition to appearing on that White House memo, Allen's name was also listed by the *New York Times* in an article announcing Van Devanter's retirement, among a list of possible replacements.[44] But Roosevelt instead selected Hugo Black, a Democratic Senator from Alabama (and former Klan member) as the new justice. Roosevelt was known for selecting political friends, rather than legal experts—Black had repeatedly voted to support the New Deal legislation and endorsed the court-packing plan. He would go on to author the opinion in *Korematsu v. United States*,[45] upholding the constitutionality of an executive order demanding that Japanese Americans move into relocation camps as a matter of national security, and the dissenting opinion in *Griswold v. Connecticut*,[46] rejecting the majority's decision to extend the right to privacy to married persons surrounding their use of contraception.

Van Devanter's retirement was only the first of many vacancies for Roosevelt. Justice Sutherland retired in January 1938,[47] and, as with the previous vacancy, Allen again was floated as a possible candidate to fill the position. Allen herself seemed surprised at the mention of her name as a possible contender for the Court, as if the idea came out of the blue. She wrote in her memoir, "All of a sudden my name was mentioned to fill an existing vacancy in the United States Supreme Court."[48] Roosevelt ultimately nominated Solicitor General Stanley Reed to the Court, and he was confirmed on January 15, 1938. Interestingly, Reed did not even hold a law degree. Despite Allen's apparent surprise at being a contender for the vacancy, she was also somewhat hopeful about the possibility. However, "on the morning of the announcement of Reed's appointment to the Sutherland seat, Judge John Gore told Judge Allen to smile when she entered the courtroom, so that the watching reporters could not impute to her a disappointment."[49] Disappointing as the announcement may have been personally, Allen also began to speculate that there probably would not be a female Supreme Court justice during her lifetime. She was right in this prediction; Sandra Day O'Connor's appointment did not occur until fifteen years after Allen's death.

In July of that same year, Justice Benjamin Cardozo passed away, and President Roosevelt nominated Felix Frankfurter, an adviser to the president and founder of the American Civil Liberties Union. Although Allen's gender surely played a role in keeping her off the Court, the discrimination she experienced was not always explicitly based on this factor. Instead, there is some speculation that one impediment to her appointment in this instance was related to severe criticism of her judicial record. This criticism, which alleged that she had an overwhelming number of decisions overturned by the higher courts on appeal, was actually untrue. According to Allen, this misinformation was intentionally conveyed to Attorney General Frank Murphy, who played a pivotal role in the appointment process, to undermine her credibility. A significant amount of media attention perpetuating the untruths was dispersed across the country and, despite Allen's best efforts to correct the record, the damage was done.

While the nomination in this instance did not go to a woman, it did go to the man who would be the first justice to hire a female clerk at the Supreme Court—Frankfurter hired Lucile Lomen in 1944.

A succession of male nominations followed in the later years of Roosevelt's presidency. Justice Louis Brandeis retired in February 1939. Again, Allen's name surfaced. The nomination went to William O. Douglas, just forty years old at his confirmation. Attorney General Murphy evolved from vetting nominees to becoming the nominee on January 4, 1940, to fill the vacancy after Justice Pierce Butler died on November 16, 1939. (This phenomenon of the vetter becoming the nominee surfaces again later in the book.) Upon Chief Justice Evan Hughes's retirement in June 1941, Roosevelt nominated Justice Harlan Fiske Stone to the position of chief justice, and for Stone's former position, Roosevelt nominated Robert H. Jackson, his former solicitor general and attorney general. Finally, the last of Roosevelt's appointments to the Court occurred when Justice James Francis Byrnes resigned in October 1942; he tendered his resignation at the order of the president in order to head the Office of Economic Stabilization (Truman later appointed Byrnes to secretary of state in 1945). In 1943, Roosevelt nominated Wiley Rutledge, a Democrat, in his place. Rutledge was a supporter of Roosevelt's court packing plan and had served on the D.C. Court of Appeals for just three years before his appointment to the Court.

By the end of Roosevelt's presidency, he had replaced almost every sitting justice on the Court but he never nominated a woman, even though Allen must have been on his mind—his wife, Eleanor, was a strong, supportive voice for her. During her time in the White House, she invited Allen to work on various commissions. On a number of occasions, Mrs. Roosevelt used her daily news column, *My Day*, as a platform to highlight Allen's accomplishments. She wrote about Allen's excellence on the bench and mentioned events at which the two women's lives intersected. Sometimes the references were off-handed, such as mentioning that she attended a dinner honoring Allen. Other times she was much more direct. On November 17, 1948, Mrs. Roosevelt actually endorsed

Allen as a contender for the Court. She wrote, "I would like to add, that if a President of the United States should decide to nominate a woman for the Supreme Court, it should be Judge Allen. She will be a nominee with a backing, on a completely nonpartisan basis, of American women who know her career and her accomplishments."[50] The women shared personal correspondence; a handful of letters between the two are preserved in Allen's archives located at the Western Reserve Historical Society.[51] Additional examples of presidents' wives advocating for female candidates are found throughout the chapters that follow.

Throughout Roosevelt's service in the executive branch, Allen's name surfaced repeatedly as someone eminently qualified for the Supreme Court. Certainly, with eight vacancies, he had ample opportunity to appoint her. Some historians have noted that Allen's greatest professional achievement was her judicial experience. However, Roosevelt was known to appoint Supreme Court justices not for their accomplishments on the bench, but rather their involvement in politics.[52] And, given that he had appointed her as the first woman on a federal appellate court, he may have felt that he had done enough to support the cause of women.

Would Truman or Eisenhower Finally Nominate Allen?

Harry Truman, who replaced Henry Wallace as FDR's running mate in his fourth and final campaign for president in 1944, served with FDR for just eighty-two days before Roosevelt died and Truman ascended to the presidency. Truman, like Roosevelt, could have made history as the first to name a woman to the Supreme Court, but he did not do so.

Despite the path that Roosevelt forged for women to serve on federal courts with his appointment of Allen to the Sixth Circuit, progress for women in the judiciary stalled in the years that followed. Truman did elevate some women into leadership roles in the federal government during his tenure in the Oval Office. He appointed Frances Perkins, who served as secretary of labor under President Roosevelt, to the

U.S. Civil Service Commission. (Perkins famously helped craft the Fair Labor Standards Act and Social Security Act.) Truman also appointed the first woman to serve as a United States ambassador, making Eugenie Anderson the ambassador to Denmark in 1949. And Truman appointed a woman, Georgia Neese Clark, as U.S. treasurer. Unbeknownst to Truman, he started a trend; since her appointment, as of early 2020, every U.S. treasurer has been a woman. Bess Truman was credited with her husband's female appointments. It was thought he would not have done so but for his having a "smart wife."[53]

Nonetheless, Truman and other male leaders in his administration seemed to be of the mind that judgeships should be held by men.[54] However, Truman did eventually succumb to pressure from Democratic leader India Edwards, who implored him to nominate a woman in October 1949 in the midst of making a significant twenty-seven judicial nominations. A powerhouse in Democratic politics, Edwards served in multiple leadership roles, as the associate director (1947–48) and then executive director (1948–53) of the Women's Division of the Democratic National Committee, the vice-chair of the Democratic National Committee (1950–56), and consultant to the Department of Labor (1964–66). She convinced Truman that public reaction would be unfavorable if there was not *at least* one woman among the appointment of so many new federal judges.

Truman nominated Burnita Shelton Matthews to the United States District Court for the District of Columbia in 1949 as a recess appointment.[55] She "was a last-minute choice" after "the President was bombarded by letter, wire and telephone, and personally by representatives of women's organizations all over the country, who were backing the candidacy of Mrs. Matthews."[56] Matthews was the first woman to serve as a federal district judge and she faced blatant sexism on the bench. As one district judge commented on her appointment, while "'Mrs. Matthews would be a good judge,' there was 'just one thing wrong: she's a woman.'"[57] Judge Matthews would remain the only female judge appointed by Truman during his entire presidency. Like Allen, she occupied a token role as she carried out her judicial service. But she would work to change this status, advancing women's legal rights in many ways. Matthews served with organizations like the National Association of Women Lawyers (of which she was president from 1934–35) and drafted laws sponsored by women's groups related to female jury service, equal pay, and elimination of male inheritance preferences.

In addition to the lower-level judicial appointments, Truman was presented with four high court vacancies. His first opportunity occurred when Justice Owen Roberts retired in 1945. Allen's name resurfaced amidst a very long list of men prepared by Truman's soon-to-be-confirmed attorney general, Tom Clark.[58] Responding to the political shift created by Roosevelt's eight appointments, Truman felt significant pressure to nominate a Republican to balance the Court when Justice Roberts retired. This pressure ultimately led to Harold Burton's nomination. When Chief Justice Harlan Stone died the following year, Truman's first instinct was to elevate Justice Robert Jackson to chief justice. However, there was conflict behind the scenes between Jackson and the other justices. Concerned that the promotion of Jackson might divide the Court, he ultimately nominated Fred Vinson, then secretary of the treasury.

Truman's appointment sealed the fate of any female until his departure, as Chief Justice Vinson was adamantly opposed to the presence of a woman. India Edwards later reflected, "I tell you we would have had a woman on the Supreme Court if it hadn't been that Fred Vinson vetoed it."[59] Specifically referencing Florence Allen as a possible candidate, Edwards recalled:

[W]hen there was a vacancy on the Supreme Court I went over and talked to the President about appointing Florence Allen to the Supreme Court and he said, "Well, I'm willing. I'd be glad to. I think we ought to have a woman." And he was perfectly sincere. He really did feel that we should have women serving more and more. He said, "But I'll have to talk to the Chief Justice about it and see what he thinks." Then he had

Matt call me and I went over to the office and he said, "No, the Justices don't want a woman. They say they couldn't sit around with their robes off and their feet up and discuss their problems." I said, "They could if they wanted to."[60]

Years later, Justice Ginsburg reflected on the outcome of President Truman's nomination efforts in much the same way: "President Truman was discouraged by the negative reaction of the Chief Justice (Fred Vinson) and the associate justices Vinson consulted. Allen had gained universal respect for her intelligence and dedicated hard work. But the Brethren feared that a woman's presence would inhibit conference deliberations where, with shirt collars open and sometimes shoes off, they decided the great legal issues of the day."[61] Breaking with gendered traditions proved too much for Truman.

Justice Murphy died in 1949, providing another vacancy. At the time, Murphy held the Court's unofficial "Catholic" seat before his unexpected death, as did his predecessor, Pierce Butler. Truman broke with tradition in his nomination of a non-Catholic, Tom C. Clark, his own attorney general who had vetted previous nominees including the shortlisted Allen. He ignored political pressure to appoint a woman. Although women, including those influential in the Democratic Party, readily promoted Allen for these vacancies along the way, their voices never amassed enough political pressure to sway Truman.

When Wiley Rutledge, a Democrat appointed by Roosevelt, died just a few months later in September 1949, Justice Burton was once again the only Republican on the Court, and, after the death of Murphy, there was still no Catholic justice. Many people surrounding Truman urged him to nominate someone to fill one of the two gaps (if not both). Again, he departed from tradition—though not the gendered one—and instead nominated Sherman Minton, an atheist Democrat, to reward the loyalty he had shown to Truman earlier in his career.[62] Judicial appointments at that time were essentially an extension of the "old boys' club" to which Judge Allen clearly did not belong.

In 1953, Dwight D. Eisenhower was elected president, and just nine months into his term, he had to appoint a new chief justice to the Supreme Court upon the death of Fred Vinson. After two Democratic presidents, the judiciary was still heavily Democratic. Eisenhower chose former governor of California Earl Warren, a Republican known for his liberal views. Warren would go on to lead the Court in its landmark decision in *Brown v. Board of Education*, which ruled public school segregation unconstitutional and ushered in the era of the fight for civil rights.[63] The president used a recess appointment to appoint Warren, a tool infrequently used in the past but deployed two more times by Eisenhower. The following year, in October 1954, Justice Robert H. Jackson died, and Eisenhower nominated John Marshall Harlan. Harlan's nomination was heavily influenced by Attorney General Herbert Brownell, who was so determined to have Harlan nominated that he did not even compile a list of nominees after the death of Jackson.

Justice Minton retired two years later, in October 1956. After Minton's retirement, Eisenhower expressed a desire to restore the "Catholic seat." He also wanted to maintain his expressed belief that the Court should remain neutral and told Brownell to include Democrats in a list of possible nominees. William Brennan, a Catholic and a Democrat, met Eisenhower's conditions, and he was ultimately nominated, again via a recess appointment. Next, Justice Stanley Reed retired in February 1957. Eisenhower nominated Charles Evans Whittaker to fill this vacancy. (Whittaker assumed his role on the Court, but soon called Attorney General William Rogers and complained of being overwhelmed by the job, even expressing a desire to quit.) When Harold Burton retired in October 1958 due to health issues, Eisenhower nominated Potter Stewart, who was just forty-three years old, via a third recess appointment. As with the earlier Harlan nomination, Eisenhower initially relied heavily on his attorney general to come up with names for judicial vacancies. But in 1958, he became more engaged in the process himself and asked that Attorney General Rogers loop him in to the selection of a new judge before bringing him a formal recommendation.

Although he decided to take a hands-on approach to his federal bench nominations, Eisenhower only wanted to nominate justices to the Supreme Court who "reflect[ed] a middle-of-the-road political and governmental philosophy."[64] In this way, he asked Rogers not to consider any individuals whose legal or philosophical views were too extreme. Eisenhower did not appear to have a sophisticated understanding of the role of the courts, as evidenced by his reliance on his attorney general not just in producing nominees, but also in explaining recent decisions of the Supreme Court and their consequences. In an effort to prevent politics from entering the appointments process, Eisenhower requested that the American Bar Association (ABA) play a role in vetting judicial candidates. Beginning in 1953, an independent judicial committee formed by the ABA began rating nominees. Some presidents relied upon the ABA rating process more than others, and its role in this process became yet another obstacle for female candidates.

During President Eisenhower's tenure, the Republican National Committee published a report, *Women in the Judicial Service*, noting that the only judicial office in which a woman had not served was the United States Supreme Court. Despite this reality, Eisenhower did not respond to pressure "for a token appointment of a woman to a major constitutional court."[65] This might be explained in part by differences in the role of women within the respective political parties: "Women seemed to have less clout within the Republican president's party than they had had with Democrats under Roosevelt and Truman."[66]

Our research did not uncover documentation of Allen being seriously considered by Eisenhower like we found with the three presidents who preceded him. The references we did uncover simply described support for her generally or efforts to persuade Eisenhower to appoint her to the Court. "But even into the 1950s, Allen's supporters did not give up: a large group of female lawyers (most of them lesbians—since they apparently felt most deeply about the issue) continued to urge President Eisenhower to appoint Florence Allen as the first female Supreme Court justice."[67]

When Allen retired from the Sixth Circuit in 1959, there was no effort made to fill her vacancy with another woman. The only judicial appointment of a woman by Eisenhower was that of Mary Donlon to the U.S. Customs Court. The *New York Times* featured Judge Donlon's appointment on the "woman's page," connoting a lack of seriousness. Rather than appearing next to political matters or breaking news of the day, the announcement found its place with articles about fashion and wedding engagements.[68] The inroads into judicial politics made by Allen at that time were not enough to elevate the accomplishments of women in the judiciary (and presumably in other fields) beyond the pages dedicated to stereotypically feminine interests.

* * *

Florence Allen's professional accomplishments are rivaled by few. She exists among a select group of lawyers whose hard work and intellect propelled her into prestigious positions throughout her career. Her success is even more significant given the historical context in which she lived, a time when white middle- and upper-class women and men occupied separate spheres, and women were excluded from professional life. Allen defied such rigid categories. She explained, "I don't cook, or sew, or shop for the simple reason that I haven't the time or energy for these things, any more than men judges have."[69] Given the historical timeframe in which Allen's career flourished, her success is somewhat shocking, as she did not fit into a typical heterosexual stereotype. At that time, however, "[s]ingle career women living and working, especially in careers like law that were the domain of men, were not thought to be homosexual but rather asexual."[70] She not only defied gendered expectations in terms of her education, work, and position in public life, but she also pushed back against the "proper" role of woman as wife and mother. Allen was neither. Yet, as she ascended into roles previously reserved for men, she was threatening perhaps in part because she appeared to be, in the words of one historian, "genderless."[71]

Allen achieved the final "first" of her career in 1958, when she became the first woman to hold the role of chief of a federal appellate court, an honor bestowed shortly before she retired from active judicial status. Although Allen unquestionably carved out a path for women in law to follow, her success remained anomalous for years to come. There was not one additional woman placed on a presidential shortlist when subsequent vacancies arose until decades later. Allen died in 1966.

2

The Shortlists before the First Nominee

SOIA MENTSCHIKOFF, SYLVIA BACON, MILDRED LILLIE,
CARLA HILLS, AND CORNELIA KENNEDY

... survey the field, and don't exclude women from your list.[1]
—President Gerald Ford to Attorney General Edward Levi
on selecting a nominee for the Supreme Court, 1975

Nearly three decades passed and twenty-seven Supreme Court vacancies occurred between the time Florence Allen's name appeared on Roosevelt's memorandum in 1937 and the nomination of Sandra Day O'Connor in 1981, all filled with men. In 1962, Soia Mentschikoff made the list prepared by an assistant attorney general in John F. Kennedy's administration and again later that same year for a vacancy that arose during Lyndon B. Johnson's presidency. In 1971, Sylvia Bacon and Mildred Lillie both landed on Richard Nixon's shortlist submitted for vetting to the American Bar Association. In 1975, Gerald Ford included Sylvia Bacon, Carla Hills, and Cornelia Kennedy on his shortlist.

The shortlisting of the women from Allen to O'Connor set the stage for future female representation on the Court. Several forces helped drive change, including pressure induced by educational institutions, civil rights organizations, media coverage, and the women closest to the presidents—their advisers, daughters, and wives. The shortlisting processes of Presidents Kennedy, Johnson, Nixon, and Ford are as compelling as the stories of the women who made it onto their lists, and both the presidential and the personal histories are explored in this chapter.

The Shortlists: Kennedy, Johnson, Nixon, and Ford

Kennedy (in office 1961–63)

John F. Kennedy was the first president to make an explicit, public promise to include female candidates in his selection of judges, pledging to "choose men and women of unquestioned ability"[2] as he signed a new law that resulted in the creation of seventy-three federal judgeships on May 19, 1961. But that promise was met with the selection of only one woman. That same year, Kennedy appointed Sarah Hughes to the United States District Court for the Northern District of Texas, making her the third woman to ever serve on a federal court. (It was Hughes who later administered the presidential oath to Lyndon B. Johnson in Dallas after Lee Harvey Oswald assassinated Kennedy.)

Kennedy faced two opportunities to fill Supreme Court vacancies during his brief presidency. The first occurred when Charles Evans Whittaker announced his retirement in March 1962. Nicholas Katzenbach, an assistant attorney general in the Office of Legal Counsel, prepared a list of potential names along with then Deputy Attorney General Byron White. Katzenbach included the name of Soia Mentschikoff.[3] He placed her among the "most serious candidates" and described her as "an outstanding woman."[4] Katzenbach knew her well, having taught with her on the faculty at the University of Chicago Law School. (A similar Chicago connection occurred decades later when President Obama nominated Elena Kagan. The two were also faculty colleagues at the University of Chicago in the 1990s. We return to Kagan's nomination in chapter four.) As it turned out, White himself was selected to fill the vacancy. As unusual as it might seem for the individual responsible for vetting candidates to be selected himself, White has not been the only member of an administration to be selected for the Court in this way. This happened with Roosevelt's nominees, and recurs again later in the book with the nominations of William Rehnquist and Harriet Miers.

The second Kennedy vacancy occurred when Felix Frankfurter retired on August 23, 1962, following a stroke. Kennedy nominated Secretary of Labor Arthur Goldberg to fill the opening without much, if any, consideration of other candidates. The vacancy was seen as a "Jewish seat," having been held by Benjamin Cardozo before Frankfurter. As of early 2020, eight of the justices who have served on the Court since its inception have been Jewish; two of the eight have been women. (While presidents have been reluctant to preserve a seat for gender, they have taken into account geography, political affiliation, race, and religion when selecting their nominees in order to achieve some semblance of balance and representation.)

Johnson (in office 1963–69)

Though President Johnson was known for approaching appointments with a single candidate in mind, his staff still prepared shortlists for Supreme Court vacancies. The first seat Johnson filled belonged to Arthur Goldberg, whom Johnson enticed to retire by offering him the role of ambassador to the United Nations. Goldberg apparently believed the president would reappoint him to the Court after service with the United Nations, though that never occurred. He resigned from the Court on July 25, 1965. Katzenbach, who became deputy attorney general after White was confirmed to the Court, again shortlisted Mentschikoff, describing her as "the only woman worth of consideration for appointment to the Supreme Court."[5] Instead, Johnson's close adviser, or as some said, "crony," Abe Fortas was confirmed easily on August 11, 1965,[6] though he would become quite a controversial figure over time.

With Tom Clark's retirement in 1967, Johnson tapped civil rights lawyer and then–Solicitor General Thurgood Marshall, who became the first African American to join the Court. Lady Bird Johnson pressed for a female candidate, stating that "Lyndon has done so much" for African Americans, so "why not indeed fill the vacancy with a woman."[7] Of course, her husband could have selected a qualified nominee who was both black and female. Jewel Lafontant, for example, would have been more than qualified, having argued and won a case before the U.S. Supreme Court in 1963.[8] She served many years as an assistant U.S. attorney for the Northern District of Illinois after being the first black woman to graduate from the University of Chicago Law School in 1946. (Nixon reportedly was later intrigued by the idea of nominating her to the Court, though he never placed her on his shortlist. He did, however, go on to appoint Lafontant to the Department of Justice as the deputy solicitor general in 1973.)

When Chief Justice Earl Warren expressed his intention to retire in 1968, Johnson hoped to promote Fortas into this leadership position. Homer Thornberry, appointed by Johnson in 1965 as a member of the U.S. Court of Appeals for the Fifth Circuit, was announced as the nominee to fill the Fortas seat. But Fortas's nomination for chief justice was withdrawn amidst a scandal about ethics issues involving bribery and illegal wiretapping, rendering Thornberry's appointment moot. Fortas then resigned, and his seat remained unfilled for most of the 1969–70 term until President Nixon took office. Though Johnson did appoint the first African American woman to a federal court, placing Constance Baker Motley onto the U.S. District Court for the Southern District of New York in 1966, his legacy would not involve putting a woman on the Supreme Court.

Nixon (in office 1969–74)

Four vacancies fell to Nixon during the years from his inauguration in 1969 to his resignation after the Watergate scandal in 1974. Two of the seats needed to be filled as soon as he entered office—a chief justice to replace Warren and an associate justice to replace Fortas. He immediately appointed Warren E. Burger as chief justice, who was sworn in on June 23, 1969. (Burger had been appointed by Eisenhower to the United States Court of Appeals for the D.C. Circuit in 1956.) Nixon next turned to filling the Fortas seat, which, despite the urgency, would remain vacant for nearly a year. His first choice, U.S. Court of Appeals for the Fourth Circuit Chief Judge Clement Haynsworth, was rejected by the Senate in a vote of 55–45 because of concerns about racism and financial conflicts of interest. Nixon next nominated Fifth Circuit Judge G. Harrold Carswell, but in the face of allegations of racism and opposition to women's rights, he too was rejected by the Senate in a vote of 51–45. The third nomination would prove the charm, with Harry Blackmun's unanimous confirmation in May 1970.[9] The idea of placing a woman on the Court, however, was not seriously contemplated during this initial set of nominations in the Nixon administration.

In the aftermath of the struggle to fill the Fortas seat, Nixon tasked Attorney General John Mitchell with the job of gauging interest among particular favored candidates when two more vacancies occurred in 1971 with the retirements of John Marshall Harlan and Hugo Black. Nixon faced increasing pressure on multiple fronts to place a woman on the Court—including the press, women's organizations, academics, government officials, his wife Pat, and daughters Julie and Tricia. Law school deans from across the country wrote Nixon to support the appointment of a woman. Even former Supreme Court Justices Tom Clark and Arthur Goldberg acknowledged that it was time.

Nixon himself did not share the view that a woman belonged on the Court. He told Attorney General Mitchell in the Oval Office: "I don't think a woman should be in any government job whatever. I mean, I really don't. The reason why I do is mainly because they are erratic. And emotional. Men are erratic and emotional, too, but the point is a woman is more likely to be."[10] Despite his personal views, he nonetheless understood the political value of nominating a woman for the Court, believing that it could help him pick up one or two percentage points in the upcoming 1972 election. He explained to Mitchell, "I lean to a woman only because, frankly, I think at this time, John, we got to pick up every half a percentage point we can."[11] His observation emphasizes a lesson that Florence Allen knew well: the votes of women count.

Following the practice established under Eisenhower, Nixon decided to send his shortlist to the ABA Standing Committee on the Federal Judiciary for vetting. He was the first president to include not one but two women on this list. He wanted independent evaluations to play a role in the process of evaluating the fitness of his potential nominees, but also counted on the ABA to deal with his "woman problem." The committee included a representative from each judicial circuit and was tasked with rating nominees as "extremely well-qualified," "well-qualified," "qualified," or "not qualified." Among the list of six names, Sylvia Bacon and Mildred Lillie appeared with Robert Byrd, Charles Clark, Herschel Friday, and Paul Roney.

Lillie and Friday were the favored candidates. Though it was supposed to be a confidential process, the shortlist was leaked to the media, with all six names appearing in the headlines. Concern arose over the idea that the ABA committee—all white men—might not support Lillie.[12] Despite her objectively excellent qualifications, including two decades on the bench,[13] the ABA committee voted Lillie "unqualified" 11–1 and Friday somewhat more favorably as "not opposed" after a 6–6 vote, even though he had no judicial experience at all.[14] Because of the non-qualified rating on Lillie, the president's staff believed it was not even worth seeking an ABA rating for Bacon.[15]

After the leak, the Nixon administration "abruptly terminated tonight its agreement to check the judicial qualifications of potential Supreme Court nominees" with the ABA and instead decided to first announce the nominees and then allow vetting.[16] The media reported that Nixon found the "talent pool small" for women, thus necessitating the nomination of two more men.[17] Behind the scenes, it was known that even with Nixon's personal views about women on the Court, he intended to nominate Lillie but for the ABA's disapproval. Yet, it turned out to be the result Nixon hoped for after hearing that Chief Justice Burger "wrote [Mitchell] a three-or four-page letter . . . letting it be known he [was] not anxious to have a woman."[18] "No more anxious than I am," replied

Nixon, observing that the ABA "may take us off the hook on the damn thing."[19]

Nixon was determined to have his subsequent candidates succeed. In the face of the ABA's double-rejection of Friday and Lillie, he selected Lewis Powell, a corporate law partner at the Virginia firm Hunton & Williams and past president of the ABA, as one of the nominees. For the other, Nixon took a page out of prior presidents' playbooks and selected a member of the team vetting potential nominees, Assistant Attorney General William Rehnquist. Once again, an individual charged with vetting candidates became the nominee—Rehnquist carried Lillie's suitcase when she interviewed with Nixon for the Court and went on to fill the seat that should have been hers.

The media subsequently described the deflated hopes felt by women when Nixon announced more men for the Court, as Dorothy McCardle wrote in the *Washington Post*: "Disappointment, laced with resignation, was the mood last night among 3,000 Republican women over President Nixon's failure to appoint the first woman to the U.S. Supreme Court."[20] An article in the *New York Times* reflected on the lack of women lawyers available as candidates, speculating that women were not hired or promoted by law firms for a variety of blatantly stereotyped reasons. These included the fear that they would just get pregnant and quit working, assumptions that juries did not like women because "they are too shrill," that women were not tough enough to handle the "strain of litigation" and inevitably "they fall apart," and because "[c]orporate law work requires long trips out of town, and long sessions at night in hotel rooms, writing briefs and otherwise preparing cases. The partners' wives would not stand for women in such jobs."[21]

At the Convention of the National Federation of Republican Women, Nixon made his annoucement of Rehnquist and Powell as nominees. In the context of his remarks, Nixon acknowledged the potential of appointing a female justice: "While I know that a great number in this audience, including my wife, felt very strongly that not only should a woman be considered but that a woman should be appointed, let me say that at least we have made a beginning, and there will be a woman on the Supreme Court in time."[22] Nixon wanted to have it both ways, giving the politically advantageous nod to women by putting two on his shortlist but preserving the male-only world that the chief justice (among others) preferred.

Women's rights organizations and political leaders quickly critiqued Nixon's choices. The National Women's Political Caucus (which had opposed Lillie) called him out for refusing to meet with them to discuss female nominees or to even acknowledge their correspondence. After the release of Rehnquist's and Powell's names, the caucus sent Nixon a telegram noting "the empty lip-service which appears to have marked the Administration's attitude toward consideration of distinguished women for the Supreme Court vacancies."[23] Senator Strom Thurmond, then a member of the Senate Judiciary Committee, observed that Nixon "had let the American Bar Association exercise a veto on his choices," recognizing that "the President was seriously considering a woman."[24] Thurmond expressed regret: "I am sorry he let the American Bar Association have a veto on the Court. I would have liked to have seen a woman. There are plenty of well-qualified women."[25]

Patricia Roberts Harris, who would become the first African American woman to serve in a presidential cabinet both as secretary of housing and urban development and secretary of health, education and welfare under the Carter administration, reflected, at the time, on the lack of pipeline opportunities: "We have generally not been permitted to achieve the external signs of eminence that are considered qualifications for the Supreme Court. We are not part of the little group that is asked to publish. We are not partners in the large law firms from which Secretaries of State are drawn. Women haven't been considered—so they aren't considered."[26] Mary Kelly, who had recently graduated from New York University Law School when Nixon made his selections, commented, "The idea that women could step into their shoes is still alien to them."[27] She further observed, "The legal world is still run by men who have no peer experience with women. They went to Harvard when there were no women students there or to other prestige schools when there were a token few. They had no women professors. They view the entire legal world as male."[28]

Clearly, Nixon was no fan of equality for women on the Court as an aspiration in and of itself. As he said when discussing Thurgood Marshall's presence on the Court: "There's a hell of a lot of stuff that has to do with women. I'm not for it. I don't think women should ever be allowed to vote even," but "if we say the Negro viewpoint should be on the court, why not the woman's?"[29] At best, he seemed to view the inclusion of women on his shortlist as a politically expedient move to capture votes and quell the rising pressure from women in the public and in his own home. But doing anything more, including making an actual appointment, was not viewed as "much of a political plus," in Nixon's words.[30]

Even so, Nixon carved a notch toward progress as the first president to place two women on his shortlist simultaneously and to make the list public. Admittedly, it is disheartening that the shortlisting of two women might be deemed progress and yet, given the historical framework, it was quite extraordinary. Nixon's record on filling Supreme Court seats likewise is notable for his uncanny ability to nominate male candidates that were rejected by the Senate, even in the face of imminently qualified female options. Nixon also laid some groundwork for future progress by assigning staff assistant Barbara Hackman Franklin to the task of adding more women to upper levels of the federal government. In an interview about her time working for Nixon, she reflected that excitement brewed about a woman nominee, but "[t]he crucial thing was that Nixon wanted someone who was philosophically compatible with his point of view. And many of the women in the judiciary were Democrats and/or were not strict constructionists. Finding candidates became a problem."[31] Nixon's fidelity to "strict constructionists" or "conservatism" became a proxy for sexism that continued to haunt the Republican Party decades later, most notably in the Miers nomination, which we take up in chapter four.

Ford (in office 1974–77)

President Gerald Ford encountered only one vacancy during his time in office. Justice William Douglas sent a resignation letter to Ford after months of illness, and Ford turned to Attorney General Edward Levi and White House counsel Phil Buchen for help. "Survey the field," he told Levi, "and don't exclude women from your list."[32] Levi offered a dozen names, which were eventually narrowed "down to five or six names, including Department of Housing and Urban Development Secretary Carla Hills and Detroit Federal District Court Judge Cornelia Kennedy."[33]

As with Nixon, family members, politicians, and women's rights organizations called for Ford to select a female nominee and flooded his office with telegrams and letters. Democratic U.S. Representative Charles Rangel, then chair of the Congressional Black Caucus, wrote Ford asking him to appoint a black woman to sit on the Court as "a most important contribution to our progress as a nation."[34] Additionally, Rangel asked Ford to include the National Bar Association, a historically black organization, in the vetting done by the ABA. Republican representative Ralph S. Regula also wrote to Ford, urging him to consider a woman for the vacancy: "My reasoning for advocating the nomination of a woman to the High Court is based upon my conviction that the time has indeed come to recognize women as equal, not only in the traditional setting of marriage, but in our governmental institutions as well. Throughout the country, there are many well-qualified women who could make thoughtful contributions in the interpretation of the nation's laws."[35] Regula further noted that "there are six women who are currently serving as federal judges. In addition, there are thousands of female lawyers, many of whom, through their education as well as experience, possess the capacity and stature needed in the nation's highest court."[36] Vernon C. Loen, deputy assistant to the president, offered Regula only a cursory reply: "The President has stated that the appointment will be based on the qualifications of the individual regardless of sex."[37]

Ford's exchange of correspondence with Audrey Rowe Colom, the first black female chair of the National Women's Political Caucus, reflects a typical tension in shortlisting, where leaders pay lip service to equality and diversity but fail to act. In July 1975, Ford wrote to Colom congratulating her on her new role as chair: "Our Nation has come a great distance since 1920 and the Nineteenth Amendment. Still, we have much to do to insure [sic] that equal rights, responsibilities, and rewards are really for every American woman."[38] But Ford subsequently stonewalled Colom on her push for a female justice. In the wake of the Douglas retirement announcement, she repeatedly contacted Ford to no avail. In November 1975, she sent a telegram advocating the appointment of a woman to the Supreme Court. She wrote, "There are many exceptionally qualified woman jurists who would bring experience, knowledge and intellect to the Court. We urge you to consult with womens [sic] groups, congresswomen and legal experts before you exercise your awesome power of appointment."[39] She promised to prepare a list of candidates and followed up the next day with a list of legal scholars, judges, and women in public life.[40] Her list of sixteen names included three of our shortlisted women—Hills, Kennedy, and Mentschikoff— and one who would, eventually, surmount the shortlist—Ruth Bader Ginsburg. Like Congressman Regula, Colum received only a brief note from Phil Buchen, counsel to the president, thanking her for expressing her views.[41]

Ford built on Nixon's efforts and formalized the process for gathering names of qualified women to appoint to senior government roles, even if not for the Court. Anne Armstrong, named by Nixon as counselor to the president with cabinet rank in 1973, remained with Ford during the early days of his transition. She held numerous responsibilities in her role, including creating the first Office of Women's Programs, later known as the White House Council on Women and Girls until it was discontinued by President Trump in 2017. Patricia Lindh joined Ford's administration in 1974, first as a special assistant to Anne Armstrong. (She would go on to lead the Office of Women's Programs when Armstrong became U.S.

ambassador to the United Kingdom.) Armstrong resigned in November 1974, leaving Ford's cabinet devoid of women until Carla Hills became the HUD secretary in February 1975.

Among the responsibilities of the Office of Women's Programs was an *official* role whereby the Office compiled information on qualified women to fill senior leadership positions in the federal government. In that capacity, Lindh sent to Ford's personnel director Doug Bennett "an unrefined list" of eighteen women on November 13, 1975, "for information and consideration" to be included on the president's shortlist, including from our study here Sylvia Bacon, Cynthia Holcomb Hall, Carla Hills, Cornelia Kennedy, Soia Mentschikoff, and Susie Sharp.[42] The next day she would send an additional name—Sandra O'Connor, Superior Court Judge of the Court of Maricopa, Arizona.[43] Lindh also wrote the president directly on November 17, 1975, noting that the attorney general's list of candidates not only omitted a female candidate, but included two or three men opposed to the Equal Rights Amendment which, in her words, "really puts us in double jeopardy."[44] Meanwhile, she observed that "[l]etters and phone calls have been coming in from women's organizations and from leaders throughout the country urging the appointment of a woman to the Supreme Court."[45] Like Colom, Lindh tried to persuade Ford to make good on platitudes about women: "You have been forthright in your many statements concerning the status of women in our society. International Women's Year and our Bicentennial have served to highlight both the achievements and aspirations of women. I realize that you have many factors to consider in making this appointment. But, all else being equal, your nomination of a properly qualified woman for the Supreme Court would be appropriate and just."[46]

Ford resumed the practice (abandoned by Nixon in the wake of the Friday/Lillie debacle) of submitting a list of names to the ABA for review before announcing the nominee. A list of ten names was sent, reportedly including Carla Hills[47] and Cornelia Kennedy.[48] Ultimately, President Ford selected John Paul Stevens, who was confirmed unanimously by the Senate in December 1975, and served until retiring in 2010. His selection angered Colom and the National Women's Political Caucus, who continued their letter writing campaign:

> Your failure to nominate a woman to the Supreme Court of the United States has disappointed a generation of women who are striving to make "equal justice under law" a living reality. The Court will not be truly representative of the American people until a woman serves in the constitutionally unique position of U.S. Supreme Court Justice. You might have played a significant part in this historical process by selecting a woman for this position. We are dismayed that instead, you chose the path of political expediency. We intend to continue our efforts to assure that women are included at all levels of our government and we expect you to appoint more women to major positions within your administration as more opportunities arise in the coming year.[49]

Colom followed up with a telegram expressing concern over Stevens and his reliance upon the Fourteenth Amendment's Equal Protection Clause to do the work of what would be guaranteed under an Equal Rights Amendment:

> The courts have not categorically declared women, like blacks, to be a suspect classification which would mandate the Court's close scrutiny of sex-based discrimination laws. Accordingly, some claims of sex-based discrimination, relying on the 14th Amendment protection, have been lost before the Supreme Court. These cases would most likely be turned around by the enactment of the ERA. Judge Stevens' indifference to the most significant pieces of legislation concerning women today is an affront to the women of this country. We urge the committee to examine him at great lengths to determine if he has sufficient sensitivity to the legal needs of the 53 percent of this country's population who are women.[50]

A letter from the president's director of correspondence dodged her concerns and justified the selection of Stevens because of his "careful and thorough consideration of a wide range of views" and "outstanding legal career . . . [with] personal and professional qualities of the highest order."[51]

Betty Ford expressed similar disappointment but commented to the press that she was "confident that he picked the most capable and best prepared person."[52] When asked whether a woman should have been selected, ABA president Lawrence Walsh conceded, "It seems to me that the President should pick the best person available and the sex of the person should not be a factor; if it's a woman, appoint a woman; if it's a man, appoint a man."[53] Elaine Latourell, vice president of the National Organization for Women, "said she was 'basically pleased' by the nomination although NOW had submitted its own list of qualified women candidates . . . 'I'm confident the Court will continue to recognize the injustices women have suffered . . . women don't have anything to fear because our issues stand up to intellectual scrutiny.'"[54]

Latourell's observation proved prescient, at least to the extent *Roe v. Wade*[55] can be viewed as a measure of support for women's rights. The men who made it off the shortlists of Johnson, Nixon, and Ford would help form the 7–2 majority legalizing abortion in 1973. As then, men can certainly represent women's interests, but this is not always the case. As Ruth Bader Ginsburg noted in an interview following the oral arguments of *Safford Unified School District v. Redding*, none of the men on the bench know what it is like to be a thirteen-year-old girl.[56] The case involved a strip-search of a young female student while at school. Although the Court ultimately sided with the female student, this might not have occurred without the perspective of Justice Ginsburg. We return to the difference a woman's perspective makes on the Court in chapter seven. But first, it is important to reflect on the personal and professional aspects of the women's lives given the time and sociopolitical context within which their shortlisting arose.

TABLE 2.1. Women Shortlisted for the Supreme Court before Reagan

Name	Birth-Death	Presidential Shortlist	Law School	Significant Professional Achievement
Florence Allen	1884–1966	Hoover Roosevelt Truman	New York University; University of Chicago	Judge, Ohio Supreme Court and Sixth Circuit Court of Appeals
Soia Mentschikoff	1915–84	Kennedy Johnson	Columbia	First female professor, Harvard and University of Chicago, and dean, Miami University School of Law
Sylvia Bacon	1931–	Nixon	Harvard	Judge, Superior Court for District of Columbia
Mildred Lillie	1915–2002	Nixon	University of California, Berkeley	Presiding judge, California Court of Appeals
Carla Hills	1934–	Ford	Yale	HUD secretary
Cornelia Kennedy	1923–2014	Ford	University of Michigan	Judge, Sixth Circuit Court of Appeals

The Women Shortlisted between Allen and O'Connor:
SOIA MENTSCHIKOFF, MILDRED LILLIE, SYLVIA BACON, CARLA HILLS, AND CORNELIA KENNEDY

Revisiting the history of shortlists prepared by Kennedy, Johnson, Nixon, and Ford is valuable in and of itself to cultivate an understanding of the dynamics at play when a particular individual is or is not selected, as well as when an excluded group seeks access to power. But what of the women themselves? Much like Allen, each woman shortlisted pre-O'Connor was a formidable trailblazer in her own right. Their individual and collective stories offer insight into ways women continue to remain on the shortlist rather than be selected from it. We introduce them individually in the pages that follow, and in part two delve into greater detail about shared experiences that remain relevant to women today.

Soia Mentschikoff

Soft spoken and informal in appearance, she could be devas-
tating in legal dispute, crushing her opponents with precise
reasoning.[57]
—Reporter for the *New York Times* on Mentschikoff's death,
1984

Soia Mentschikoff had planned to become a lawyer since she was a child.
Born in 1915, she recalled how, when she was just twelve years old, a
"girlfriend and I put down what we wanted to be on a piece of paper and
sealed it in an envelope. Years later, after I moved and was in law school,
I came across the envelope and opened it. The piece of paper was still
inside and mine said: 'I want to be a lawyer.'"[58]

The same year Allen's name appeared on Roosevelt's list, 1937, Soia
Mentschikoff graduated from Columbia Law School at age twenty-

FIGURE 2.1. Soia Mentschikoff
(Credit: Stephen Lewellyn, public
domain)

two. (Recall that Columbia was Allen's first choice, but at the time, as a woman, she was prohibited from attending.) As a student, she met the man who would later become her lover and husband, the prominent legal scholar Karl Llewellyn, though at the time they met he was married to someone else. After graduation, she practiced law at Scandrett, Tuttle and Chalaire in New York City from 1937 to 1941.[59] The public was fascinated by the novelty of a female lawyer, and in 1940 the *New York Post* ran a multi-page article about her daily life titled "Dates, Clothes and Play Relevant, Not Material," including a full-length photo of Mentschikoff in a ballgown.[60] Part two of the book further examines the *Post* article and similarly sexist media coverage of the other shortlisted women.

In 1945, Mentschikoff became one of the first female partners on Wall Street at the firm Spence, Windels, Walser, Hotchkiss and Angell, where she remained until 1949. While there, she served as an assistant reporter for the American Law Institute, aiding Llewellyn in writing the Uniform Revised Sales Act, and then as associate chief reporter, again working with Llewellyn on the Uniform Commercial Code (UCC). Though associate chief in name, she was widely thought to be the primary driver for the implementation of the UCC. The two married in 1946 and both began teaching at Harvard Law School in 1947. Her first appointment at Harvard was as a visitor; she became a professor in 1949, three years before women were even admitted as students. Harvard Law School's announcement of her appointment stated that "it is her specialized professional competence rather than her sex which will entitle her to sit in the chair once ornamented by the great Williston," referencing Samuel Williston, an acclaimed scholar of commercial law.[61]

Mentschikoff remained at Harvard until 1951, when she left to become the first female professor at the University of Chicago. She was hired along with Llewellyn at a time where simultaneous "hiring of a husband and wife on the same faculty had not as yet been done by any major law school."[62] Dean Edward Levi set out to recruit Llewellyn as his faculty's "most wanted hire," but soon learned when telephoning references that "Karl would be fine, but Soia might even be better."[63] Though she had "made a greater impact than her husband" as an academic at Harvard Law School, Chicago's anti-nepotism rules prevented hiring both of them as tenured faculty. Thus, she was given only an untenured position as "professional lecturer" and hired at "a sum very close to the top salary" but not equal to that of Llewellyn, who "was to be given the 'top salary' even higher than" the dean of the law school.[64] By the 1960s, "[r]umor had spread that she and Karl . . . were the highest paid law professors in the nation."[65] We explore this sort of influence from lovers and partners in the careers of the shortlisted women more fully in part two.

After teaching at the University of Chicago, Mentschikoff was named the first permanent female dean of Miami Law School in 1974, making her the second ever female dean of an accredited law school.[66] She also became the first female president of the Association of American Law Schools in 1974. She was often described as "one of the best legal minds in the country" with a "personality as formidable as her intellect."[67]

Mildred Lillie

People will see that she's not one of these frigid bitches, you know?[68]
—Attorney General John Mitchell on his interview with Justice Mildred Lillie, October 11, 1971

That's right, I know, the terrible ones.[69]
—President Richard Nixon's response to Mitchell

I couldn't have lived for going on to 76 years, with my background and all the things that I have done, and my exposure to the critical comments, prejudices, and biases of others,

without being aware of the inequalities suffered by females
from the beginning of recorded history.[70]
—Mildred Lillie, from her oral history

Mildred Lillie was born in 1915, the same year as her shortlisted sister
Soia Mentschikoff. After her parents divorced, she moved from Iowa to
California, where she was raised on her uncle's farm by a single mother
who struggled financially. The home did not have electricity or indoor
bathrooms. Lillie did not have much time for normal childhood activities because she worked to provide financial support and helped cook
family meals. Nevertheless, she excelled in high school, earning a scholarship to the University of California, Berkeley. She majored in political
science and supported herself through various jobs, such as working as
a domestic cook. Lillie's father, from whom she was mostly estranged,
actively discouraged her from going to law school when she wrote to
him to tell him her plans. Ascribing to the ideas of traditional gender
roles, he offered his opinion on her decision: "Well, he wrote to me—I
think it was about the third letter I ever received from him—and told me
what a ridiculous idea it was, that I was on my own, that it was a waste
of money, that all I would do would be to get married and have a batch
of kids, that I would never use my law degree, even if I got through law
school, and that I was wasting my time and I ought to get smart and get
a job. I decided that since I had been living all this time without any help
from him, that I could continue to do so. So, I entered law school."[71]

Lillie remained at Berkeley for law school and graduated in 1938.
Alexander Kidd, Lillie's criminal law professor, referred to her only by
the title "mister."[72] He could not tolerate the presence of women in law
school and therefore rendered them invisible by refusing to acknowledge them in accordance with their gender. Lillie recollected, "He ignored us until he called on us, and if we did not answer correctly, he
became insulting and threw tantrums."[73] Lillie's grades were strong during law school except for the semester when her uncle died—she received one D and one F, according to White House Counsel John Dean

FIGURE 2.2. Mildred Lillie (Credit: Center for Sacramento History, Sacramento Bee Collection, 1983/001/SBPMP05010)

and his assistant David Young, who interviewed her in October 1971 while vetting candidates for the U.S. Supreme Court.[74] After her uncle's death, Lillie supported herself and her mother "by grading international law papers for the Dean while continuing her cooking job. Incidentally, the only other woman in her law school class was 20 years her senior."[75] Reflecting on whether she was discriminated against in law school, Lillie confessed that she had little time to be concerned about discrimination because she was busy studying, working to support herself, and taking care of her mother. She observed, "The fact of the matter was that we three women were largely ignored. No one paid much attention to us or took us seriously."[76]

Lillie's first job out of law school was with the Alameda City Attorney's Office from 1938–39; she then moved to private practice before becoming an assistant U.S. attorney in 1942. She left that position in 1946 to return to private practice, marrying Cameron Lillie in 1947. That same year she was appointed to the Municipal Court, City of Los Angeles in

1947, followed by the Superior Court, County of Los Angeles in 1949. She remained at the Superior Court until 1958, when she was elevated to the California Court of Appeals. Cameron died in 1959, and she later married Alfredo Falcone in 1966, but kept her first husband's name, which was so controversial at the time that Dean and Young asked her about it when they interviewed her for the potential Supreme Court appointment.

Lillie came the closest any woman had before her to being selected for the Supreme Court. Her presence on President Nixon's publicly revealed shortlist garnered both support and controversy. Numerous letters and telegrams poured into the president's office in support of her nomination, including a letter from the Board of Supervisors of Los Angeles County describing her "keen mind which cuts through 'legal entanglements' like a laser beam. She would be considered a conservative. Her good judgment, integrity, stability, fairness, pleasing personality and physical attractiveness make her a 'natural' as your appointee as a first woman to become a United States Supreme Court Justice."[77] A memorandum written by Dean and Young for Attorney General John Mitchell and John Ehrlichman after interviewing her for the nomination stated that they "were reasonably impressed with her as an articulate woman of considerable breadth and experience from a legal as well as a personal point of view."[78] Apparently the men were taken by her appearance much in the same way the author of the New York Times article noted her bathing beauty figure. They observed that "she is a rather handsome woman with excellent hearing; rather large but not overweight."[79] They concluded with a favorable recommendation: "She appears to be a most able woman and [our] impression is that she is not an intellectual lightweight. Her philosophical views of justices have been borne out of experience and are accordingly stern and strict. She is not afraid to dissent, and [we] think confident enough to hold her own on the Court."[80]

But support for Lillie was not universal. A letter signed by more than twenty law professors from the University of California Los Angeles (including only one woman—Barbara Rintala) "strongly opposed the nomination of Justice Lillie" based upon her lack of competence for the Court.[81] Ultimately, the ABA sealed her fate when it deemed her "not qualified."[82] It was widely speculated that Nixon succumbed to pressure to nominate a woman, even though he privately hoped that the ABA would reject her: "Nixon decided that if Lillie's ratings were negative as expected, he could take credit for having considered a woman for the Court and blame the ABA for its low rating, making it impossible for him to go forward with her nomination."[83]

Long after Lillie's shortlisting, John Dean offered an opinion on the ABA's decision: "I later—after Sandra Day O'Connor was selected—I lined up the credentials of these two women and Mildred Lillie was every bit, if not more, qualified to be a Justice than Day O'Connor."[84] Dean elaborated in a radio interview, explaining the disconnect: "But what happened was the American Bar Association at that time was made up of all men and the old boys did not think that it was time for a woman to be on the high court. But the principal person who really objected to Nixon selecting a woman was none other than the Chief Justice himself, Warren Burger, who threatened that he would resign if Nixon put a woman on the court."[85] As Dean observed, reflecting on a conversation with Lillie shortly before her death, "Justice Lillie's five decades on the bench, with 44 years on appellate courts (including an occasional case when she had been designated to sit on the California Supreme Court), resulted in thousands of learned written opinions notable for their intelligence, clarity and logic, further putting the lie to the ABA committee's smear to keep her off the U.S. Supreme Court."[86]

When Lillie died in 2002, she was the longest serving judge for the state of California.

Sylvia Bacon

Bacon probably would appear to be just a little too young. I don't know, what do you think? She isn't by my standards. I wonder if something could be said, John, for appointing a

woman who represents the younger generation, not only a
woman, but the youngest [justice] ever appointed.[87]
—President Nixon to White House counsel John Dean

Born in South Dakota on July 9, 1931, Sylvia Bacon was raised by a family with ties to the Republican Party who published a local paper, the
Watertown Public Opinion. (Though she could not have known this as a
child, the family business would later become an asset during the vetting
process for judicial appointments. Their political ties and publishing
background were discussed favorably in White House memoranda
advocating for her nomination to the Supreme Court.) Bacon flourished
in high school, "almost a 'straight A' student and ranked second in her
class of 138."[88] She was active in extracurricular activities and known to
be "the outstanding debater on the squad, a winner in Declamation, and
a leader in the school's radio club."[89] She also acted in and directed plays,
and served as editor-in-chief of the school newspaper.[90]

Bacon fled the Midwest after high school, graduating from Vassar
College in 1952 with a degree in Economics but maintaining her political
roots. While there, she served as vice-chair of the New York State College Young Republicans. She then attended the London School of Economics for a year. She received her law degree from Harvard Law School
in 1956 and her LLM from Georgetown University Law Center in 1959.[91]
At Harvard, Bacon again pursued political interests as the secretary of
the Harvard Law School Young Republicans.

Judge Burnita Shelton Matthews of the United States District Court
for the District of Columbia hired Bacon as a clerk from 1956–57. (Recall
that Matthews was appointed by President Truman in 1949, the first ever
woman on a federal district court.) Matthews long endured personal
discrimination in the legal profession, including having her application
and dues check rejected by the District of Columbia Bar Association
because she was a woman. Perhaps as a way to fight back against these
sexist practices, she hired only female law clerks during her time as a
federal judge. Matthews went on to become president of the National

FIGURE 2.3. Sylvia Bacon (Credit: Richard M. Nixon Presidential Library, public domain)

Association of Women Lawyers and was undoubtedly influential in Bacon's career trajectory.[92]

Bacon worked at the United States Department of Justice for several years early in her career, where, among other notable accomplishments, she was an author of the District of Columbia's no-knock crime bill, a "controversial crime and court reorganization law."[93] Through her work at the Department of Justice, she earned a reputation of being tough on crime, and was appointed by President Nixon to the Superior Court of the District of Columbia in 1970 at a time of "pressure on the Administration to appoint women to high positions."[94] (Nixon appointed another one of the shortlisted sisters to the federal bench that same year, Cornelia Kennedy.) The Nixon administration considered Bacon for a range of potential judgeships, based upon what an internal memorandum described as "the unusual extremely high qualifications of Miss Bacon to serve as a Federal judge."[95] Among the positions for which she was deemed "qualified to serve" were the U.S. Court of Appeals for the District of Columbia Circuit and the Eighth Circuit (where no woman had ever served), the U.S. District Court for the District of Columbia (where her mentor Matthews served from 1948–68 and Julie Green served at the time Bacon was considered) and for South Dakota (where no woman had ever served), the U.S. Court of Customs and Patent Appeals (where no woman had ever served), and the U.S. Court of Claims (where no woman had ever served).[96] But she was never appointed to any of these roles.

She was also regarded for her work on victims' rights. In 1976, she testified before Congress about the flaws of rape laws:

> Unfortunately, these logically "shaky" rules have had a far-reaching effect on enforcement of the rape laws. Although it is difficult to separate social attitudes, police practices and rules of evidence, many rape victims refuse prosecution because of the potential humiliating inquiry into most personal matters. . . . The number of occasions on which the United States must dismiss prosecutions because the witnesses are most reluctant to come forward are numerous. . . . I daily observe the terror with which women come to the witness stand and the experience they have in the courtroom.[97]

Bacon famously signed the consent order requiring Georgetown University "to give homosexual student groups the same privileges as other student groups."[98] On the bench, Bacon was known as "one of the court's ablest and hardest-working judges," though it was reported in the mid-1980s that she also struggled with a "lengthy period of pain and depression after both legs were broken when she was hit by a car" and "encountered problems trying to care for her seriously ill mother."[99] She underwent treatment for alcoholism in 1986[100] and later returned to the bench, where she served until 1991.

Bacon's name surfaced as one of six potential nominees to the Court when she was just thirty-nine years old.[101] She was widely discussed during the same time that Lillie was also shortlisted by President Nixon, her name appearing among other possible contenders on the front pages of the *New York Times* and *Washington Post*.[102] She was described as having a strong law-and-order background that led her to be seriously considered by Nixon. But she was also critiqued for having "little trial experience,"[103] which hardly seems disqualifying considering that a significant number of justices had minimal or no trial experience prior to their appointments. (O'Connor, for example, had authored only thirty opinions as a state judge, and Kagan had never even served as a judge, when each was nominated.)

Nixon's archives are filled with numerous letters advocating for Bacon's placement on one of the federal courts of appeals and the Supreme Court. Marjorie Longwell, chair of the National Women's Party, praised her extraordinary qualifications:

> We know Judge Bacon to possess an extraordinary dedication and intense loyalty to the law as well as a remarkable capacity for the discernment and application of sound legal principles. Her career reflects her great vitality, industry and courage, and her ability to fulfill responsibility expertly and expeditiously. You realize just as we do that when you create the precedent of naming a woman jurist to the Supreme Court, the eyes of the country will concentrate on your precedent. We are convinced that Judge Bacon would do you honor and would serve on the Court with distinction. She would indeed grace the Court with her poise, dignity and wisdom.[104]

Politicians including Kansas Senator Robert Dole wrote on her behalf, noting her excellent judicial temperament and long history of support for the Republican Party.[105] The archives also include a letter Bacon graciously sent to Nixon in support of Powell and Rehnquist, the men who filled the seat she had been shortlisted for. Nixon responded to her letter, writing back that she was "very kind to write me, expressing such generous support for my nominations."[106]

After being shortlisted for the Court, Bacon was recommended by John Mitchell for the role of associate judge, District of Columbia Court of General Sessions, a new position created by a federal law approved in 1970.[107] Notably, the Standing Committee on Federal Judiciary of the American Bar Association declared her qualified for this position.[108] (Recall that Nixon declined to advance her name after the Lillie debacle with ABA ratings.) Bacon again appeared on a list of Supreme Court candidates prepared for President Ford in filling the Douglas opening, recommended by Pat Lindh,[109] as well as on a "preliminary" list of "strong candidates for review" circulated within the Reagan administration in July 1981.[110] Bacon was the second woman to serve on the ABA Board of Governors, a role she took on in 1988. As she assumed the position, she cautioned the recently formed ABA Commission on Women in the Profession: "Let's not think we are in the mainstream because we have a budgeted commission and a women's caucus. To be in the mainstream we're talking about the House of Delegates, the Board of Governors . . . The ABA should be a leader . . . in the profession by an example."[111] (At that time, no woman had ever presided over the ABA. Roberta Cooper Ramo put her hat in the ring that same year, but did not become the first female president of the ABA until 1995. The first woman of color did not become president until 2015—Paulette Brown.) After leaving the bench, Bacon continued her dedicated service to the legal field, teaching at Columbus School of Law, Catholic University of America, for many years.

Carla Hills

She's willowy, brunette and capable of turning on a Mary Tyler Moore smile. She's also our new secretary of Housing and Urban Development.[112]
—Reporter for the *Los Angeles Times*, 1975

Carla Hills, similar to her predecessors Lillie and Mentschikoff, encountered pervasive sexist commentary based on her appearance that accompanied—and often supplanted—discussions of her professional accomplishments and qualifications. Born in 1934, her childhood nickname was "Butch" because of her tomboy ways.[113] Her family was

FIGURE 2.4. Carla Hills
(Credit: Department of Housing
and Urban Development, public
domain)

affluent, living in Beverly Hills where she attended private school and
excelled in tennis to such an extent that she later became the captain
of the Stanford collegiate team. She graduated from Stanford *magna
cum laude* in 1955. She initially planned to remain at Stanford for law
school, but instead went to Yale on the advice of Carl Spaeth, who was
the dean of the Stanford Law School at the time but nonetheless advised
her to pursue her degree elsewhere.[114] Hills was one of only a handful
of women at Yale Law School when she arrived. Despite her family's
affluence, her father initially refused to pay for law school on the east
coast (he favored Stanford), so Hills paid for law school tuition with her
savings from working summers at Bank of America as a bookkeeper and
teller until her father finally agreed to help her.

When Hills graduated from law school in 1958, there was not one
female partner in a law firm in Los Angeles County. Though she graduated among the top of her class from Yale (twenty-first in a class of

167), she struggled to find employment. "Sorry, there are no 'separate facilities' for women lawyers," was the response she received from one firm.[115] She began her career as an assistant U.S. attorney in Los Angeles, then moved into private practice before eventually becoming the assistant U.S. attorney general for the Civil Division of the Justice Department in 1973. During her early years of law practice, she experienced overt discrimination in court with "some judges who would remark on the fact that they would rather not have a woman in the courtroom."[116]

President Ford appointed Hills as the Housing and Urban Development secretary in 1975, and in this capacity she was the youngest person (let alone the only woman) ever to occupy that role. Her four children ranged in ages from four to thirteen at her swearing-in, the youngest of whom held her hand during the ceremony. She was the sole woman in the cabinet during her tenure, and the third woman in United States history to serve in a president's cabinet.[117] The only other women to hold that rank before Hills were Francis Perkins as secretary for the Department of Labor under Franklin Delano Roosevelt, Olveta Culp Hobby as Dwight Eisenhower's secretary of Health, Education, and Welfare, and Anne Armstrong as counselor to Nixon and Ford. Hills almost declined the job. She told the president, "You know I'm not an urbanologist. You'll probably get some push back on this and actually I think you need me at the Justice Department because that is what I've been doing all my life, being a lawyer."[118] He replied, "I'm told you are a good manager. HUD needs a good manager. I'd like you to go."[119] Hills decided that "when the president asked you to do something, you do it. So I acquiesced."[120] (That would not be the case when Ford later broached the topic of the Supreme Court.)

Media coverage surrounding Hills's appointment reflected women's admiration for her intellect and capacity to balance her roles as a professional and a parent. "She's an executive, a good one," remarked one attendee at a reception held by the Executive Women in Government (an organization she founded) in Hills's honor following the swearing-in ceremony.[121] Another shared, "What excites me . . . is that she's a mother with younger children and getting such a job. This is happening more and more."[122] In that same article, Pat Lindh commented, "Now for the Supreme Court. We've only just begun."[123] Betty Ford publicly claimed responsibility for Hills's appointment: "I think I've done a good job . . . I got a woman into the Cabinet."[124] Her position did cause stress for entertaining, given that her husband also held a prominent but not superior role in the administration: "The Washington hostess who entertains the new chairman of the Securities and Exchange Commission Roderick M. Hills may have trouble with the seating at dinner when his wife comes, too. She is the only woman in the President's Cabinet. As Secretary of Housing and Urban Development, Carla Anderson Hills outranks her husband."[125] She might have outranked him in government, but when she formed the law firm Munger, Tolles, Hills and Rickershauser with her husband (among others) in 1961, she was "paid far less" because she was a woman, though eventually negotiated a "full salary."[126]

Hills spoke little about her consideration for the Supreme Court except to acknowledge in an oral history that she did in fact know she had been shortlisted upon the retirement of Justice Douglas. She denied any actual formal conversations on the topic, but did note that Ford asked her to consider the role in the 1970s, which she declined.[127] Public commentary surrounding her shortlisted status focused explicitly on her gender, with one reporter from the Washington Post concluding that her qualifications were not sufficient on their own to elevate her to the Court. In his opinion, it was her gender, not her accomplishments, that set her apart: "Hills is a gifted and imaginative administrator at an agency much in need of her abundant talents. But were she not a woman she would not be considered for the nation's highest bench."[128]

Commentators also speculated about her potential as a running mate for Ford: "Carla Hills the Secretary of Housing and Urban Development recently was asked about the possibility that she might become the first woman vice presidential candidate. She replied with a big smile: 'I don't think you have to hold your breath on that.'"[129] An editorial dismissed the idea of Hills as a candidate because selecting her "would look like playing a wild card—an act not in keeping with the sense of stability the president needs to communicate."[130] Hills remained at HUD until 1977, and returned to cabinet-level rank when she served as U.S. trade representative for President George H. W. Bush from 1989 to 1993.

Cornelia Kennedy

If you want to know about Judge Cornelia Kennedy . . . and
the future of women in general, ask her husband.[131]
—Reporter for the *Washington Post*, 1970

Cornelia Kennedy was born in 1923. When she was just eleven years old, her mother passed away while a second-year law student at the University of Michigan Law School. Kennedy and her sister were then raised by their father, a lawyer in Detroit, who helped cultivate her interest in the legal profession. He made sure she had female role models: "As a high school senior, Kennedy was so intrigued by the election of the first female judge in Michigan, Lila Neunenfelt, she asked her father to arrange for her to interview the judge for her school newspaper. She did, and it was a moment that Kennedy would not soon forget."[132] Cornelia Kennedy and her sister, Margaret Schaeffer, both became attorneys and judges. Margaret served on the 47th Judicial District in Farmington Hills, Michigan. They were, quite literally, sisters in law.[133]

Kennedy graduated third in her class from Michigan Law in 1947, which only included five women. There were no women on the faculty at that time. There were no dormitory rooms available for women law students, so unlike her male peers, she was required to make her own living arrangements. Upon graduation, Kennedy found law firms were unwilling to hire women; in a speech she remembered, "One prominent firm had the audacity to tell me that they hired women lawyers during the war, but too bad for me the war was over."[134] Nevertheless, she persevered to become the first woman to clerk for the United States Court of Appeals for the District of Columbia Circuit, hired by Chief Judge

FIGURE 2.5. Cornelia Kennedy (center), her father, and her sister (Credit: University of Michigan Law School)

Harold W. Stephens from 1947 to 1948. Following her clerkship, she practiced law with her father from 1948 to 1952 and then with her sister, Margaret Schaeffer, for a year before becoming a partner at Markle & Markle, where she remained until 1966 when she was elected to the Wayne County Circuit Court. She lost her first campaign for that office by less than one hundred votes, but that did not stop her from running again to become only "the third woman elected to a court of general jurisdiction in the state of Michigan."[135]

Like all of the shortlisted women, Kennedy achieved numerous "firsts" during her career, even earning the nickname "First Lady of the Michigan Judiciary."[136] The official certificate documenting her first judicial appointment had the pronouns "he" and "his" erased and exchanged for "she" and "her,"[137] evidencing how unprecedented the presence of a woman on the bench was in those years. Kennedy was also the first woman to head the Detroit Bar Association. President Nixon appointed her to the U.S. District Court for the Eastern District of Michigan in 1970, and in 1977, she became the first woman to serve as chief judge of a U.S. district court.[138]

Kennedy was elevated to the U.S. Court of Appeals for the Sixth Circuit by President Jimmy Carter two years later in 1979, where she remained until her death in 2014. The fact that her ascendance in the federal judiciary came at the behest of presidents representing opposing political parties speaks volumes about her judicial temperament. She would display this balanced temperament over the course of her career, voting "in sync, when they sat on the same panel, with Judge Bailey Brown" who "was a Tennessee Democrat."[139] Kennedy explained, "He didn't have any kind of agenda. We only disagreed on one case in 20 years."[140] It was a copyright case involving comedian Johnny Carson's famed slogan, "Here's Johnny!" Kennedy disagreed with the majority who held "that Carson had exclusive rights to the phrase."[141]

At the time of her confirmation to the Sixth Circuit, the presence of women in the judiciary remained a novelty. The male judges excluded Kennedy, like Florence Allen before her, from their regular daily lunches at the University Club of Cincinnati, which banned women during that era. Allen, whom Kennedy had argued a case before during her time practicing law, gave her the very hot plate she used to warm her lunch while the male judges savored the club's culinary offerings.[142] Kennedy displayed it with pride atop a marble table. Eventually the male judges decided that they would stop frequenting the club unless it changed its exclusionary ways, which the club finally did.

Kennedy also grappled with informal discriminatory practices and institutional policies that impacted women disproportionately. At the time, there was no provision for the husbands of federal judges to collect pension benefits in the way that wives were entitled to do so. Kennedy successfully worked to change this provision.[143] She was also the first to preside over an "all-female, three-judge panel" in the Sixth Circuit.[144]

Justice John Paul Stevens, in memorializing Kennedy, identified her as an inspiration: "You cannot help but aspire to be a judge when you have the opportunity to clerk for Judge Kennedy. She was the consummate role model."[145]

When Kennedy was asked about the possibility of a woman on the Supreme Court, she concluded, "I think there should be women—in plural—on the Supreme Court. Two or three would be just fine."[146] Kennedy was shortlisted by Ford and Reagan. Sometimes she learned about being considered for the Court from "people sending [her] articles from East Coast newspapers."[147] Her personal archives at the University of Michigan are filled with newspaper clippings and hundreds of letters of support of her nomination from friends, admirers, and strangers in Michigan and across the country. Reacting to Ford's consideration of her for the Court, she observed, "I guess I knew that I could be considered for it, but as a Republican, it's not too often that the President appoints someone of the opposite party when there are probably good candidates of his same party."[148] In 1975, Kennedy was distraught after reading a news article suggesting that the ABA rated her unqualified to serve on the Court, *and* that she was no longer under consideration because of her liberal leanings. In response, she wrote directly to Warren Christopher, the ABA Federal Judiciary Committee chair, asking him to clarify the rating issue: "These political characterizations don't bother me, but I am concerned when my judicial qualifications are impugned."[149] The ABA in fact had been asked to screen Kennedy preliminarily, and in doing so gave her its "qualified" rating; while this was a step up from their review of Mildred Lillie years before, "it was still lower than their rating of several men on the list."[150]

Although Kennedy would not make it off the Supreme Court shortlist, she removed the "Mr." from "Mr. Justice" for the woman who would. Justice John Paul Stevens credited Kennedy with inspiring an 8–1 vote among the justices to change the brass name plates on the chamber doors after the two of them participated in a law school moot court competition in the mid-1970s.[151] The competitors were all women, "excellent advocates" in the words of Stevens and "the best moot court that I attended in my years on the bench."[152] During the argument, however, he noticed Kennedy growing increasingly unhappy being addressed as "Madame Justice" by all of the female advocates. After the fourth did so, she questioned: "Why do you address me as Madame Justice? The word Justice is not a sexist term."[153] Upon Stevens's return to Washington, he raised this issue with his colleagues and, as he explained it in a memorial for Kennedy:

> Potter Stewart responded by stating that sooner or later we were going to have women serving on the Court, and that it would be wise to anticipate that change by substituting the simple term "Justice" for the term "Mr. Justice" that had formerly been the only accepted form of address to a Member of the Court and which then appeared on the brass name plates on the door to every Justice's chambers. His suggestion was promptly endorsed, and by an eight-to-one vote put into effect. Thanks to the firm position expressed by one of the pioneer female members of the federal judiciary, an all-male institution anticipated and avoided one of the problems that might have confronted Sandra Day O'Connor (and the rest of us) when she joined the Court.[154]

If only Kennedy had complained about the lack of toilets for women in the Supreme Court. (There were no suitable facilities when O'Connor first went to the Court.) Perhaps she did not think about it since Florence Allen had secured that privacy for her in the Sixth Circuit along with the hot plate to warm her lunch. Addressing that challenge for the Supreme Court would be left to the first woman to join it.

3

From Shortlisted to Selected

Last week, he apparently discovered women.[1]
—Secretary of Education Shirley Hufstedler on Ronald
Reagan's campaign promise to nominate a qualified woman
to the Supreme Court, October 17, 1980

Looking back at the historical pattern of shortlisting, it seems the writing was on the wall in the 1980s for a woman to join the United States Supreme Court. In the final days of Ronald Reagan's presidential campaign, he committed to not only shortlist but select the first woman justice. This assertive declaration set him apart from most of his presidential predecessors and appealed to some of his competitor's base, given President Jimmy Carter's extraordinary efforts to place more women in the judiciary. While Carter never faced a judicial vacancy on the nation's highest court, his record for appointing women and minorities to the federal bench was exemplary. He went further than any of his predecessors in selecting diverse candidates for these positions. Carter added forty female federal judges during his term to the mere ten appointed by all presidents before him.

Not everyone was convinced of Reagan's expressed intentions. Shirley Hufstedler, a former Ninth Circuit Court of Appeals judge who had served as Carter's secretary of education, was one such skeptic, as evidenced in the quote above. Hufstedler was also widely believed to have been his choice for a Supreme Court nominee had a vacancy arisen during his time in office.[2] Hufstedler's wariness of Reagan was not entirely unfounded. Only twelve of the 600 appointments he made to the judiciary in California during his eight years as governor were women.[3] Reagan's poor record on women would follow him from the governor's mansion into the White House, but Hufstedler's skepticism proved to be only partially warranted.

Potter Stewart gave Reagan the opportunity to make good on his campaign promise just a few months into the presidency. Attorney General William French Smith was the first to learn of the impending vacancy in a private meeting with Stewart on March 26, 1981. After that meeting, Smith assumed the task of creating a shortlist and vetting potential candidates. He knew Reagan planned to keep his campaign pledge, but because of the assassination attempt on Reagan's life on March 30, 1981, the president did not actually hear of the imminent vacancy until almost a month after Stewart confided his intentions to Smith.

When Stewart publicly resigned in June 1981, Cornelia Kennedy's name appeared yet again on the shortlist to replace him, along with several other women: Judge Amalya Lyle Kearse, Judge Joan Dempsey Klein, Chief Justice Susie M. Sharp, and Judge Sandra Day O'Connor. This represented the largest cohort of women ever shortlisted simultaneously for a seat on the Court.

TABLE 3.1. Women Appearing on Reagan's First Supreme Court Shortlist

Name	Birth/Death	Law School	Significant Professional Achievement
Amalya Lyle Kearse	1937–	University of Michigan	Judge, Second Circuit Court of Appeals
Cornelia Kennedy	1923–2014	University of Michigan	Judge, Sixth Circuit Court of Appeals
Joan Dempsey Klein	1924–	University of California Los Angeles	Presiding judge, California Court of Appeals, Second Appellate District
Sandra Day O'Connor	1930–	Stanford	Judge, Arizona Court of Appeals
Susie M. Sharp	1907–96	University North Carolina–Chapel Hill	Chief justice, North Carolina Supreme Court

The Women Shortlisted Alongside O'Connor

AMALYA LYLE KEARSE, JOAN DEMPSEY KLEIN, SUSIE M.
SHARP, AND CORNELIA KENNEDY (AGAIN)

Amalya Lyle Kearse

There were a lot of firms on Wall Street that had no women
lawyers. There was no firm on Wall Street that had any black
lawyers. So when I went looking for a job I had two things
to overcome.[4]
—Amalya Lyle Kearse, Academy of Achievement interview,
1984

Amalya Lyle Kearse was born in 1937 and grew up in New Jersey. Her
mother was a doctor, and her father a postmaster. Like other women in
this book, Kearse would go on to live out the aspirations of her father.
Kearse reflected, "My father always wanted to be a lawyer. . . . The
Depression had a lot to do with why he didn't. I got a lot of encouragement."[5] As a child, she read countless Perry Mason mysteries, and these
books influenced her decision to go to law school. (She was not the only
female jurist influenced by fiction mysteries; Sonia Sotomayor credited
Nancy Drew with fueling her interest in the law.)

Kearse was among only three African Americans in her Wellesley
College freshman class, where she completed her undergraduate education in 1959. Like Kennedy, she attended law school at the University
of Michigan, though her advisers at Wellesley counseled against it. At
Michigan she was one of only eight women in her law school class, graduating near the top with the academic distinction *cum laude* in 1962.
She was an editor on the *Michigan Law Review* and served as a research
assistant for Professor John Reed, who spoke well of her. Not only did he
find her academic work of the highest quality, but "Reed was impressed
by Kearse's creativity and breadth of interest, and describes her as a Re-
naissance person with many talents."[6] Outside of law school, Reed in-

FIGURE 3.1. Amalya Lyle Kearse (Credit: Rick Kopstein, NY Law Journal)

vited Kearse to join him and other members of the faculty on the tennis court, another place where she exhibited excellence.

Kearse lived out the intersectionality that impacts minority women.[7] For any woman, let alone a young, black woman, finding a job on Wall Street at that time was not an easy endeavor. During those early days when Kearse was looking for a job after law school, no Wall Street lawyer looked like her. She understood the difficulties that exist for individuals who bear not just one but many facets of their identities that deviate from white, male, heterosexual norms. But she did not let this hold her back.

Despite these challenges, Kearse secured employment at a Wall Street firm, Hughes Hubbard & Reed in 1962. Not long after that, she became both the first female and the first African American partner of this major Wall Street law firm in 1969. In doing so, she joined a small legacy of women partners in Manhattan firms, including Mentschikoff, who had become partner of her firm in 1945. Kearse ran the firm's hiring committee from 1973 until she became a judge in 1979. Her early influence is likely why Hughes Hubbard & Reed remains a leader among law firms in diversity hiring, regularly recognized as a top firm for minority attorneys.[8]

As a litigator, Kearse handled antitrust, banking, and commercial and product liability cases. In January 1979, she successfully argued a critical antitrust case before the United States Supreme Court, *Broadcast Music, Inc. v. Columbia Broadcasting System, Inc.*[9] Deciding unanimously for Kearse's client, the Court held that Broadcast Music had not engaged in illegal price fixing through their system of collecting fees and issuing licenses to perform copyrighted musical compositions. That same year, Kearse became the first woman inducted as a fellow of the American College of Trial Lawyers. She is also an elected member of the prestigious American Law Institute (similar to a number of the other women who were shortlisted before O'Connor, including Cornelia Kennedy, Soia Mentschikoff, and Susie Sharp, along with all of the women who made it off the shortlist—Ruth Bader Ginsburg, Elena Kagan, Harriet Miers, Sandra Day O'Connor, and Sonia Sotomayor).

Kearse's judicial career commenced when President Carter appointed her to the U.S. Court of Appeals for the Second Circuit in June 1979, though Senator Jacob Javits (New York) tried to convince her to accept a district court clerkship several years before. Kearse self-shortlisted on that opportunity, believing that she lacked the requisite experience to be a trial judge. Javits testified on her behalf during the Senate confirmation hearings: "I can only give her the best recommendation of any that I know of. Some 4 to 5 years ago, I offered her a district court judgeship. She then said she thought her talents and experience needed to be more matured and that she hoped ultimately to go on the bench, but she hoped she would be appointed to an appellate court. Here she is, her talents matured and her appointment before the Senate."[10] She was just forty-two, making her the second-youngest person appointed to a federal circuit court at the time. Despite President Carter's strong commitment to appointing diverse judges, Kearse was the only black woman appointed to a federal appellate court during his presidency. She remained the only woman on the Second Circuit for almost twenty years until Rosemary Pooler was appointed by President Clinton in 1997 and confirmed to the bench the following year.

Kearse was the first woman and second African American (following Thurgood Marshall) to serve on the Second Circuit, a position she still held four decades later in 2020. Her Senate confirmation hearings occurred in tandem with another judge, Jon O. Newman, who would later urge her consideration as a candidate for the Supreme Court. During their confirmation process before the Senate, Judge Newman received an "exceptionally well-qualified" rating from the ABA's Standing Committee on the Judiciary, while Judge Kearse only received a "well-qualified" rating. One can only guess about the difference in ratings, but Judge Newman did have previous judicial experience as a United States District Court Judge for the District of Connecticut, whereas Kearse came directly from private practice. Both were educated at prestigious undergraduate and law schools, though Newman's pedigree (Princeton and Yale) might be interpreted by some as more impressive. Others speculate that the rating had more to do with her gender and race than her qualifications.

President Reagan was the first to consider Kearse for a Supreme Court vacancy, for the seat eventually filled by O'Connor, and in later years, President Clinton included her on his shortlist as well. Kearse's appearance on the shortlists of presidents from both political parties is noteworthy and an anomaly in the context of most judicial appointments, though she shares this attribute with other shortlisted sisters including Florence Allen and Cornelia Kennedy. As an article in the *Wall Street Journal* explained, "Judge Kearse has won the support of liberals and conservatives because she doesn't fit conventional definitions. She is seen by Republicans as a cautious judge who is well-versed on securities issues, and Democrats note that she isn't afraid to take their side on social issues."[11] Early in her life she was a registered Republican but later changed her political affiliation to independent.

Despite the prominence of her judicial appointment, and the re-peated public recognition she received from three presidents as they vetted candidates for the Court, Judge Kearse rarely makes public ap-pearances and maintains a very private life. One reporter wrote, "By all accounts Judge Kearse is brilliant, if somewhat enigmatic. The fiercely private jurist rarely writes legal articles or gives speeches. But she is well known in the bridge world: She has translated French books on the game and will be competing this month to represent the U.S. in the world bridge championships."[12] Her preference for privacy, while understandable, has resulted in limited knowledge about her personal life outside of the law, other than that Kearse has never married or had children.

Judge Kearse was the only woman of color shortlisted for a vacancy on the Court in the years leading up to and contemporaneous with O'Connor's nomination in 1981. This trend reversed to some extent with the appointment of Justice Sotomayor when, as a part of President Obama's legacy, a minority woman went from shortlisted to selected for the Court. Media reports suggest President Obama shortlisted two black women when filling his vacancies: former Georgia Supreme Court Chief Justice Leah Ward Sears and Judge Kentanji Brown Jackson, a district court judge for the District of Columbia. However, there has yet to be a black woman who has actually ascended to the role of Supreme Court justice.[13]

The intersectionality of Kearse's identity as a black woman was a focal point of media discussion of her presence on presidential shortlists. As an article in the *Washington Post* highlighted, Kearse's race was news-worthy, and it seemed to take precedence over other parts of her iden-tity, qualifications, experience, or political ideology. One report on the shortlist mentioned two possible female candidates: "The others were Judge Cornelia G. Kennedy of the 6th U.S. Circuit Court of Appeals, who is considered a conservative Republican, and Judge Amalya Lyle Kearse of the 2nd Circuit Court of Appeals, who is black."[14] Although her appointment to the federal appellate bench was incredibly significant, one reporter contrasted Kearse with Justice Thurgood Marshall, and noted that that she "has not in the past been particularly identified with the causes of women or blacks."[15] The assumption that she should automatically be an activist simply because of her race or gender is a common but unfair burden imposed on outsiders, and we explore the burdens of this token status further in the second half of the book.

Years after O'Connor was nominated to the Court, Kearse's name was again floated during a vacancy that arose under George H. W. Bush. The nomination of Clarence Thomas became complicated by sexual harassment allegations made by a number of women during the confirmation process, including Professor Anita Hill. At that time, the possibility of Kearse's selection as a replacement nominee was considered by some as a solution to "end the controversy that cannot be satisfactorily defused."[16] Apparently they felt, as a qualified minority candidate, Kearse would further the president's diversity agenda and provide a way around the inherent problems with the Thomas nomination. Ultimately, Thomas survived the controversy and was confirmed by the Senate, dissipating the potential for Kearse's nomination at the time.

It is interesting to note, however, that Judge Newman, who himself was later seriously considered by President Clinton alongside Stephen Breyer for the vacancy left by Justice Byron R. White, wrote a letter published by the *New York Times* on October 10, 1991, urging Kearse's nomination in place of Thomas. This letter might well have been Newman's undoing, at least insofar as it relates to his consideration for the Court. He and Breyer were regarded as very similar to one another and some seemed to think the nomination could easily be given to either man. However, Newman's letter was deemed inappropriate by many who believed a sitting judge should not weigh in on such matters and that to do so was a violation of judicial ethics. Ultimately, Breyer was the chosen one to be nominated to the Court.

Susie M. Sharp

Oft a bridesmaid—never a bride.[17]
—Susie Sharp on being considered for the U.S. Supreme
Court

Susie Sharp was born on July 7, 1907, making her the oldest among the women shortlisted with O'Connor, a factor that undoubtedly hindered her chances of a nomination. As a young child, Sharp's parents encouraged her to find the means to support herself without reliance on anyone else, including a spouse, but a career in law was likely not what they had in mind. Although not explicitly unsupportive of her professional legal ambitions, Susie Sharp's father did not initially provide her with encouragement, even though he was a lawyer himself. Nonetheless, she later worked with him for a time after law school.[18] She began her education studying chemistry at Woman's College in Greensboro, North Carolina,

FIGURE 3.2. Susie M. Sharp
(Credit: Courtesy of the State
Archives of North Carolina)

but ultimately left for the University of North Carolina Chapel Hill and matriculated into law school after two years of college there. She was the only woman out of sixty law students in the graduating class of 1929.

Sharp excelled in law school—earning straight A's—but her experience was, like many of her shortlisted sisters, marked by difficult interactions with her male peers. At the beginning of her time in law school, several of her male colleagues were so hostile to her presence that they left notes on her seat making reference to legal cases such as the North Carolina decision in *State v. Black*,[19] where the state supreme court upheld a man's right to physically punish his wife. (Such affronts continue to be hurled at women who dare to enter roles traditionally held by men. Hillary Clinton's experience on the 2018 campaign trail was rife with public insults. At one rally, several men yelled, "[i]ron my shirt," before being removed by law enforcement.[20]) Sharp felt her law school classmates resented her presence, and viewed her as taking a seat that a man could have filled, another common sentiment experienced by other shortlisted sisters. Despite the hostility, the novelty of her presence did not impede Sharp's ability to excel at her legal pursuits. And not all of Sharp's interactions with men in the legal profession were characterized by such negativity. In fact, the male lawyers present in her life as family, friends, lovers, and mentors all had profound impacts on her personal and professional life. We explore the complexities of these relationships for Sharp and other shortlisted women more fully in the second half of the book.

After law school, Sharp initially went into law practice with her father. A brief article appearing in the *New York Times* on February 18, 1929, announced her arrival into his office: "A father and his daughter have become law partners in the adjoining county of Rockingham. Former State Senator J.M. Sharp is the senior partner of the firm and Miss Susie Sharp is associated with him under the name Sharp & Sharp."[21] This announcement did not compare to the sexist report appearing the *Greensboro Daily News*. The North Carolina paper, reflecting the separate spheres that dominated that era, reported Sharp would be joining her father in his law practice, where she would use her brain, unless she decided to pursue marriage instead, where she would use her beauty.[22] Sharp's decision to join her father was informed in part by his need for help as a solo practitioner, but also by the fact that it was very difficult for a woman to find a legal job at that time. While he may not have initially supported her choice of law as a career, he did help her launch her practice. Sharp's biographer notes, "She did not have many options if she wanted to practice law. In the absence of a father—or a husband—to take her into his practice, the chances of a woman earning her living as a lawyer were remote."[23] That same year, at only twenty-one years of age, Sharp argued a case before the North Carolina State Supreme Court.

Several years into practice, Sharp became frustrated with the low pay she earned and the resistance from clients who were reluctant to be represented by a female attorney. She struggled with the decision, but ultimately left practice with her father to accept a position at her alma mater as the secretary to the dean of the law school. Although she stretched the bounds of the secretarial position to make it more meaningful and challenging, it was not the kind of work she envisioned doing long-term and she missed practicing law. She described a sense of failure from working in such a subordinate role given her credentials. Sharp's biographer suggests that her decision, while influenced by money, was also complicated by the affair she was engaged in with a former professor. (We examine this relationship further in chapter six.) Sharp's presence in Chapel Hill allowed that relationship to continue somewhat seamlessly. She eventually returned to work with her father after two years, and the city of Reidsville subsequently hired her as an attorney in 1937, making her the state's first-ever female city attorney.

Sharp entered the judiciary in 1949 when she was appointed to serve as a special judge on the state's superior court; she remained in judicial service throughout the rest of her life until she retired in 1979, which was required by law, at age seventy-two. Sharp encountered odd and offensive gendered dynamics that framed women as outsiders at almost every turn. In one county, she was not able to enter the court's chambers without traipsing through the men's restroom. In another context, "she laughingly told of a deputy sheriff who, bidding her farewell at the end of a court term, told her, in all seriousness, 'I just want to tell you, ma'am, you did better than I expected.'"[24] When she remarked that it didn't sound like he expected much, he replied, "Tell you the truth ma'am, I didn't expect nothing."[25] A reporter once asked about the appropriateness that she, as a woman, preside over a rape trial. Sharp's response was that since the rape in question could not have been committed without the presence of woman, it was only fitting that a woman oversee a trial involving this kind of gendered crime.

In 1962, Sharp became the first woman elected to the North Carolina Supreme Court and, in 1975, the first woman elected to serve as chief justice on a state supreme court in the United States.[26] The *Charlotte Observer* reported on her ascendance to the state's highest court, quoting Sharp: "I just felt I not only had the burden of the law on my shoulders, but that I also had the future of women in the law."[27] In addition to coverage of her courtroom decorum (requiring lawyers to wear coats and refrain from smoking cigarettes), the article mentioned her pastimes outside of the law: "After a tiring day on the bench, she would return to her needlepoint, her collection of hi-fi operatic records, her cookbooks."[28] We know from materials found in her archives, however, that she also occupied her time sketching out elaborate make-up application techniques alongside diet and exercise routines, as well as clipping news about the British royal family and romantic poetry excerpts, which she pasted in her journals.

A reporter noted Sharp's professional legacy was characterized by breaking down barriers for women, describing her accomplishments in the context of her gender: "It's safe to say that Susie Marshall Sharp was the first N.C. Supreme Court justice to be sworn in wearing a double strand of pearls."[29] Sharp's story is reminiscent of Florence Allen's in terms of her commitment to the practice of law and presence as the first and only woman on a number of courts in a single state. The two women also shared the habit of keeping personal diaries in which they recorded myriad details about their lives. Sharp reflected on her achievement in personal notes preparing for an interview: "Wonderful experience to have been the first woman judge in North Carolina and I feel almost selfish when I realize that it is one which, in the nature of things, cannot be duplicated. I absorbed the shock and it was a tremendously exciting experience. I didn't deserve it. I just happened to be a woman at the right place at the right point in time. My only regret is that I didn't have more wisdom, learning and insight to bring to the opportunity."[30]

There was a significant outpouring of support from those who loved and admired Sharp in her home state of North Carolina when Court vacancies arose during multiple presidential administrations, though she was only *officially* shortlisted by Reagan contemporaneously with O'Connor.[31] With the retirement of Justice Charles Evans Whittaker in March 1962, when Sharp had been on the North Carolina Supreme Court for just two weeks, President Kennedy was faced with a vacancy. Just five months later, Justice Felix Frankfurter also left the Court. Both of these seats were filled swiftly by Kennedy with male nominees (Justices White and Goldberg, respectively). Shortly thereafter, North Carolina Governor Terry Sanford sent a letter to President Kennedy suggesting that he nominate Sharp should another vacancy arise. At this stage of her personal life and career, however, Sharp felt conflicted about a possible move to Washington. She actually wrote to Governor Sanford after he put forth her name to President Kennedy, declaring that she lacked qualification because she had no experience with federal cases and no desire to assume such a role (a form of self-shortlisting that we revisit in chapter eight). Serving on the Court would have taken her away from her beloved North Carolina, and from the men with whom romantic ties remained strong (though this latter reason was a deeply guarded secret).

Although Sharp was not formally shortlisted in the years of Kennedy's tenure as president, more vacancies arose during the subsequent presidencies of Johnson, Nixon, and Ford, and her friends and allies continued to rally for her appointment. The number of letters from lawyers, politicians, and governors—both from North Carolina and adjacent states—amounted to an all-out campaign. Sharp's view had also evolved even by the time her name was suggested to President Johnson; still demure, she nonetheless appeared open to the opportunity. This shift in perspective was due in part to the changing nature of her relationship with one of her lovers, John Kesler, which appeared to have cooled during this time. According to Sharp's biographer, "she was willing to ponder the possibility of becoming the first woman on the U.S. Supreme Court, even if she was not exactly on fire about it. The enormity of such a historical appointment could not fail to draw her."[32]

Even in the midst of her pervasive internal conflict about the possibility of leaving North Carolina and the men she loved, Sharp decried her perpetual shortlisted status. This contradiction characterized much of her life. In a personal letter to her sister-in-law, Sharp complained, "I am . . . getting mighty tired of being 'mentioned' for the job every time a vacancy occurs. It begins to smack of the old Listerine ad, 'Oft a bridesmaid—never a bride.'"[33] Sharp's awareness and description of her constant consideration without selection truly evidences the sting of shortlisting.

The conflict Sharp felt about serving on the Court emblemized other aspects of her identity. She spoke often to a variety of audiences on topics related to women and seemed compelled to use her power to create change. As but one of many examples, in 1959 she gave a talk entitled "Women and Their Influence" to a meeting of the Wesleyan Service Guilds of the Methodist Church's Greensboro District. But, similar to Allen and many other women of that era, Sharp vehemently opposed the Equal Rights Amendment. Her objections stemmed from a concern that such a law would require abandonment of many protections women enjoyed, like exemption from drafted military service. In her view, the kinds of rights women needed could be protected by the Fourteenth Amendment. Yet, she herself enjoyed the freedom to attend law school and become a member of the bar, and found it beyond comprehension that women were excluded from jury service. Sharp reflected, "When I got my law license, women couldn't even sit on juries. . . . I could practice law before 12 men but not 12 women. I worked my head off to get that changed."[34]

Sharp lived to see many changes unfold in the legal profession, including the appointment of not just one but two women to the Supreme Court; she passed away at age eighty-eight on March 1, 1996.

Joan Dempsey Klein

A woman on the Supreme Court would enhance the image
of women in the legal profession and strengthen the self-
image of all women.[35]
—Judge Klein in a 1975 interview

Joan Dempsey Klein was born in 1924, a descendant of California's first lawyer, John W. Kottinger.[36] Despite this significant tie to the profession, she received no family guidance about the pursuit of a law degree. Her parents, like those of many women profiled in this book, suggested that she seek a career in teaching.[37] But Klein had other ideas, informed in part by the family life in which she grew up. She spoke openly about her childhood and the factors that motivated her professional direction in her oral history: "My dream was to have a life unlike my mother's. I couldn't stand the way she was treated and the way she lived."[38] She was

FIGURE 3.3. Joan Dempsey Klein
(Credit: State Bar of California)

referring to the treatment of her mother by her father; he was extremely racist and an alcoholic. "I asked my mother, 'Why the hell are you still with this man?' But she was still with him—because she had given him an ultimatum: 'either you stop drinking or I'm out of here.' She had a guy in the wings ready to take all of us crazy kids, the whole family. And, when he knew that, and she finally got the guts to say that to him, he quit drinking cold turkey. Then she felt she owed him the obligation to stay with him the rest of his life."[39] Klein's pursuit of a career in law reflected her desire to lead a different life than her mother.

Klein did not earn high grades in high school, and she was not encouraged to attend college by her parents or teachers. A fellow student put the idea in her head that college would open doors for her, so she attended San Diego State University and graduated in 1948 with a teaching degree, though a career in teaching was not her desired path. Eventually, Klein decided to attend law school, and she credited UCLA Law Dean L. Dale Coffman for guiding her legal career. He had a reputation as being somewhat unfavorable toward women but offered her admission to the school nonetheless. When she entered law school, her class of approximately 200 had only eight women in it, and that number had decreased to two by the time she graduated in 1955.[40] At the time, there were no female professors on the law school faculty, which would remain the case until 1971.

Not unlike other early female law students, Klein faced pervasive hostility from male faculty and students. When asked about the perspective of men in her class regarding her presence, she reflected, "Many of them expressed openly to me that they felt I had no business being there because I was only going to get married, have kids, stay home and waste a seat for some guy who could have had a career. They made generally negative comments, that were pretty much sexist and reflected a very biased attitude. And for the most part I just ignored them, although I did do a little responding here and there . . ."[41] Male students asked her questions like "What are you doing here?" or "How come you're taking a place that a male student should have?"[42] Klein also took a somewhat untraditional path—she ignored the advice of the law school administration, taking a job out of necessity and working throughout law school to make ends meet. She ended up graduating a semester later than the students with whom she entered law school, and earned her degree in 1955.

Unsurprisingly, simply holding a law degree did not result in immediate job offers from prestigious firms—or from any legal employers, for that matter. In fact, UCLA allowed private firms to determine what type of candidates they would interview for jobs. Klein recalled, "No one came to law school and said give us your women graduates."[43] Instead, like many women in this book, her first job as a lawyer was in government. "We were led to believe that because government is government and, supposedly, represents all the people, and, supposedly, is more open-minded and tolerant, that maybe we had a better chance [for positions] with the public law offices."[44]

In her early career, Klein worked as a state deputy attorney general in California. She formed friendships among some male colleagues who carpooled with her and looked out for her during her pregnancy. Even so, much like Kennedy who challenged the use of the title "madam" before justice during the University of Michigan moot court arguments with Justice Stevens, Klein was also subject to and ultimately cast off this label during a trial. A judge had been repeatedly referring to her as "madam" rather than "counsel," as he was calling her male counterpart, and Klein confronted the judge: "Your honor, I am not a madam. I would appreciate your referring to me as counsel just as you do my co-counsel."[45] During her time at the attorney general's office, Klein had two children, and also went through a divorce and a remarriage. In those days, flex-time and work-life balance were not a part of workplace culture. We return to the struggles of being forced to balance career and child care in chapter seven.

Klein began her judicial career in 1963 when Governor Pat Brown appointed her to the Los Angeles Municipal Court. She would later be elected to the Los Angeles Superior Court and served there until Governor Jerry Brown appointed her to the California Court of Appeals, Second Appellate District, Division Three in Los Angeles in 1978. Brown appointed her as the court's presiding justice; she was the first woman to occupy that role and she served in this capacity until she retired in January 2015. At the time, the three men on the court were not initially welcoming to her, especially because she entered the court in a leadership role as the presiding justice. Klein described the dynamic this way: "So here were these three guys who had crew-cuts and here was I a young female PJ."[46] Although her recollection of the interactions with her fellow justices suggested collegiality, she did in fact decline to assert her right to select which judicial chambers she would occupy, leaving the large corner office to one of her male colleagues. Klein credits Governor Brown's appointment of Rose Bird to the position of chief justice of the California Supreme Court as helping pave the way for her own appointment into this leadership position. Once on the bench, Justice Bird suggested that a woman should serve on every appellate court in the state of California.

Klein gave back to the legal profession and provided mentorship to other women lawyers by creating professional organizations for women lawyers and judges. She urged women who had become judges to take an even more active role in the bar, "so that our male peers can be aware of us as judges who do not have two heads but who do have brains, education, ability, egos—yes, egos—and ambition."[47] Unlike Amalya Kearse, who spent much of her judicial life outside of the public eye, Klein worked diligently through leadership roles in professional organizations to create change for women lawyers by addressing the problem of gender inequality in the profession head on. To this end, Klein served as the founding president of the National Association of Women Judges (NAWJ), as well as the founding president of California Women Lawyers. She frequently spoke to audiences of lawyers and law students about gender bias in the legal profession and was of the mind that the appointment of a woman to the Supreme Court would make a measurable difference for women in the legal profession.

Though never nominated to the Supreme Court, in a somewhat ironic twist, Klein testified before the Senate Judiciary Committee on behalf of Sandra Day O'Connor's nomination. At the time, she was the president of the NAWJ, as well as the presiding justice of the California Court of Appeals. Who better to speak on behalf of O'Connor than someone with the expertise, stature, commitment, and prominence of Justice Klein?

Klein's brief remarks to the Senate Judiciary Committee began with a short historical overview of women in law over the years. She stated, "As you might well imagine, the appointment of a woman to assume a place on the highest court has had top priority on our agenda. It seems to have been such a long time coming but, when considered in a historical perspective, perhaps the 191 years is an understandable period of time."[48] Klein referenced the case of Myra Bradwell and her unsuccessful appeal to the U.S. Supreme Court to engage in the practice of law despite meeting the requisite qualifications. She also emphasized to the committee that while there was understandable excitement at the mere prospect of a woman on the Court, she and the members of her organization were "emphatic that the woman selected be of the highest caliber."[49] After all, Klein continued, "her performance will reflect on all of us lesser judicial luminaries, and we want to be assured that she has the capacity to succeed."[50] She reported that the NAWJ considered Sandra Day O'Connor to be "exceptionally well qualified."[51]

Sandra Day O'Connor (and Cornelia Kennedy, Again)

President Reagan has chosen a woman for the Supreme Court—and more. Other presidents have had the will, or the opportunity, but never both.[52]

—Reporter for the New York Times, 1981

The appointment of O'Connor to the Supreme Court in 1981 made history, but her story must be contextualized by the very serious consideration of Cornelia Kennedy. Profiled in chapter two, we include Kennedy here yet again because her name resurfaced as a viable nominee when Ronald Reagan worked to fill this vacancy. In fact, in the end, it came down to O'Connor and her. As Kennedy acknowledged: "I don't think they interviewed anyone except Justice O'Connor and myself."[53]

Like O'Connor, Kennedy received a visit from Jonathon Rose and Ken Starr on behalf of President Reagan. While Rose and Starr met with O'Connor in her home over a salmon mousse she prepared for them days after undergoing a hysterectomy, they interviewed Kennedy in her judicial chambers. They asked about many of her judicial opinions, including a case involving an Ohio abortion statute which she voted to uphold. The next day she flew to Washington, D.C., for more interviews, by herself. Her husband did not accompany her because "he remembered a time when he was interviewing someone for a position at his former firm, and they brought their mother with them and it was not a good thing. He thought they might treat a husband the same way."[54]

President Ford wrote a letter to President Reagan regarding the possibility of a Kennedy nomination dated June 25, 1981. He shared with Reagan his impressions that she would be an excellent addition to the Court, and included in his correspondence a letter he received during his presidency from five Michigan circuit court judges endorsing her candidacy. Ford wrote:

> Over the years, I have closely observed the judicial performance of Judge Cornelia Kennedy as she has served both Michigan and the United States court systems. She has carried out her judicial duties with great distinction and, in my judgment, would serve this nation exceedingly well as a member of the United States Supreme Court.[55]

Ford genuinely supported Kennedy for the Court (even if he did not appoint her himself). Reagan soon thereafter replied to Ford, in a letter dated July 11, 1981, affectionately referring to him as "My Dear Mr. President" and acknowledged that Kennedy was one of a handful of individuals whom he gave the "closest consideration."[56]

Kennedy revealed in her oral history that she really did not think she would be selected. For her, the fact that she was a Democrat, and Reagan a Republican, was decisive. She could not fathom the president crossing party lines when he did in fact have excellent Republican choices available to him. It was not unheard of, however, for presidents to do so, for example Kearse was shortlisted by presidents from both parties and Nixon, a Republican, shortlisted Lillie, a Democrat. Kennedy herself was initially appointed to the federal district court by Nixon and then elevated to the court of appeals by Carter. Sound as such a theory may have been, the self-doubt expressed by Kennedy and the other shortlisted women is notable. Other factors surely were at play. O'Connor fit the norms most comfortable for what one scholar calls "Benchmark Men," i.e., men "who remain the primary decision makers [and] prefer to appoint women who espouse values most like their own. That is, they should be white, able-bodied, heterosexual, middle class and politically right of center."[57] Age was also a likely factor, a conclusion supported by a memo in Reagan's archives listing several potential female nominees with their ages handwritten in blue ink in the margins. Kennedy, at fifty-seven, was not as appealing as O'Connor at age fifty-one. We consider the implications of age further in chapter six.

When Reagan revealed O'Connor as his nominee instead of Kennedy, the front page of the *Detroit Free Press* ran an above-the-fold headline similar to every newspaper in the nation: "1st Woman for Supreme Court."[58] But Kennedy's home state newspaper also included a unique article entitled "Many Here Wish It Were Kennedy," as a tribute to the state's beloved Sixth Circuit judge.[59] The story described a certain "bewilderment" at the choice of O'Connor, suggesting that Kennedy "was widely regarded as a leading choice for the nomination," and also expressed a preference that Kennedy had been selected instead.[60] Kennedy herself was interviewed for the story, and the author reported, "Kennedy said she was pleased a woman had been nominated. She added, 'I would have been more pleased if it were I.'"[61]

If Kennedy felt disappointment at the news that she did not receive the nomination, O'Connor was understandably elated. After all, as Kennedy confessed in her oral history, "I think every judge would like to be on the Supreme Court and every lawyer would like to be on the Supreme Court."[62] Any appointment to the Supreme Court is significant, but the selection of the first woman to occupy this role even more so. Although feminists long prioritized the importance of selecting a woman, a goal shared by Reagan if for no other reason than political expediency, the issue appeared to be of much less import to the general public, at least according to a *New York Times*/CBS News poll which found that "72 percent of the public believed that it made no difference whether a man or a woman was appointed."[63]

Much has been written by others about the political process of selecting O'Connor as the first woman on the Court. It is well known that Chief Justice Warren Burger reportedly brought her to Attorney General Smith's attention after the two met on an overseas trip with several judges.[64] Smith quickly became very fond of O'Connor and lobbied on her behalf, ultimately becoming a driving force behind her nomination.[65] Smith was also a contender for the seat on the Court himself, along with White House counselor Edwin Meese III, and Deputy Secretary of State William P. Clark. A *Washington Post* article revealed how the choice of these men would not have served Reagan well. The reporter noted:

> The naming of any one of them would open Reagan to charges of cronyism, particularly Smith, who headed the presidential transition team and wound up picking himself as attorney general. And Reagan would miss the presence of Meese, on whom he relies heavily for counsel. Some White House officials say that Clark, whose California State Supreme Court service gives him the best judicial qualifications of any insider, would be missed equally because he has played a vital role in easing tensions between the White House staff and Secretary of State Alexander M. Haig Jr.[66]

These men ultimately withdrew their names from consideration.

The administration invited O'Connor to Washington, D.C., to meet with Reagan on July 1, 1981. In recent years, abortion has dominated the Supreme Court appointment process, though nominees rarely confronted questions about it before *Roe v. Wade* became the law of the land in 1973. O'Connor's vetting was the first to be touched by the issue, perhaps because she would be the first justice who could actually receive an abortion to decide whether women hold autonomy over their own bodies. During her meeting with Reagan, O'Connor disclosed a strong pro-life ideology sufficiently reassuring for him to settle on her as the nominee by the end of their discussion. After news of her selection leaked to the public, organizations on both sides vocally opposed her candidacy. The White House regularly tracked messages received by mail and telegram, and during July 1981 reported 2,907 messages supporting O'Connor's nomination and 3,547 opposing it.[67] However, Reagan was not persuaded by public opinion, at least that as measured by his mailbox. Undeterred, Reagan announced her as his choice on August 19, 1981. The Senate unanimously confirmed her on September 21, 1981. Over a decade later, validating the fears of the pro-life organizations who opposed her nomination, Justice O'Connor joined the three-justice plurality in *Planned Parenthood v. Casey*,[68] the 1992 case that chipped away at but nonetheless upheld the central holding of *Roe v. Wade*.[69]

Long before O'Connor's confirmation to the Court, she clipped newspaper articles in the 1970s speculating about the possibility of a woman holding a seat. Did she imagine it might be her? She even wrote to President Nixon and "urged him to put a woman on the Court."[70] Instead, he gave the spot to her law school boyfriend—and near-fiancé—William Rehnquist. He proposed marriage to her soon after both graduated from Stanford Law School in 1952. While the two never did marry, they would go on to enjoy a lifelong friendship. The first time O'Connor stepped foot into the Supreme Court was for Rehnquist's swearing-in ceremony. Both called Arizona home and, once reunited on the Court, they were often referred to as the "Arizona Twins." Clearly as qualified as Rehnquist for the Court, her appointment came a decade after his.

Like other women of her time graduating at the top of their law school class, O'Connor initially struggled to find an employer willing to hire a woman lawyer. She declined a secretarial position and found her first legal job only by agreeing to work for free as a deputy county attorney in the San Mateo County Attorney's Office while her husband John finished his law degree. When he went into the army, the couple subsequently moved to Germany; there, she worked as a civilian lawyer. After returning to the U.S. and moving to Arizona, she spent several years in private practice and then became an assistant attorney general. While O'Connor did not adhere to the same rigid ideas about the separation of spheres as Allen and Sharp, after the birth of her children she reduced her law practice to part-time for four years, allowing her to devote time to their care as well as other civic activities. The attorney general for whom she worked noted that she was the only person he knew who would do a full-time job for half-time pay.

O'Connor's career also included a stint in the legislative branch of government; she served in the Arizona State Senate beginning in 1969 when appointed to fill a vacancy. She then ran for reelection for two additional terms and became the nation's first female majority leader in a state legislature. O'Connor spent only six years on the bench before Reagan plucked her off his shortlist, first as an elected judge on the Maricopa Superior Court from 1975 to 1979, and then on the Arizona Court of Appeals for just two years.

Reagan promised to select a woman for the Court during his campaign, but once a vacancy arose, he faced significant criticism for suggesting that he would *only* select a woman. He qualified his very public misstep, remarking, "Now, this is not to say I would appoint a woman merely to do so. That would not be fair to women, nor to future generations of all Americans whose lives are so deeply affected by the decisions of the court. Rather, I pledged to appoint a woman who meets the very high standards I demand of all court appointees."[71]

O'Connor lacked extensive judicial experience at least insofar as not having spent her entire career on the bench, and those critical of Reagan's choice exploited this "shortcoming." We know, however, that the competency and qualifications of female nominees, and female candidates in general, are often evaluated more closely and assessed more stringently than those of men. Not surprisingly, the news of O'Connor's historic nomination dominated the front page of news media sources across the country, and many of those headlines were infused with this kind of gendered critique.

For example, an opinion piece in the *Washington Post*, "The Nomination of Mrs. O'Connor," declared that "[r]arely, if ever, has a president reached so far down into the state judiciary to find a Supreme Court justice. Most of them have come from higher ranks of the judicial system, from national political positions or from the nationally known law firms."[72] The article, although generally expressing praise for the president's pick and acknowledging the plight of women lawyers, nonetheless failed to address O'Connor's potential for success and instead levied criticism against her ostensibly less-than-perfect professional credentials. Despite the justices' own rejection of the use of honorifics before their names in writings and deliberations, the media continued to describe women by referencing their marital status and gender rather than professional qualifications. Judge or senator would have been a more appropriate and respectful descriptor, rather than "Mrs." Similarly disrespectful was another reporter's characterization of O'Connor's visits to meet senators before the confirmation hearings as if she was a "debutant at a ball."[73] The article belittled her appointment, reducing it to something akin to a beauty pageant instead of the intense, rigorous, and grueling intellectual experience that it most certainly was.

During the years leading up to O'Connor's appointment, many of the male nominees possessed similar, or sometimes even less impressive, credentials than she. For example, Stanley Reed, appointed by President Roosevelt in 1938, did not even hold a law degree (though he did serve as an apprentice to a lawyer and was admitted to practice in Kentucky), and he was not the only justice to lack such a qualification. During O'Connor's confirmation hearings, Judge Klein spoke to the gender inconsistency in the evaluation of qualifications: "Judge O'Connor's experience on the appellate bench serves to prepare her for the work ahead. By contrast, at least 15 of the prior 101 Supreme Court justices had no judicial experience whatsoever, or a bare minimum prior to their appointments. These numbers include three of the justices currently serving with distinction."[74] Second-guessing the qualifications of women, holding them to exceedingly high standards, and/or selecting them only after they have proved their worth, as opposed to banking on their potential, continues to hamper women's professional trajectories. Klein also spoke to the excessive scrutiny women face in their professional lives, particularly when they shatter gender norms. More of her testimony appears in part two of the book.

Much like Allen, Kennedy, and other early women judges, O'Connor continued to endure gendered stereotyping even after ascending to the bench. As just one example, among O'Connor's initial responsibilities after her confirmation was an assignment by Chief Justice Burger to serve as a delegate to the cafeteria committee. She was the first justice ever placed in such a role. Maybe Burger had heard about the salmon mousse she prepared for Rose and Starr when they visited her in Arizona to interview her for the nomination.

O'Connor retired from the Court in 2006 so that she would have the time to care for her husband, who was suffering from Alzheimer's disease. In her retirement, she also dedicated much of her time and passion to civics education. O'Connor was routinely asked about regrets she had from her time on the Court. She sidestepped making any definitive remarks on this subject until an interview with the *Chicago Tribune*, in which she spoke about casting the deciding vote in *Bush v. Gore*,[75] the case that stopped the recounting of ballots in Florida and effectively handed the presidency to George W. Bush in 2000. O'Connor suggested in that interview that the Court should not have taken on that case after all, due to the damage it caused to the country. She also expressed regret over retiring early, as her husband's health faded much more rapidly than expected and he passed away in 2009. She could have easily served nearly another decade. On October 23, 2018, O'Connor announced in a letter released to the public from her family that she was withdrawing from public life due to her own diagnosis of dementia.

* * *

President Reagan's selection of Sandra Day O'Connor as his choice for the Court finally changed the practice of placing women on shortlists as an endgame. O'Connor's ascent to the nation's highest court concluded the longstanding and previously impenetrable gendered tradition of men's dominance in this realm. It is sobering, in retrospect, that so many executive branch leaders considered and subsequently rejected qualified women for all the vacancies that arose in that time.

Unlike many campaign promises that so often go unfulfilled, Reagan actually made good on his by shortlisting several women and selecting one. Reagan's record, however, was fairly disastrous as relates to the selection of women and minority judicial candidates overall. As the next chapter reveals, he was taken to task by the Senate Judiciary Committee in 1989 for his shortcomings. His own administration was aware of this problem early on, as evidenced by an August 11, 1981, memo from Diana Lozano, special assistant to the president for public liaison, to Elizabeth Dole, then director of the White House Office of Public Liaison (and later a U.S. senator). The memo suggested that the administration was potentially going to be in trouble regarding the appointment of women to the judiciary. Lozano cautioned, "If we don't pay attention to this process, we could find ourselves in an embarrassing situation."[76] Further, she acknowledged how the benefit derived from the O'Connor nomination would be for naught and become merely a token "if women are seen as taking a giant step backward in the lower courts."[77] The memo concluded with a request to study the situation more closely and take action: "If the numbers look potentially embarrassing, it may not be too late to influence the process."[78] Whatever wisdom lurked in this recommendation and the surrounding discussions, Reagan did not heed the warning. His legacy as someone who forever changed the gendered dynamic of Supreme Court with the appointment of O'Connor is tempered by his shortfalls in working toward gender parity in the judicial branch. He rode the tokenism of the O'Connor appointment as far as it would take him.

Although women appeared on presidential shortlists with most of the subsequent vacancies on the Court, including the two later openings that arose during Reagan's time in office, O'Connor remained the solitary female Supreme Court justice for more than a decade. Not until the Clinton administration would another woman be elevated from the shortlist and placed on the Court.

4

The Shortlists following O'Connor

A Long Way from Nine

People ask me sometimes, when—when do you think it will be enough? When will there be enough women on the Court? And my answer is when there are nine.[1]
—Ruth Bader Ginsburg, speech at Georgetown Law School, 2015

Sandra Day O'Connor spent over a decade as the only female on a court unprepared for her presence. No restrooms for women existed near the courtroom, so she had to use one located in a male justice's chambers.[2] Even though the justices dropped the honorific "Mr." several months before her appointment, two years later, the *New York Times* still referenced the "nine men" sitting on "SCOTUS" in an editorial. O'Connor fired back with a letter observing, "According to the information available to me, and which I had assumed was generally available, for over two years now, SCOTUS has not consisted of nine men."[3]

This chapter examines the backgrounds of the few women who appeared but remained on Reagan's subsequent shortlists and the women who, like O'Connor, eventually made it off the lists and onto the Court during future presidential administrations. O'Connor's ascendance to the Court marked the end of decades of women being passed over and discounted. But the story does not end with the achievement of this "first," no matter how historic it was. To the contrary, her nomination marked the beginning of a new chapter in a decades-old saga of persistent gender inequality. Before further exploring the dynamics that keep women on the shortlist, there is more to the story; other women were shortlisted by Reagan.

Reagan's Post-O'Connor Shortlists

CYNTHIA HOLCOMB HALL, EDITH JONES, AND
PAMELA RYMER

After the appointment of O'Connor, Reagan faced two more opportunities to nominate justices from an ever-growing list of qualified women.
In addition to the five women he considered for O'Connor's seat, Reagan
later shortlisted Cynthia Holcomb Hall, Edith Jones, and Pamela Rymer
for vacancies.[4] Despite the ample number of women with impeccable
credentials, the Reagan administration returned to Nixon's tradition of
shortlisting women as a political strategy without selecting any of them.
With a woman finally on the Court, it seemed, the men in power were
satisfied that the gender "box" had been checked. As one commentator
noted, "The women, particularly Judge Hall and Judge Rymer, reflect
another White House strategy: mentioning certain names to score political
points, while not taking them seriously as contenders."[5] O'Connor effectively became a token, a dilemma we unpack more fully in chapter five.

Reagan's "strategy" and the resulting dearth of women selected for
federal judicial vacancies did not go unnoticed. In fact, the Senate conducted Oversight Hearings on Judicial Selection toward the end of his
presidency in an effort to make sense of his dismal record in appointing diverse candidates. As an introduction to the hearings, Senator Ted
Kennedy revealed statistics related to the appointment of women and
minorities to the judiciary under Reagan's watch. He explained:

> These statistics make it clear that the Reagan administration has aban-
> doned all pretense of promoting diversity in the Federal judiciary. Indeed,
> we will hear testimony today that the Reagan administration has never
> made a real effort to find qualified women and minorities to nominate to
> the Federal bench. The record suggests that in making nominations, the
> administration looks largely to a narrow cadre of white males who share
> its hardline judicial philosophy. While the President is surely entitled to

appoint nominees who are mainstream conservatives, he should not be permitted to homogenize the Federal judiciary.[6]

The hearings included extensive and detailed testimony from several senators and outside experts. Senator Kennedy's agenda for these hearings is best expressed by his insistence that "it is vitally important that all Americans have confidence that the Federal judiciary is not an exclusive club open only to white males."[7]

Of the 343 federal judges appointed by Reagan by the time of these hearings, only five were black. (President Carter, by contrast, appointed 38 black judges among his 265 total appointments.) Similarly, only 8.4 percent of Reagan's appointed judges up until the hearings were women, as compared to Carter's 15.5 percent. According to Senator Patrick Leahy, "It did not have to be that way. This Administration could have reached out to nominate more minorities and women—skilled, experienced, talented men and women— who would make outstanding federal judges. The result would have been a federal bench no less excellent than the federal bench that makes up the Reagan legacy. But this Administration chose the easy way out. It chose the Reagan legacy, as our nation enters its third century, a federal court system that many Americans perceive as unprepared to provide equal justice to an increasingly diverse American population."[8] Reagan's gubernatorial record of not appointing women followed him and similarly tainted his presidency.

Not all of the testimony in these hearings, however, expressed disapproval of Reagan's record. Senator Alan Simpson's remarks to the committee focused almost exclusively on the import of finding *qualified* candidates for the judiciary and resisted the idea of imposing a quota system.[9] His observations implied that maybe there were not enough women and minorities who possessed the requisite qualifications to justify appointment to the federal judiciary. He praised Reagan's efforts, highlighting that his record exceeded that of Ford, Nixon, and Johnson. Additionally, the testimony of Stephen Markman, assistant attorney general in the Office of Legal Policy, expressed a discernible defensiveness regarding the president's record of diversity in judicial appointments.[10]

Reagan could have established an authentic legacy of equality on the Supreme Court. But instead he filled the additional vacancies of his term with men. When Chief Justice Burger announced his retirement in 1986, Reagan elevated Rehnquist to chief justice without considering any other potential nominees. Reagan replaced him with Antonin Scalia after also shortlisting Robert Bork. Scalia was confirmed 98–0. The final opportunity came with Justice Powell's resignation in 1987. For this seat, Reagan initially shortlisted two women—Cynthia Holcomb Hall and Amalya Kearse—along with Bork again, whom he ultimately nominated. The Senate rejected Bork, however, with a vote of 42–58 after a fiercely contested battle led, in part, by civil rights and women's rights groups. Renowned academics, including Judith Resnik (who would go on to serve Anita Hill's legal team against Clarence Thomas), testified against him. Years later, Resnik wrote that "Bork's belief that the Equal Protection Clause of the US Constitution did not protect women was an important factor in the Senate's decision not to confirm him. So were several of Bork's decisions involving women's rights."[11] Interestingly, in contrast, Carla Hills testified before the Senate Judiciary Committee on Bork's behalf.[12] After Bork's failed nomination, Reagan revised the women appearing on the shortlist, this time including Cynthia Holcomb Hall, Edith Jones, and Pamela Rymer. He also named Anthony Kennedy, who he selected and the Senate confirmed 97–0, though the additional women shortlisted by Reagan post-O'Connor—Hall, Jones, and Rymer—certainly did not lack in qualifications.

TABLE 4.1. Women Shortlisted for the Supreme Court by Reagan after O'Connor

Name	Birth–Death	Law School	Significant Professional Achievement
Cynthia Holcomb Hall	1929–2011	Stanford	Judge, Ninth Circuit Court of Appeals
Pamela Rymer	1941–2011	Stanford	Judge, Ninth Circuit Court of Appeals
Edith Jones	1949–	University of Texas	Chief judge, Fifth Circuit Court of Appeals

Cynthia Holcomb Hall

I know it helped that I was a woman, a Republican, and a judge. If I had been a bra-burning liberal, I probably wouldn't have gotten the job.[13]
—Cynthia Holcomb Hall, *Los Angeles Daily Journal* (undated)

Cynthia Holcomb Hall credited her father with inspiring her to pursue a career, albeit not one in law.[14] He encouraged her to choose a teaching career, something more in line with traditional gender roles. He was adamant that she figure out how to make a living on her own, wanting to make sure she could support herself should a future husband die at war. Hall did indeed pursue a career, though not the role he believed more suitable. His guidance about financial independence was wise, however; while she did not lose her husband at war, they did divorce, leaving her as a single parent until later remarrying. She attended Stanford University for college (graduating in 1951) and then law school (graduating in 1954), while also serving in the United States Naval Reserve from 1951 to 1953.

FIGURE 4.1. Cynthia Holcomb Hall (Credit: U.S. Court of Appeals for the Ninth Circuit, public domain)

Hall entered law school having never stepped foot into a courtroom or known a lawyer growing up. When she told her father she planned to attend law school, he responded, "Well I'd never marry a lawyer but I guess it's no sin to raise one."[15] Hall was a year behind Sandra Day O'Connor at Stanford Law School and in the same class as John O'Connor, whom Hall befriended. He taught her how to annotate her lecture notes and, in her words, she "would not have gotten through it without him."[16] O'Connor had been Hall's friend as an undergraduate at Stanford, regularly sharing meals along with William Rehnquist's wife as well. The camaraderie from law school did not extend to the same sort of professional development networks men enjoyed, however, according to Hall: "I didn't have people I'd studied with in law school, which the men did."[17] She was also criticized for "taking a good man's place" and "wasting one of the few valuable spots" because presumably she would get married and never practice law.[18]

Following graduation, she became the first female clerk at the U.S. Court of Appeals for the Ninth Circuit, hired by Judge Richard Chambers in 1954. But even with the prestigious clerkship and her other impeccable credentials, the job search proved difficult. She received advice from one law partner to obtain a specialty degree, and so she attended NYU Law for an LLM in Taxation, graduating in 1960. She left her daughter behind with her parents because housing options did not accommodate a single parent. Hall recalled, "I couldn't get into a law firm when I got out of law school. After getting a Master's degree in the area of tax law, after spending—being a law clerk to a judge in the Ninth Circuit, after spending four years as a trial lawyer in the Tax Division of the Department of Justice, after spending two years on the staff of the Secretary of the Treasury in Tax policy, I then went out to look for a job in private practice."[19] Like most of the shortlisted women, private practice was not an immediate option until putting in years of service elsewhere.

Hall's persistence paid off, however, and President Nixon nominated her to the Tax Court in Washington, D.C., in 1972. To entice her to take the position, her husband John was nominated at the same time as a

THE SHORTLISTS FOLLOWING O'CONNOR | 107

deputy assistant secretary for tax policy so that they would not be forced to navigate a cross-country marriage. Apparently, such dual appointments were unprecedented in government, though it was not dissimilar to the double recruitment of Soia Mentschikoff and her husband Karl Llewellyn by the University of Chicago Law School. Hall was aware of the pervasive gender bias of the era, reflecting, "I don't suppose anyone would ever have reached out to me had there not been an effort by the White House to look for women."[20] Her hiring was part of the initiative spearheaded by Barbara Hackman Franklin to bring more women into senior positions during the Nixon administration.

Reagan later nominated Hall to the U.S. District Court for the Central District of California in 1981, a year after her husband died in an airplane crash. She was sworn in by Sandra Day O'Connor. In 1984, Reagan elevated her to the United States Court of Appeals for the Ninth Circuit.

When Justice Powell retired in 1987, a White House memorandum circulated describing her superb "confirmability":

Judge Cynthia Hall is second in seniority (after Sandra Day O'Connor) among women federal judges appointed by President Reagan. Prior to her appointment in 1981, the *Washington Post* observed that she was the "sole woman known to be a strong contender for a judgeship" in the Reagan Administration. Her ten years as a federal trial judge preceding her appointment to the Ninth Circuit Court of Appeals make her, at the age of 56, one of the longest-sitting Republican women judges. Her academic, professional and intellectual qualifications are first rate. Throughout her tenure as a federal trial and appellate court judge, she has consistently evidenced a solidly conservative judicial philosophy . . . Throughout Judge Hall's career, she has not attracted any negative publicity. To the contrary, she has been consistently mentioned in articles otherwise critical of the Reagan Administration's judicial appointments. For example, she was a lonely bright spot in an otherwise dour article appearing in the *Washington Post* on September 10, 1982, entitled "Reagan's Judiciary: Mostly White, Mostly Men." . . . The National Women's Political Caucus has criticized the President's record in appointing women to federal judgeships as "abysmal" . . . Overall, Judge Hall appears to be the perfect Reagan judge. Moreover, she would have little problem with confirmation. She is a woman head of household with two bright children (she has been quoted in the press as wondering whether "women who give up a husband or a family to have a career, or give up a career to have a family . . . get to a point when they realize they've missed something. I liked having a husband, I love my children, and I wouldn't give up my career for all the world, although I've worked hard to manage them all") . . . Indeed, it is tough to find any shortcomings in Judge Hall save that she is 56 instead of 46 . . .

Judge Hall is an excellent prospect for the Supreme Court. As it happens, she is a woman, and the most qualified in the country of her gender. But more importantly, she stands shoulder-to-shoulder with the small group of male Supreme Court candidates, based solely on her merits.[21]

That same memorandum resurfaced during the George H. W. Bush presidency when other vacancies arose. Despite her pristine Supreme Court credentials, Hall remained on the U.S. Court of Appeals for the Ninth Circuit until she passed away in 2011.

Pamela Rymer

The women, particularly Judge Hall and Judge Rymer, reflect another White House strategy: mentioning certain names to score political points, while not taking them seriously as contenders.[22]
—Reporter for the *New York Times*, 1987

Pamela Rymer was born in Knoxville, Tennessee, and attended Vassar College, like Sylvia Bacon, graduating in 1961. She immediately enrolled at Stanford Law School and graduated in 1964—just over a decade after Hall and O'Connor—and subsequently worked on Barry Goldwater's

FIGURE 4.2. Pamela Rymer
(Credit: Steve Gladfelter)

presidential campaign. She entered private law practice in 1966 and became the first female partner of Lillick, McHose & Charles. She eventually founded her own firm, Toy and Rymer, where she worked from 1975 to 1983.

Rymer was nominated to the U.S. District Court for the Central District of California in 1983 by President Reagan. She soon became a contender for a seat on the California Supreme Court, but she removed herself from consideration to remain viable for a seat on the U.S. Court of Appeals for the Ninth Circuit. That decision was wise, as President George H. W. Bush elevated her to the Ninth Circuit in 1989. She was forty-eight years old at the time and remained unmarried without children. Her judicial appointment filled the opening left by Justice Kennedy when Reagan appointed him to the Supreme Court—Rymer stayed on the shortlist. Her reputation as a judge was for "her carefully reasoned decisions" and she "was considered one of the toughest sentencing judges on the U.S. District Court in Los Angeles."[23] The ABA rated her "exceptionally well qualified," but conservatives objected to her potential views on women's rights and abortion. Throughout the duration of her career on the bench, Rymer authored more than 300 opinions.

Among her notable work on the bench, Rymer wrote for the majority in *Planned Parenthood v. American Coalition of Life Activists*,[24] decided by the Ninth Circuit in 2002, which held that the First Amendment does not protect internet threats against physicians who perform abortions. She joined the more liberal judges on the court, in a deeply divided 6–5 vote upholding a jury verdict and judicial injunction against an anti-abortion group. Rymer poured much energy into supporting Stanford University throughout her career, including service on the Board of Trustees, and was known to be an extraordinary mentor to her clerks. She was also described as "very elegant and always perfectly coiffed" and at the same time "something of a mystery outside of the courtroom, [leading] a very discreet private life."[25] No funeral services were held when she passed away in 2011, and no survivors were listed in a press release issued by the Ninth Circuit.

Edith Jones

Judge Jones has been on the shortlist longer than most contenders have been on the bench.[26]
—Reporter for the *Wall Street Journal*, 2005

Edith Jones was appointed by Reagan to the U.S. Court of Appeals for the Fifth Circuit in 1985. She studied economics at Cornell University, graduating with honors, and earned her law degree from the University of Texas Law School, where she served as a law review editor and graduated Order of the Coif. She began her professional life in 1974 at the firm now known as Hunton Andrews Kurth. Jones became the first female partner of the firm in 1982, an honor bestowed upon her while on maternity leave with her second child. While "an unknown commodity to most Houston practitioners when she was appointed"[27] to the Fifth Circuit, she quickly established a reputation as a strong and outspoken conservative. Her judicial opinions have called into question the *Roe v. Wade*[28] abortion decision, supported expediting death penalty

FIGURE 4.3. Edith Jones (Credit: University of Houston Law Center)

executions, and she has also spoken openly about the importance of "moral values."[29] Additionally, she supported the creation of stricter bankruptcy laws, and in a 1997 opinion overturned a federal ban on the possession of machine guns.[30] According to a White House memorandum vetting her potential candidacy for the Court, she was "tough on drugs" and "genuinely concerned with protecting the rights of mentally retarded and handicapped citizens."[31]

Not only was she shortlisted by Reagan, but, like Hall, she resurfaced when President George H. W. Bush needed to fill a vacancy with the resignation of William Brennan. She must have come extremely close to being selected. The Bush presidential archives contain an official speech printed on heavy, formal paper that reads:

My oath to the Constitution charges me to faithfully execute the Office of President and to the best of my ability preserve, protect, and defend the Constitution of the United States. Few duties are more important in discharging that obligation than my responsibility under Article II, Section 2 of our Constitution to select, from among all possible choices, one nominee to fill a vacancy on the Supreme Court of the United States. The task of narrowing the selection to one highly qualified jurist committed to the rule of law and faithful to the Constitution could never be easy, but I have found it enormously satisfying. My choice, I think, will serve the Court and the Constitution well.

I am most pleased to announce that I will nominate as Associate Justice of the United States Supreme Court a remarkable woman of vigorous intellect and first-rate ability—a firm Judge, a fair Judge, and a Judge committed to interpreting the law—Judge Edith Jones of the United States Court of Appeals for the Fifth Circuit. Judge Jones, I believe with all my heart, will prove a worthy Member of the Court. Let me pay tribute to the man whose retirement from the Court created the vacancy I will nominate Judge Jones to fill, Justice William Brennan.[32]

Jones joked in a handwritten thank-you note to President Bush after meeting with him to discuss her candidacy that it "was the first 'job interview' I'd had in 17 years—since I first went to Andrews & Kurth."[33] Some were surprised by Bush's selection of David Souter over Jones. Others speculated that she would be the choice when another vacancy opened. Instead, Jones served as chief judge of the United States Court of Appeals for the Fifth Circuit from 2006 to 2012, and, in 2019, remained on the court after stepping down from this leadership role. (She was subsequently shortlisted by George W. Bush in his eventual selection of John Roberts, Harriet Miers, and Samuel Alito.)

George H. W. Bush shortlisted no women when he faced another vacancy, and he selected Clarence Thomas to fill Justice Marshall's seat in 1991, though, as noted previously, Amalya Kearse's name was floated as a possible back-up plan had Thomas's nomination failed in the wake of the Anita Hill controversy. Bush instead appointed "rich, white men" to the federal judiciary, giving him a "lackluster record . . . all the more disappointing because the pool of qualified women and minority candidates increased greatly."[34] A report by the Alliance for Justice found "[o]nly 7 percent of the president's court appointees are black or Hispanic . . . and 14 percent are women."[35] Nan Aron, executive director of the Alliance for Justice, critiqued his record, saying "Bush judges could not be less representative of the American people in whose name they render judicial verdicts."[36] Of course, this was an improvement, however modest, over previous administrations other than Carter.[37]

The Handful of Women Who Made It Off the Shortlist after O'Connor

During the Senate hearings critiquing Reagan's record of appointments, Senator Leahy addressed the committee in the following way: "The Reagan legacy of a federal bench largely closed to minorities and women was an avoidable disappointment. Over the last few decades, the legal profession as a whole has benefited from an influx of talented members of previously excluded groups. This trend has accelerated during the 1980s. But as the bar has become more diverse, more reflective of American society as a whole, the federal bench has become less diverse."[38] Leahy was correct that law schools were graduating more women and minorities than in the past, but the coveted power positions in law and elsewhere were still reserved for white men. While the judiciary has, over time, become a place of greater diversity than other parts of the legal profession, it still has a long way to go.

After Reagan, every president shortlisted at least one woman for the Supreme Court during his time in office, though not for every vacancy—as we note above, George H. W. Bush created an all-male shortlist when he nominated Thomas. What once was unimaginable—a woman on the shortlist, let alone the bench—is now accepted as the norm. Women regularly appear among the official pool of Supreme Court contenders.

In some ways, this represents progress to celebrate, since one must be on the shortlist in order to be selected. In other ways, however, the shortlists for the Supreme Court and other positions of leadership or power have become political tools. They function as nothing more than hollow nods toward equality while legitimating prejudice and bias as more white men are selected. We explore the consequences of shortlisting in law and other professions in the second half of the book.

Unlike the shortlisting process, which occurs behind closed doors through networks of private relationships, the confirmation process is very public. Candidates are assessed by bar association committees, paraded through the halls of Congress, scrutinized by the media, and subjected to long days of countless questions in Senate hearings. The public nature of the confirmation process affords greater detail about the unequal experiences of women. Four women join O'Connor in receiving the honor of being nominated for the Supreme Court, three of whom were confirmed.

TABLE 4.2. Women Nominated for the Supreme Court after O'Connor

Name	Birth–Death	Presidential Shortlist	Law School	Significant Professional Achievement
Ruth Bader Ginsburg	1933–	Clinton	Columbia; Harvard	Judge, D.C. Circuit Court of Appeals
Harriet Miers	1945–	G. W. Bush	Southern Methodist University	White House Counsel
Sonia Sotomayor	1954–	Obama	Yale	Judge, Second Circuit Court of Appeals
Elena Kagan	1960–	Obama	Harvard	U.S. Solicitor General

Ruth Bader Ginsburg

We should not be held back from pursuing our full talents, from contributing what we could contribute to the society, because we fit into a certain mold, because we belong to a group that historically has been the object of discrimination.[39]
—Justice Ruth Bader Ginsburg in an interview with journalist Lynn Sherr, 2001

Twelve years and four vacancies passed after O'Connor was appointed before a second woman would go from shortlisted to confirmed. President Clinton was just three months into his presidency when

FIGURE 4.4. Sandra Day O'Connor, Sonia Sotomayor, Ruth Bader Ginsburg, and Elena Kagan (Credit: Steve Petteway, photographer for the Supreme Court of the United States, public domain)

notified of Byron White's retirement. This occurred on the heels of the debacle of the Thomas confirmation, where Anita Hill's highly credible accusations of his sexual harassment ushered in 1992's "Year of the Woman," during which women swept into political offices in unprecedented numbers. Ruth Bader Ginsburg rode that wave, but she was not Clinton's first choice, and women's groups—both conservative and liberal—opposed her. Feminist law professor Catherine MacKinnon critiqued Ginsburg's philosophy that men and women should be treated equally under the law as ignoring the historic oppression of women. Additionally, abortion opponents and champions alike expressed concern about her appointment.

Clinton's top pick was reportedly New York's governor Mario Cuomo, whom he courted for months. When Cuomo let the opportunity pass, Clinton mused about other possible candidates, including his own wife, Hillary Rodham Clinton. At the same time, Marty Ginsburg was working behind the scenes to secure support for his wife's candidacy from across the country, seeking letters authored by lawyers, legal scholars, and political organizations. Ruth Ginsburg had an impeccable background that made her particularly well-suited to be elevated to the Court. She attended Cornell University for undergraduate and started law school at Harvard, where she was one of nine women in a class of 500. She transferred to Columbia Law School, and tied there for first in her class at graduation, where she later served as a tenured professor after beginning her academic career at Rutgers School of Law. She became general counsel for the American Civil Liberties Union in 1973 and was appointed by President Carter to the U.S. Court of Appeals for the District of Columbia in 1980. Ginsburg argued six cases—and won five of them—in front of the Supreme Court before she became a judge, all of which dealt with gender discrimination in some way.[40]

After Clinton selected her from his shortlist as the nominee, the media attention immediately focused on her gender. One article encouraged senators to "Treat Judge Ginsburg Like a Man."[41] Another reporter noted that Ginsburg's "whole career, not only her gender," rendered her qualified for the position.[42] The media also focused on Ginsburg's personal life, particularly on her relationship with Marty and their seemingly unconventional but unquestionably loving and supportive marriage, in which he supported her career and handled domestic tasks. In "The Man Behind the High Court Nominee," a reporter for the New York Times wrote that "[e]ven though she had established an extraordinary record as a lawyer and teacher, Ms. Ginsburg has acknowledged that without the strong personal and political support of her husband, she may never have become President Clinton's choice for the Supreme Court."[43] In the Washington Post, Ginsburg's husband was named "The Spouse of Ruth; Marty Ginsburg, the Pre-Feminism Feminist."[44] Among

the more interesting passages from this article is a reflection on Ginsburg's skills as a new wife, describing her as a "complex young woman
with large ambitions, [who] placed a lumpy mass of tortured protein on
a plate in front of the person she had recently married," insisting it was
"tuna fish casserole."[45] Ginsburg was "phased . . . out of the kitchen at a
relatively early age" because her children found their father to be a better cook.[46] The *Washington Post* called Ginsburg "motherly enough for
traditionalists."[47]

Notably, in our media study that examined articles written by the
New York Times and the *Washington Post* about Supreme Court nominees from 1970 to 2010, not one of the male nominees' domestic abilities,
such as cooking skills, received attention. By contrast, details about the
domestic capabilities (or lack thereof) for all of the female nominees
made the headlines.[48] Fortunately, the Senate did not require excellence
in the kitchen as a prerequisite to confirmation, and voted 96–3 to appoint Ginsburg in 1993, making her the second woman, and first Jewish
woman, to join the nation's most prestigious judicial body.

After giving the country its second female justice, Clinton later shortlisted Amalya Kearse, who previously appeared on Reagan's shortlist, but
he ultimately selected Stephen Breyer for Justice Blackmun's seat in 1994.
Like Reagan, President Clinton was happy to check the woman box for
the shortlist but not willing to actually select more than one woman for
the Court. One token female Supreme Court nominee per president was
apparently the limit.

Harriet Miers

So conservatives are caught between loyalty to their ideas
and loyalty to the president they admire. Most of them have
come out against Miers—quietly or loudly. Establishment
Republicans are displaying their natural loyalty to leadership. And Miers is caught in the vise between these two
forces [conservatism and Republicanism], a smart and good

woman who has been put in a position where she cannot succeed.[49]

—David Brooks, *New York Times* op-ed, 2005

Harriet Miers was the third woman officially nominated for the Supreme Court in 2005, making it off President George W. Bush's shortlist that included three other women: Edith Jones (yet again!) and two other judges from the U.S. Court of Appeals for the Fifth Circuit—Edith Clement and Priscilla Owen. When O'Connor announced her retirement, she and others, including Justice Ginsburg and first ladies Hillary Clinton and Laura Bush, publicly expressed hope that the president would name another woman to the Court. Instead, he nominated John Roberts, then a judge on the U.S. Court of Appeals for the D.C. Circuit. (Perhaps not coincidentally, Roberts, while working in the Office of Legal Counsel in the 1980s, had helped prepare O'Connor for her own Senate confirmation hearings.) But, just over a month after the announcement, Chief Justice Rehnquist passed away, leaving Bush with two simultaneous vacancies to fill. Bush then nominated Roberts to fill the role of chief justice, and obliged the wish of his wife and others for a woman by selecting White House Counsel Miers. Similar to Justices Clark, Murphy, Rehnquist, and White, Miers had worked to vet candidates when Roberts was selected only to then find herself the nominee. Unlike those men, however, her candidacy would be fraught with controversy.

As with many of the women profiled in this book, Miers overcame significant family hardships in her youth before she accomplished many firsts as a female lawyer. Her family fell into debt after her father suffered a stroke during her first year as an undergraduate at Southern Methodist University (SMU). She persevered and secured admission to SMU's law school, one of seven women in a class of almost one hundred. Miers excelled in law school, landing a spot on the law review and then a judicial clerkship with Texas District Judge Joe Estes after graduation in 1970. She then joined the Dallas firm Locke, Liddell & Sapp, where she was eventually named the first female managing partner.

FIGURE 4.5. Harriet Miers, with
President George W. Bush
(Credit: White House Photo by
Paul Morse, public domain)

Miers practiced law for decades and was the first female president
of both the Dallas Bar Association and the Texas State Bar Association
before serving George W. Bush during his time as governor of Texas in
1995. She also chaired the Texas Lottery Commission, leaving that role in
2000 as Bush anticipated a White House campaign. After his inauguration, she held several roles in the administration, including assistant to
the president, deputy chief of staff for policy, and White House counsel,
the position she held when Bush announced his intention to place her
on the Court in 2005.

Miers's many years of government service providing legal counsel to
a governor and president are what led Bush to select her for the vacancy.
Indeed, some might say that she had been on a decades-long interview
and vetting for the role. While she did not graduate from one of the
more prestigious law schools that recent nominees claim as their alma
mater, like Yale or Harvard, she was at the top of her class at a well-
regarded institution at a time where women were rarely present in any
law school. She consistently rose to the highest leadership roles in her
firm and bar organizations.

However, even with these strong credentials, Miers was critiqued
as being inexperienced for not having served as a judge, though others on the Court over the years lacked this experience, including William Rehnquist (the seat Miers would fill) and Elena Kagan, who would
later make it off President Obama's shortlist. Conservatives questioned

Miers's commitment to their values, much like they had done to Mildred Lillie. Similarly, the media focused endlessly on her appearance and status as a single woman. The *New York Times* and the *Washington Post* reminded readers of Harriet Miers's fondness for "girls' nights out"[50] and engaging in "a lot of girl talk"[51] with "Condi and the other single girls,"[52] referencing then-Secretary of State Condoleezza Rice. Reporters noted that "Miers enjoys the absolute confidence of the president, who once called her 'a pit bull in size 6 shoes,'" and that in her youth, "Harriet was blond, pretty and athletic—she captained the tennis team as a senior, and was voted 'best all around in sports'—but she was known as more serious than social. While the cool girls wore bouffant hairdos, she wore a long braid wound modestly around her head."[53] Another article reported that "[h]er red Mercedes-Benz was such a fixture in the West Wing lot that colleagues called it an abandoned car; she has never married or had children, and some of her friends believe she has sacrificed her personal life for work."[54]

Robert Bork, whose own confirmation process derailed, wrote a scathing op-ed in the *Wall Street Journal*, complaining that "[t]he administration's defense of the nomination is pathetic: Ms. Miers was a bar association president (a non-qualification for anyone familiar with the bureaucratic service that leads to such presidencies),"[55] even though Justice Powell's service as president of the American Bar Association had been touted among his exemplary credentials for securing his seat on the Court. Nixon, for one, lauded Powell's experience as "President of the American Bar Association, and [noted] in that . . . role he provided leadership in the provision of legal services for the needy and with revision of the standards for criminal justice."[56] An asset for a male nominee was characterized as a liability for a female nominee, a phenomenon that by now is all too familiar for readers of this book.

Rather than emphasize her actual qualifications as a skilled lawyer and leader, the administration touted her religious convictions—an evangelical Christian who, by implication, would vote to overturn *Roe v. Wade*[57]—in an effort to appease conservative critics. This strategy failed. Miers withdrew her name from consideration after only twenty-four days. In her place, Bush nominated Samuel Alito, who was confirmed with minimal controversy by a vote of 58–42, mostly along partisan lines. The media focused little on his personal life and, to the extent it did, highlighted lawyerly qualities: "As a parent, Judge Alito appears to follow his parents' model. Hilary Monaco, a friend and neighbor, said she and Judge Alito spent many hours coaching the high school mock trial team. He taught the students, including his son Philip, the rules of evidence and how to write opening and closing statements. In 2001, the team made it to the county semifinals—its best performance, she said."[58] There was no mention of Alito's boys' nights out, hairstyles, or shoe size.

Sonia Sotomayor and Elena Kagan

Here we go again. For the second time in a year, a childless, unmarried woman in her 50s has been nominated to be a justice on the Supreme Court and the critics have come out swinging.[59]
—Reporter for the *New York Times*, 2010

President Barack Obama broke with the token tradition of his predecessors, not only shortlisting numerous women[60] but selecting two women for seats on the Court: Sonia Sotomayor in 2009 (also the first Latina) and Elena Kagan (the second Jewish woman) in 2010. Sotomayor's education places her among the most well-pedigreed justices, having graduated *summa cum laude* from Princeton in 1976 and from Yale Law School in 1979. She worked in government and private practice, first as an assistant district attorney in New York County followed by time at Pavia & Harcourt. She became a judge of the U.S. District Court, Southern District of New York in 1992, appointed by President George H. W. Bush, where she remained until President Clinton appointed her to the United States Court of Appeals for the Second Circuit in 1998. Ten years later, President Obama nominated her to the Supreme Court, where she was confirmed by a vote of 68–31 in 2009.

Equally well-pedigreed, Kagan also attended Princeton, graduating *summa cum laude* in 1981, and then Harvard Law School, graduating *magna cum laude* in 1983. She clerked for Justice Thurgood Marshall and worked for many years in government. She was the first female solicitor general, appointed by Obama in 2009. Kagan also taught at the University of Chicago Law School (with Obama) and Harvard Law School, serving as Harvard's dean from 2003 to 2008. Like Miers, Kagan had no experience as a judge. She had not even argued a case in any court until she did so in 2009 as solicitor general. Just a year into that role, she was confirmed to the Court by a vote of 63–37.

While the selection of two women by the same president signaled significant progress, the gendered media coverage of their professional and personal lives rivaled that describing Mildred Lillie in her bathing suit in the early 1970s. Criticism leveraged against the two women regarding beauty, fashion sensibility, marriage, motherhood status, and sexuality accompanied the usual assessment of qualifications and experience for Supreme Court nominees. As one commentator wrote when Obama contemplated filling his first vacancy:

Consider the two women widely considered the frontrunners for the nomination: former Harvard Law School dean and current Solicitor General Elena Kagan, and federal appellate judge Sonia Sotomayor. Within hours after the news broke that Souter was resigning, concerns arose that Kagan and Sotomayor might be too fat to replace him. A commentator on the site DemConWatch.com noted that of the three most-mentioned candidates "the oldest (federal judge Diane Wood) is the only one who looks healthy," while Kagan and Sotomayor "are quite overweight. That's a risk factor that they may not last too long on the court because of their health." The author further quipped, "For some men, the only thing more intolerable than the sight of a powerful woman is the sight of a powerful woman they don't want to sleep with." The author went on to observe, however, that the news coverage about the female candidates' weight and health is "destructive" and that if "we were really concerned about medical risk factors that actually do have a significant negative correlation with a candidate's life expectancy, the most relevant is one that has afflicted 108 of America's 110 Supreme Court justices: being a man."[61]

Much attention was devoted to Sotomayor's lack of a personal life, similar to that which surrounded Harriet Miers. One headline declared "Sotomayor: A Single Supreme?," and the article reported, with exuberance, that there was yet "[a]nother first on the Supreme Court! If Sonia Sotomayor is confirmed, she'll be its first . . . bachelorette."[62] The article went on to describe her first failed "college marriage," her subsequent "fizzled" engagement to Peter White, and her current single status.[63] The author projected pity on Sotomayor: "Who's going to accompany her to those fancy White House dinners?"[64] Similarly, an additional article appearing in the New York Times, titled "A Trail Blazer and a Dreamer," reported that Sotomayor, "[d]ivorced and with no children, . . . enjoys the ballet and theater"[65] instead of a robust domestic life. The Washington Post ran the headline "Friends Provide Glimpse Into Nominee's 'Very Full Life,'" noting that, "[a] 54-year-old divorced woman who never had children, Sotomayor is said to be a workaholic who fills her free time with a huge network of close friends, extended family members, colleagues, former classmates and just about anyone else who has entered her circle."[66] The article interviewed her friends as saying that "[o]ut of deference to her privacy, the one topic [of] Sotomayor's [they] won't discuss is her personal relationships."[67] But the reporters made sure to confirm "that Sotomayor 'does date.'"[68]

The novelty of the nomination of the first single woman to the Supreme Court did not wear off even after Sotomayor's confirmation. The New York Times headline "Then Comes the Marriage Question" appeared during Kagan's nomination.[69] The author wrote, "This time Elena Kagan, the former dean of Harvard's law school, who is now solicitor general, has been described as having sacrificed a home and personal life in her quest for a brilliant legal career."[70] The *Washington Post* ran a similarly-themed article with the following headline: "The Supreme Court Needs More Mothers."[71] The story articulated how alive and well the prejudice surrounding motherhood continues to be, even into the twenty-first century: "Motherhood offers a one-word verifier. It signals a woman with an intensity of life experiences, jammed with joys and fears, unpredictability and intimacy, all outside the workplace. Much of the time, it's the opposite of being strategic and assiduously prepared."[72] The role that kept generations of women from the workplace—motherhood—was now deemed essential for a "respectable" nominee. Two days later, the *New York Times* published an article entitled "Judging Women," in which the author observed, "If Elena Kagan is confirmed by the Senate, there will be three women on the Supreme Court for the first time. This is a measure of how far women have come. Two will be single and childless. This may be a measure of something else entirely."[73] What exactly that "something else" might be is left unsaid, but the author seems to imply a world where women cannot be both justices and mothers. "She really is a thinker," a colleague said of Kagan.[74] "She is not married and she doesn't have family in her life. Her books are, in many ways, her companions. She has a lot of friends. But she's lived alone, and the world of books and ideas is her world."[75] One reporter observed that "double-entendre wisecracks about Kagan's softball prowess were all the rage on Fox News and MSNBC."[76] An article in the *Washington Post* explained about Kagan, "[s]he's not gay, okay? Actually, the all-too-public discussion about the ought-to-be private topic of Elena Kagan's sexuality would be easier if the Supreme Court nominee were gay."[77]

President Obama faced a third vacancy about a year before the end of his second term when Justice Scalia passed away unexpectedly. Obama shortlisted[78] three women and three men, and nominated Merrick Garland, a judge on the U.S. Court of Appeals for the D.C. Circuit. Republicans, controlling both houses of Congress at the time, refused to hold confirmation hearings or a vote, leaving the seat vacant until after the 2016 presidential election. President Donald J. Trump filled the seat along with that vacated by Justice Kennedy soon after taking office, both seats going to men even though several women appeared on the short-list. We return to Trump's shortlists and selections at the end of the book in chapter eight.

* * *

As this book went to press, an entire decade had passed since a woman was last nominated to the Supreme Court. It bears repeating, and remembering, that *less than half of one percent* of Supreme Court jus-tices since the founding of this nation have been women. We are a very long way from Ruth Bader Ginsburg's nine. But what might we learn from the shortlisted women profiled here? The second half of the book turns to an exploration of the personal and professional lives of these extraordinary women to illuminate and address solutions to the contin-ued gender inequities that persist for positions of power and leadership not just on the Supreme Court, but throughout the legal profession . . . and beyond.

PART II

Their Stories Are Our Stories

Transcending Shortlists

A system of justice is the richer for the diversity of background and experience of its participants. It is the poorer,
in terms of evaluating what is at stake and the impact of its
judgments, if its members—its lawyers, jurors, and judges—
are all cast from the same mold.[1]
—Ruth Bader Ginsburg, speech at Southwestern University
School of Law, 2003

Justice Ginsburg's observation above is true not only for the legal system,
but for all institutions of power that have historically lacked diverse participants. While most women will never find themselves shortlisted for
the Supreme Court, they will be considered for important roles throughout their careers. Inevitably, a list of qualified candidates emerges for a
given position, and while women's names sometimes appear on that list,
men are more likely to be selected. The effects of this shortlisting fall
exceptionally hard on women of color.

We now turn from the historical narrative about how women found
their way onto presidential shortlists for the Supreme Court and change
course to explore their experiences in the context of themes that cut across
generations. We examine how these women navigated challenges in their
personal lives and professional careers. These stories teach others how to
transition from shortlisted to seriously considered to finally *selected*.

Telling stories is essential to the practice of law. Before law schools
provided legal education, aspiring advocates apprenticed with senior
lawyers. Storytelling, like the evocative tales of Abraham Lincoln, offers

lessons few casebooks could match. Critical legal theorists have recently reclaimed this historic practice by sharing the stories of those on the margins. Few of the women profiled in the book chronicled their own lives and experiences. An exception is Florence Allen, who wrote two books. One is devoted to the law, *This Constitution of Ours*,[2] and the other is more personal, a memoir, *To Do Justly*.[3] Her memoir took her twenty-five years to complete and was published a year before she died. Historians have speculated that had Allen completed the book sooner, it would have garnered readership from those like Eleanor Roosevelt and may have even helped her secure the nomination for the Supreme Court. Three of the four women confirmed for the Court have written autobiographies, but none of the others who appear in these pages have done so.[4] Our shortlisted women suffered both indignities and triumphs, unaware that their lives would inspire future generations of women. These women are unwitting mentors to all of us.

The consequences of systemic shortlisting extend beyond the fact that women are denied positions of distinction; their tales are also routinely subjugated. We should all be familiar with their stories, as they reflect not only fascinating details of their lived experiences, but also an unfairly stifled but important national identity, and an imagination of what we might become.

Part two weaves together many stories and narratives from the lives of the shortlisted women to help identify lessons at both individual and societal levels, and to develop remedies for the gendered consequences that follow from shortlisting. We hope that these lessons will serve as a guide for those who are underrepresented to more successfully navigate the barriers, challenges, and obstacles that impede advancement through the pipeline to power in the legal profession and elsewhere. More important, we hope that these lessons motivate those in power to implement structural changes to further diversity, equality, and inclusion.

5

After Shortlisted, Tokenism

We should not think or speak of the desirability of a token woman at any level in the judiciary, including the Supreme Court. Rather, the object is women—lots of women—at all levels of the judiciary, including the Supreme Court. Yes, there is a dearth of women judges. And isn't it ironic that justice is portrayed as a woman.[1]
—Cornelia Kennedy, remarks to the Women Law Students Association, October 21, 1978

I've always said it's fine to be the first, but you don't want to be the last. I was acutely aware of the negative consequences if I arrived here and did a poor job. It made me hesitant to say yes when the president called.[2]
—Sandra Day O'Connor in a rare interview with the *Chicago Tribune*, 2003

Although Justice O'Connor did not invoke the word "tokenism" to describe her trepidation about accepting President Reagan's offer to join the Court, she captured the pressures it caused in her quote, above. Often, when a member of an underrepresented group is shortlisted, nominated, appointed, hired, or promoted, he or she becomes a token. Tokenism is defined by the *Oxford English Dictionary* as "[t]he practice of making only a perfunctory or symbolic effort to do a particular thing, especially by recruiting a small number of people from underrepresented groups in order to give the appearance of sexual or racial equality."[3] Development of the concept is widely attributed to Harvard business professor Rosabeth Moss Kanter, who relied on it to explain the consequences for women beginning to enter the workplace in the 1970s. In her seminal work *Men, Women, and the Corporation*,[4] Kanter exposed how corporations would hire women to make clear their presence was not opposed, but women would never be integrated fully into the organizations and were always looked at as "other."

Token individuals rarely feel like they fit in or that they are part of the normal course of business in the workplace. Rather, they find themselves subjected to rigorous scrutiny and pressure, as noted by O'Connor, or are frequently ignored or overlooked. Amalya Kearse's recollection of a celebration with her family after she was sworn into the U.S. Court of Appeals for the Sixth Circuit in 1979 offers an example of this invisibility:

> A very nice induction ceremony . . . [a]nd afterwards about a dozen of us were going out to dinner. And we were going to a nice restaurant in midtown New York. . . . My mother by the way was a doctor. And I was very lucky to have her there when I was sworn in. We arrive at the restaurant and we were seated at our table, we were the first to arrive when the next person arrived. She asked, "Are Judge Kearse and Dr. Kearse here yet?" and she was told by the waiter, "No, just two ladies."[5]

So few women of color had achieved prominence in the judiciary (or the medical profession) that Judge Kearse's professional accomplishment (and that of her mother) were unimaginable.

Mildred Lillie had a similar experience while she was on the bench. In her oral history she recounts arriving to preside over the municipal court: "I presented myself to the clerk, but I did not tell the clerk who I was. I asked, 'Could you tell me where the judge's chambers are?' He said, 'I have no time for that and the judge isn't here and you'll have to wait.' Finally I said, 'I'm the judge.' He looked me all over and said, 'You're kidding.'"[6] The clerk's shock at seeing a female judge is reminiscent of a story told by Cornelia Kennedy: "In 1979, the new women judges organization met in Washington, D.C. A reception was held at the Supreme Court where 200 of us gathered in the east conference room. As Chief

Justice Warren Burger came into the room to greet us, he exclaimed in a surprised voice: 'are all of you women judges?'"[7]

Tokenism creates both individual and societal harms in a number of ways. First, the practice obstructs equality because it inhibits increased selection of the underrepresented group. In other words, the presence of only one woman or minority in a position of leadership or power leads to the mistaken belief that inequality has been eradicated. Second, tokenism results in the lone woman or minority bearing the burden of being perceived as representative of all women or all minorities.[8] The laser focus on a single member of a minority group often leads to inappropriate scrutiny of the individual's professional and personal life. Third, tokenism, as a practice, does little to correct rampant gender disparity in the workplace, thereby allowing harms like sexual harassment to proliferate in an environment that remains heavily dominated by men. All of the women profiled in this book were tokens in various ways, whether they were considered or ultimately selected for the Supreme Court. This chapter delves further into their lives to explore the harmful consequences that flow from tokenism.

Tokenism Preserves the Status Quo

Tokenism impedes equal representation by facilitating the assumption that equality has been achieved based on the presence of a woman or minority individual. Their presence signals, albeit inaccurately, that the "woman problem" or "race problem" has been solved. This misperception reduces the sense of urgency or importance of ongoing efforts to diversify the bench or the boardroom.

Recall the listing of Florence Allen on the 1937 Roosevelt administration memorandum addressing the court packing plan. Allen was unequivocally qualified, rivaling if not exceeding the judicial experience of her contemporary sisters in law—not to mention all of the men—who made it onto the Court. Yet, she was a token contender as the sole woman to appear on his shortlist and was the only woman to sit on a federal court of appeals for many years. Similarly, consider how President Nixon shortlisted Sylvia Bacon and Mildred Lillie, and then submitted Lillie's name strategically to the ABA to quiet the loud voices demanding the appointment of a woman to the Court while hoping she would be sabotaged by a poor rating. The net effect of this strategy allowed Nixon to take credit for advancing the cause of gender equality without actually following through and appointing a woman. This exemplifies the most classic kind of tokenism: placing a woman on the list to give the appearance of a commitment to diversity while perpetuating the status quo, allowing members of the dominant group to continue being selected.

O'Connor's nomination also functioned to preserve the status quo, even though it simultaneously forever changed the face of the Supreme Court. With his token female justice on the highest court, Reagan appointed few additional women to the federal judiciary during his eight years in office. As noted in part one, his own administration was well aware of this troubling reality. An internal memo prepared in fall of 1981 for Elizabeth Dole, then-director of the White House Office of Public Liaison, proclaimed, "Unless the proportion of women selected increases substantially, the O'Connor nomination may well be labeled as mere tokenism and not truly reflective of any trend in this Administration toward increased recognition and participation of women."[9] Despite the acute awareness of this problem, it was never rectified in any meaningful way by the Reagan administration. At the end of his two terms, only four of seventy-eight vacancies on federal appellate courts were filled by women, less than one percent.[10]

Tokenism Imposes Burdens

A token woman or minority in a position of leadership or power is often held out as the representative of the entire affinity group. Though there may be similarities, there is not one universal experience shared by all. And yet, when only one woman or minority occupies a position of leadership or power, she is often looked to as a proxy for all. Tokens often feel an extraordinary pressure to be all things to all people. They are assumed to speak for their entire gender or race, which results in a failure to account for the intersectional dimensions of people's lives. They are also often taxed with additional service responsibilities when an organization desires to showcase its commitment to diversity.

Amalya Kearse yet again provides an instructive example. She was the only black woman at her law firm and later the lone black woman on a court when she entered those positions. She was expected, because of her prominence, to take up the causes of women and black people in a more formal way, like Justice Thurgood Marshall, whose career began with activism in the NAACP, and when she did not, she was labeled as "not a favorite" among "affinity groups."[11] But her legal opinions did often reflect concern for women's issues and civil rights. In one case, she dissented from an opinion that upheld an executive order by President Bush banning federally funded clinics from providing information about abortions and, in another case, she authored a majority opinion preventing prosecutors from excluding minorities from juries. Later in her career, Kearse's token status came into play when her name was floated as a potential replacement had the nomination of Clarence Thomas—another token chosen to fill the apparently "black seat" vacated by Marshall—failed in the wake of the Hill harassment allegations.

O'Connor, as the first woman on the Court, in many ways set the standard for what would be deemed "acceptable" for future female nominees. Among other characteristics, she was white, heterosexual, and married with children. With only O'Connor (and later Ginsburg) as a benchmark for what a female justice could be—a white mother of children, married to a white lawyer—backlash ensued years later when President Bush and President Obama selected women for the Court. Harriet Miers, Sonia Sotomayor, and Elena Kagan were all single and childless. Their personal lives differed significantly from the token female justices, and they became fodder for media criticism, as described in the preface and chapter four. The *New York Times* and the *Washington*

Post both fretted over the women's dating lives, for example speculating about Miers's dinner companion, "a Texas Supreme Court justice,"[12] and pointing out the novelty of Sotomayor's "bachelorette" status, inquiring who might accompany the single justice to official dinners.[13] It seems O'Connor's token qualities set the expectations for what a woman justice should or could be, and that included the companionship of a husband.

When the pool of qualified women increases in size and depth, the token effect dissipates somewhat and lessens the pressure for women to conform to unrealistic and unattainable ideals. It also allows for a range of viewpoints and perspectives to flourish. This is evident with the three women who served on the Court post-Obama. Justices Ginsburg, Kagan, and Sotomayor do not universally vote as a bloc, but rather bring a diversity of views to the decision-making of the nation's highest judicial body. They represent different religions, ethnicities, lawyering experiences, personal attributes, and more. Even so, because the justices are not only female, but rather they embody complex intersectional identities, their token status may linger. Sotomayor is the only Latina who has ever served on the Court, and one of the 1.3 percent of Latina lawyers in the country.[14] The Court no longer has a token woman, but it does have a token Latina.

Tokenism can also take a deeply personal toll on the individuals who find themselves isolated as the sole woman or minority in an office or on a court. The focus on one as an outsider who ascends into a leadership position also results in an almost obsessive kind of scrutiny and distortion both of her professional accomplishments and of her personal characteristics like appearance or habits. Researchers have documented that there is a negative impact that arises from having just one woman in a list of finalists: "[I]t highlights how different she is from the norm. And deviating from the norm can be risky for decision makers, as people tend to ostracize people who are different from the group. For women and minorities, having your differences made salient can also lead to inferences of incompetence."[15] As another scholar observed in the context of the legal academy, "To treat a minority faculty member as represent-

ing his or her race and gender—as if a faculty were the equivalent of
Noah's Ark—is nothing less than unfair, disrespectful, uncomfortable,
and demeaning."[16]

When Joan Dempsey Klein testified before the Senate Judiciary Committee on behalf of Sandra Day O'Connor during O'Connor's confirmation hearings, she described this intense scrutiny that comes along with
being the sole woman in such a heavily male-dominated field: "By virtue
of the fact that so many of us have been the 'first woman judge' or the
'only woman judge' in any number of situations, we are keenly aware
of the spotlight focused on our every act and the scrutiny to which we
are continually subjected. Such attention will be greatly magnified in
the case of the 'first woman Justice on the Supreme Court.'"[17] With just
one woman in a leadership role, how she physically appears stands in
dramatic contrast to men, and she is judged on how she looks. Appearance bias has been documented by sociologists and other scholars.[18]
The excessive and inappropriate attention to the way a woman looks can
be harmful whether or not she conforms to gender norms and stereotypes.[19] Female lawyers receive far more frequent compliments on their
appearance than on the substance of their legal work, in contrast to male
attorneys, who receive almost no appearance-based comments and are
complimented almost exclusively on their substantive legal or professional contributions.[20] Our earlier research on the gendered represen-
tations of Supreme Court nominees in the media showed that women
received more attention related to their appearance than men. Appearance is not a qualification for confirmation into the role of a Supreme
Court justice, yet it is often a point of discussion for female nominees.
This distracts attention from where it should be focused—on the nominee's qualifications.

The women profiled in this book faced glaring scrutiny based on
their appearance. Indeed, our outrage at the *New York Times* coverage
of how Judge Lillie looked in a swimsuit sparked the ideas for this book.
Soia Mentschikoff's preference for donning interesting hats and lace
underwear was covered extensively by the media. When Mentschikoff

began work as an associate in a law firm, the *New York Post* published a multiple-page article describing her romantic dates, the clothing she wore, her expenses for social activities like drinking and smoking, and her family obligations. The article noted that "she gives in to femininity on two items: hats and underwear. She loves frivolous hats with eye-length veils and the like and buys about 10 a year."[21] Later in her career, Mentschikoff actually credited her hats as playing a role in her success as an attorney. She reflected, "I used to wear elaborate hats with birds and flowers on them to the negotiating sessions. The hats made men feel superior and by the time they figured out what was going on I'd have control of the situation."[22] (Her approach, of using the obsession with her appearance to her advantage, is worth considering.) The media also emphasized the appearance of Carla Hills, particularly her brunette hair, in its coverage of her professional accomplishments. The *L.A. Times* reported, "Not surprisingly, the preservation of the existing stock in this new 200-year-old nation has the endorsement of Carla A. Hills, the brunette Secretary of Housing and Urban Development."[23] How odd that the hair color of the nation's HUD secretary was relevant to her endorsement. Hills, aware of the misplaced attention and scrutiny of her appearance, seemed unfazed. She pushed back against the characterization and tried to redirect the focus where it rightly belonged: on her accomplishments. Hills responded to this attention: "My attitude has been if you don't like the way I look, just look at my work product."[24] These are just a few examples, and we return to more in chapter six.

Tokenism Allows for the Proliferation of Sexual Harassment

Sexual harassment, and other forms of gender-based violence like rape and domestic abuse, have often been overlooked as reasons for women's stalled professional progress. The #MeToo and #TimesUp movements were effective in shedding light on a problem that has gone unchecked for years. Because tokenism results in workplaces where women sometimes make up only a fraction of all employees, this gender imbalance allows harms like sexual harassment to proliferate. In such contexts, a small number of women become the focus of a large number of men, which can lead to the creation of a workplace culture where reporting harassment is uncomfortable if not impossible and can also drown out women's pleas for help. It is hard to know the exact percentage of women who have endured harassment in the workplace, as there is wide variance in research and reporting, but studies confirm with certainty that it is a pervasive and widespread problem.[25]

Sexual harassment is not new, but the attention paid to the problem and the vocalization of women's stories in public spaces certainly is. While increased public awareness of this problem represents progress, how individuals respond to the harassment when it happens can give rise to additional complications. Speaking out carries certain risks: one may be blamed for what happened, may not be believed or may be affirmatively accused of lying, and may experience retaliation like being fired, isolated, or denied promotions and quality work assignments. Remaining silent is similarly rife with problems. It reinforces the status quo as harassment continues to run rampant and it does not allow perpetrators to be held accountable for the harms they cause.

Many of the shortlisted women described outright discrimination based on their sex in their oral histories. Florence Allen, for example, could not attend her desired law school, Columbia University. Moreover, every woman experienced discrimination in employment. Mildred Lillie applied for a position with the district attorney's office and recalled of the interview, "He said, 'Well, I don't like to discourage you but I would never appoint a woman.' He said, 'I've had a couple of women in this office, one of whom worked out fairly well, but the other one created nothing but problems, and I want no part of women in the law.' So he said, 'Good luck to you. I don't encourage you very much because I think that women probably don't belong in the law.'"[26] When Kearse applied for jobs on Wall Street, one of her interviewers looked at her resume and said, "God I wish you were a man."[27] Cornelia Kennedy, like Allen before her, was excluded from lunch with her male colleagues on the U.S. Court of Appeals for the Sixth Circuit. Susie Sharp was questioned about her suitability for presiding over a rape trial because it involved a female victim. And the list goes on.

We examined the lives of the shortlisted sisters for any sexual harassment they may have endured. Joan Dempsey Klein recalled "overt discrimination that included crude remarks as well as getting chased around the mulberry bush."[28] Cynthia Holcomb Hall also described constant unwanted sexual attention: "In those days, it was not unusual to be chased around a desk by a male co-employee or boss or anything else, and you just stayed out of reach and ducked and said, 'I'm sorry, but this is not the time,' or . . . 'I'm not interested today' . . . but done in a kidding way, and you know, they got the message."[29] Hall contemplated the effect of speaking out, noting, "If you'd file suit in those days, they would have laughed at you."[30] Women routinely encounter harassment as "part of the job," deflecting unwanted advances with humor or avoidance. Rarely do they report it. And, for most of the shortlisted women, the concept of sexual harassment—at least as we know it today—did not yet exist. The behavior was real and prevalent, but it was not perceived by those in power as harmful, let alone actionable under the law.

Catharine MacKinnon gave a name to this form of abuse in 1979: "Sexual harassment, most broadly defined, refers to the unwanted imposition of sexual requirements in the context of a relationship of unequal power."[31] But it was not until Anita Hill famously testified as part of Clarence Thomas's confirmation hearings in 1991 that sexual harassment became part of a public cultural conversation. And even then, silence was more the norm until the #MeToo movement provided a platform for vocalization nearly three decades later. The shortlisted sisters lived in a time when public or legal acknowledgment was nonexistent, and silence prevailed.

When founding the National Association of Women Judges in 1979, Judge Klein named sexism and discrimination faced by women in the legal profession as significant reasons for creating the organization. In an interview, she specifically referred to the "sophomoric sex bias they face daily, the men who call them 'honey' or 'dear' instead of 'judge,' the patronizing and harassment that are only too familiar to all working women."[32] The sexism that Klein spoke of continues today, with national organizations still trying to remedy it. For example, in 2016, the American Bar Association amended its Model Rule 8.4 to include a provision banning "conduct that the lawyer knows or reasonably should know is harassment or discrimination on the basis of race, sex, religion, national origin, ethnicity, disability, age, sexual orientation, gender identity, marital status or socioeconomic status in conduct related to the practice of law."[33] While California and Vermont quickly adopted similar rules, several other state bar associations affirmatively rejected the revision with formal votes. The attorney general of Texas, for example, issued an opinion challenging the rule's validity on First Amendment grounds.

On the heels of #MeToo, in late 2017, at least fifteen women (including prominent lawyers and law professors) levied credible allegations against Judge Alex Kozinski of the U.S. Court of Appeals for the Ninth Circuit of sexual harassment.[34] The judge resigned from his post, which under special policies for federal judges allowed him to avoid formal investigation while still receiving full retirement benefits.[35] In response to widespread publicity about Kozinski and pressure from former female law clerks, the federal judiciary established committees to make recommendations for reforms to address sexual harassment and other workplace misconduct. One of us testified as part of the process and observed, "No one should have to endure sexual harassment as a rite of passage in the legal profession."[36] In March 2019, new rules were adopted to require mandatory reporting of sexual harassment and provide for the possibility of an investigation into institutional policies even if a judge retires (though still protecting the judge from further investigation in an individual capacity). While the reforms offer potential routes—which previously did not exist—for addressing harassment, the burden still remains on the victim; the judge's ability to stop an individual investigation into misconduct by retiring means in many instances victims will still find no recourse through the judicial discipline system. Notably, the new rules do not apply to the Supreme Court or state courts, or to the legal profession generally. Even with these reforms, harassment and other misconduct remain a threat.

The shortlisted sisters' stories highlight the institutional factors that place women, particularly those from underrepresented populations, into vulnerable positions fraught with coercive power dynamics in the legal profession. The pressure to endure harassment silently is fierce; a decision to make a report can harm future career prospects. An unfavorable reference letter, or even a superior's refusal to write one, can compromise or destroy career aspirations. It is sobering to consider that Judge Klein's motivation for creating an organization to address sex discrimination forty years ago is still as relevant in 2020 as it was then. Equal, not token, representation of women in positions of leadership and power would bring far more effective remedies to routine workplace sexual misconduct than more platitudes and policies.

* * *

No longer are the doors of law schools, law firms, courthouses, or other legal institutions closed to women. Gone are the days of explicit barriers and formal inequality. Women enjoy equal access to all areas of professional life, unlike those who entered the profession a century, or even a few decades, ago. After eradication of formal barriers, it was widely believed that women's advancement in the profession was just a matter of time.[37] A reporter for the *New York Times* addressed this very point on the day that Rehnquist and Powell were nominated to the Court. Lamenting the small talent pool of women available to the president, she predicted that the future would surely be one where there were more women in the legal pipeline, and therefore "the pool may contain hundreds rather than merely dozens of women because the number of women entering the legal profession and the number who appear headed for influential positions within it have started to grow very rapidly."[38]

That reporter's prediction over four decades ago was accurate in the case of tokens. Many organizations have at least one woman and one minority (sometimes a role held by the same individual) among their leadership ranks. Rather than eradicate sexual discrimination and bias, however, the presence of tokens, even if well intentioned, has led to a professional world that functions very similarly to that of the 1970s in leadership ranks. Some may find this conclusion startling, especially women who attend college and graduate school in equal if not greater numbers than men and have not yet begun their ascent into leadership roles. But statistically, women, especially minority women, remain relatively isolated today in the upper echelons of power.

In the next chapter, we look at ways the shortlisted women navigated the complexity of their personal and professional lives against the backdrop of their token status.

6

Challenging Double Binds and Unifying Double Lives

Neither forget nor remember that you are a woman, as para-
doxical as that sounds. Unconscious femininity is an aid in
public life.[1]
—Advice from Florence Allen in a speech from 1926, as
recalled by Cynthia Holcomb Hall in her oral history

Each of the shortlisted women sought meaningful professional pursuits and personal connections, sometimes in alignment but often
in seeming contradiction as they navigated double binds and, in
some instances, double lives. We previewed a few of the ways that
these issues manifested in part one of the book, but here we take the
time to explore some of the more significant complexities in greater
detail. We consider these contradictions to make a case for a whole
life, blending the personal and the professional, rather than simply
repeating what is often a hollow call for work-life balance, where one
aspect of our lives is often compromised for another. Our goal is not
to criticize, but instead to find inspiration from our shortlisted sisters
as we extract lessons for remedying the remaining gender inequality
that persists in positions of leadership and power. By challenging the
artificial dichotomies and common narratives fraught with socially
constructed myths foisted upon women throughout history and
today, we encourage everyone to live authentic, unified lives, unafraid
of professional consequences based on personal choices like how one
appears or who one loves.

One reason there is so much difficulty challenging inequality and sexism is that, as a subordinated group, women are often confronted with
"double binds," or "situations in which options are reduced to a very few

and all of them expose one to penalty, censure or deprivation."[2] Being trapped in a double bind means constantly facing a false dichotomy, where a "winning" solution is not immediately apparent, and undesirable consequences attach to either of the two choices, often at the cost of sacrificing authenticity and peace of mind. The concept of double binds has been broken into specific categories by one scholar and includes "womb/brain," "femininity/competency," "silence/shame," "sameness/difference," and "aging/invisibility."[3] As but one example, the femininity/competency double bind describes situations where women must forsake femininity if they want to be taken seriously in the workforce. But adopting more stereotypical male characteristics is not a solution either, as their gender non-conformity is seen as problematic and discrediting. Similarly, "[w]omen often face a form of glass ceiling bias that is a 'Catch 22': either they are penalized for not being competent enough or for being *too* competent."[4]

We appreciate how these lived experiences can be reduced to discrete categories in order to clarify the challenges women face, but we also see a good deal of fluidity among the categories and reject them as absolutes. This chapter is organized around similar themes that arose in the lives of the shortlisted sisters. We explore the binds, conundrums, and contradictions as they relate to (1) feminism/racism; (2) appearance/femininity/respectability; (3) professional and intimate relationships; (4) motherhood/competing careers; and (5) age.

The degree to which our research allowed glimpses into the private, intimate lives of the women in this book varied greatly. There is more readily-available material for the women who were shortlisted early on, most of whom are deceased, and many of whom left their papers and other personal documents, including lengthy oral histories, to libraries for archival purposes. For the women still living, fewer resources are available. The variance in access to material means that there is a greater focus on some of the women than on others, but this should not be taken as an indication of the absence or presence of any of these issues in the women's lives if they go unmentioned.

Feminism/Racism

The suffrage struggle itself took on a similar flavor, acqui-
escing to white supremacy—and selling out the interests of
African-American women—when it became politically expedient to do so. This betrayal of trust opened a rift between
black and white feminists that persists to this day.[5]
—Brent Staples, *New York Times* Editorial Board, 2018

One might think that the shortlisted sisters would naturally be at the
forefront of efforts to make the path easier for future women and minorities to follow in their footsteps. But the women did not universally take
up feminist issues and they did not all share the same perspectives as to
what it meant to advance women's rights or other causes. Some held outright racist beliefs and differed as to whether they let these beliefs affect
their professional lives and judicial decision-making. The viewpoints of
the women featured in this book varied markedly on social movements
and ideas.

Florence Allen came of age during and was very active in fighting a
significant political battle: the women's suffrage movement. Allen's skill
at keeping her words short, honed by her mother's advice growing up,
served her well: "In the suffrage campaigns the men in the meetings
who were friendly to us would sometimes give us a chance to speak for
five, three, or even two minutes. If we spoke more than the allotted time
it would hurt the cause, so we earnestly tried to keep within our time
limitation."[6] On the one hand, Allen's mother's advice was sage. It helped
Allen and others at that time work within the gendered power structure
and maximize their effectiveness to advance causes they cared about.
On the other hand, women's voices to this day are still often ignored,
cut off, or dismissed outright. Men are rewarded for their long-winded
monologues to such an extent that women have created names for the
occurrence: "mansplain" and "manologue" are now part of our contemporary lexicon. Professional conferences regularly featuring panels of

all-male speakers are scorned as "manels." And these notions are more than just anecdotal.

Research documents how women's voices are often not heard, and their speech is frequently interrupted by men. Scholars studied this problem in Supreme Court oral arguments, finding that the female justices are more frequently interrupted by their male peers and by counsel.[7] Ruth Bader Ginsburg faced this throughout her entire career: "I don't know how many meetings I attended in the '60s and '70s, when I would say something, and I thought it was a pretty good idea. Then [a man] would say exactly what I said. Then people would become alert to it, respond to it."[8] Even after sixteen years on the Court, she observed, "I will say something—and I don't think I'm a confused speaker—and it isn't until [a man] says it that everyone will focus on the point."[9] So while Allen's mother's advice was sound at the time, it nonetheless reinforced a specific place for women and parameters within which they must behave if they were to successfully participate in the male-dominated political and public spaces.

Despite Allen's strongly held beliefs that women deserved the right to vote, she did not always favor policy initiatives to advance women's rights. She opposed the Equal Rights Amendment. Allen's position might today seem a contradiction given the very progressive life she herself led as an activist, lawyer, and judge, but it was actually consistent with the views many women held at the time.[10] As we explore later in this chapter, Allen was a woman who herself confounded heterosexual norms because she was intimately involved in relationships with other women. The contradictions inherent in Allen's life or that of any of the shortlisted women should not automatically be taken as an affront to women or feminists. Indeed, this reflects the diversity among women, reinforces even more strongly the problems with tokenism, and further highlights the need for representation of many women on the bench, in the courtroom, and in the boardroom.

Allen was not alone among the shortlisted sisters in her position on the ERA and other women's rights issues. Soia Mentschikoff feared that the legislation would lead to "endless litigation."[11] Edith Jones said she "always opposed the ERA as being unnecessary to the fundamental distinction between men and women, and leading to unforeseeable and unfortunate consequences."[12] Mildred Lillie was also likely not a fan— when vetted by the Nixon administration for a seat on the Court and questioned about "the women's lib movement, she said she stayed far away from it and personally considered it to be somewhat dangerous."[13] And Susie Sharp, while publicly expressing a desire for equal opportunities between the sexes, strongly believed married women with children ought to stay home: "You have got to choose. When you get old and decrepit, you might rather have grandchildren than a lot of honorary degrees. You can't have both."[14] She objected to women trying to balance both family and career. Sharp so strongly opposed the ERA that she actively lobbied legislators for its defeat while she was on the bench even though, as a general matter, she was a stickler for separating politics from her role as a judge. Some in fact criticized her judicial activism on the ERA as an inappropriate merging of politics with the judiciary. By contrast, while Cynthia Holcomb Hall did not actively advocate for the amendment because of her role as a judge, she was personally in support of it: "I don't understand how anybody could be against it?"[15]

Mentschikoff also was not what one might describe as a conventional feminist. She was an active leader in professional roles, serving as a reporter for the American Law Institute, the most prestigious legal organization in the country, and the first female president of the Association of American Law Schools, a national association for members of the legal academy. But she did not promote other women unless she felt they "earned" it. According to Roberta Ramo, a lawyer who attended the University of Chicago Law School from 1967 to 1970:

> People always want to know if she was a great mentor to the other women in the law school. . . . She did not go out of her way at all for women until after the first year because she wanted to see if you were smart enough. Her theory, I believe, was that it was so difficult for a woman to make it in

the law that she didn't want to encourage anybody who wasn't going to be at the very top of their game because they would never get anywhere. . . . But she didn't really see it as her job. I think she felt—and I don't really blame her at all for this, this is the world in which she had grown up— that women had to fight to make a place in the law for themselves. And that her mollycoddling, which is how she would have viewed it, really wasn't going to give anybody much help at all.[16]

Mentschikoff was described as "not likely to initiate supportive relationships; she was often quoted as saying women were responsible for their poor representation in law school."[17] Yet, she supported meritorious women, advocating for scholars like Harvard Law Professor Mary Ann Glendon, and exchanging letters with former student Carol Mosley Braun in her early years of law practice. (Braun would go on to be elected as a U.S. senator during 1992's "Year of the Woman.") Similar to Allen refusing to take on the divorce docket, Mentschikoff declined to author an article on the subject of "Women Lawyers—Estate Planners" for the *Harvard Law School Record* in 1951 because, as she explained, "I feel deeply that women lawyers should not be limited to this type of activity."[18]

Cornelia Kennedy, too, sometimes took positions that could be perceived as at odds with the rights of women. In one case, Kennedy found against a sexual harassment victim, voting to "take away a $250,000 jury award from a woman who won," but in another context, upon learning "that the husbands of judges received fewer spousal benefits than wives did, she successfully campaigned for equality."[19] Another example of women not always supporting the same causes was Carla Hills's testimony on behalf of Robert Bork's confirmation to the Supreme Court. As noted in part one of the book, she lent her support even in the face of significant protests against him by women's rights groups. As mentioned in part one, "affinity groups" expected Amalya Kearse to take up the causes of women and blacks as an activist, but she did not.[20] Nonetheless, some of the women expressed support in unexpected ways. Kearse's judicial opinions, for example, revealed support for women's issues and civil rights.

Some of the women held openly racist views. Cornelia Kennedy's decision as a district court judge was reversed by the U.S. Court of Appeals for the Sixth Circuit when she found that a Detroit suburb's all-black school was not the product of the school district's intent to segregate. When considered for an appointment on the Sixth Circuit herself, the National Association for the Advancement of Colored People (NAACP), the National Bar Association, the Michigan chapter of the National Conference of Black Lawyers, the Wolverine Bar Association, and a number of prominent law professors compiled voluminous reports based on extensive review of her judicial opinions. These organizations unequivocally determined that she was not an appropriate pick due to her exceedingly anti-plaintiff record on cases dealing with civil rights, race discrimination, police brutality, and prisoners. Prominent attorney Dennis Archer, who would later become a Michigan Supreme Court justice and the first African American president of the American Bar Association, concluded, "A plaintiff cannot win in a civil rights case before her."[21] To smooth things over, the Carter administration packaged Kennedy's nomination with that of Nathaniel Jones, then-general counsel of the NAACP. Both were confirmed.

Susie Sharp's personal views were also racist. She believed strongly in segregation and the North Carolina constitutional ban on interracial marriage. In contrast to Kennedy, however, Sharp did not seem to let these perspectives impact her judicial decision-making. Sharp "was an admitted racist, yet she delivered irreproachable judicial decisions with race."[22] She was the first judge to issue an order ending segregation in Charlotte's public spaces. In that case, the Bonnie Brae golf course excluded black people, and sixteen plaintiffs challenged this ban in 1952, seeking an injunction to end the practice. Sharp granted the injunction based upon Supreme Court cases desegregating public spaces like beaches, state parks, and golf courses. But she didn't want to: "I could feel [NAACP lawyer Spottswood Robinson's] hatred and I had the impression that he could feel mine because I had to grant him the injunction but despised having to do so. . . . [W]asn't it the irony of fate that I, who would almost have preferred to close it down, had to *order* the course opened to them."[23] In many ways, her blatant racism is abhorrent, and yet, at the same time, Sharp was able to set aside personal views to apply the law in a way that achieved justice.

The suffrage movement Allen was such an integral part of was itself marked by massive contradiction regarding race. While advocating for women's rights, a number of the well-known suffragists embodied racist views, both implicit and explicit. Many were unwilling to involve black women in their efforts, sacrificing inclusivity for their (white) gendered priorities related to securing the franchise. Allen, however, did not seem to personally embody such explicit racist views. One historian noted, "Her stance on the rights of racial minorities to equal treatment was generally ahead of the times."[24] Allen decided one case in particular, *State ex rel Weaver v. Board of Trustees of Ohio State University*,[25] which offers some insight into her views on race. There, Allen ruled against a black college student who sued Ohio State University, claiming that she was being denied access to education as a result of an unfavorable housing arrangement. Some critiqued her position, and she was questioned about the case during her confirmation hearings for the U.S. Court of Appeals for the Sixth Circuit. One historian explained Allen's position, which on the face of it may have appeared to have racist undertones: "Judge Allen attempted to distinguish between academic rights and social prerogatives related to residence on campus."[26] Allen reflected in her memoir the internal conflict she felt, seeking validation of her decision in this racially charged case from a black college friend:

When I was in college at Western Reserve University we were seated alphabetically in classes, so I had the pleasure during the first year of sitting next to a very nice colored girl, Mary Brown, who later became a member of the Cleveland Board of Education. During the attacks made on me because of my vote in the Weaver case, Mary came to Columbus. And

I explained the matter to her. I said, "Mary, if you had been in that situation in the University and working for your Home Economics degree, what would you have done when you were assigned to live under all the same conditions as Doris Weaver in the University House?" "Why, Florence," she said, "I would have stayed right there and graduated and made it easier for some colored girl to follow me."[27]

It is significant to note that as impactful as women's advocacy can be, whether formal or informal, not all of the women profiled in this book were active in promoting causes or political agendas. For example, Kearse rarely speaks publicly outside the courtroom and did not take on leadership roles, even reportedly declining to serve as chief of the Second Circuit. But this may simply reflect a preference for how she used her time. As one reporter revealed, "Miss Kearse is a person of apparent contradictions. She loves physical activity, yet has chosen the contemplative path. Strangers are struck by her reserved demeanor, but those who know her well speak of her warmth. She is enthusiastic about her avocations and is a tournament bridge player, yet her work weeks stretch to 100 hours, leaving her little time for diversion."[28]

Appearance/Femininity/Respectability

Evening gowns bring out the Russian in her; her business clothes are neat, severe. But she goes for expensive undies of sheer, black silk. And hats! Ten a year; $3 to $10 each. . . . She's a fall guy for expensive underwear, with an unsatisfied longing for sheer black silk. For ordinary wear she pays $2 or $3 for a slip, $5 or $7.50 for a girdle . . .[29]
—*New York Post* article on Soia Mentschikoff's wardrobe as a lawyer practicing in New York, 1940

Recall the exuberance expressed in an early news story about Mildred Lillie's bathing beauty figure or Carla Hills's brunette hair and great smile. Their actual qualifications for the nation's highest court were lost in reporting about their sex appeal. Our cultural focus on the appearance of women being considered for leadership roles detracts from their actual qualifications. And women conforming—or failing to conform—to gender stereotypes often affects perceptions of competence.

As women entered the legal profession, they faced questions surrounding how to dress and present themselves, both in and outside of the courtroom. Should women dress in such a way as to highlight their femininity and risk not being taken seriously as a lawyer, or instead should they try to conform with the male norms regarding their appearance so as to better blend in and look more like a lawyer is "supposed" to look? The shortlisted sisters adopted different strategies. For Florence Allen, and other professional women of her generation, this double bind was exceedingly rigid. Digging through Susie Sharp's personal papers, one of us uncovered an article she clipped and pasted into her journal about Allen: "Law as a Career for Women Urged."[30] The reporter praised Allen's judicial appointment and quoted advice offered by other male judges for female attorneys that reflected a quintessential double bind: "She must not assume the attitude of a man, either in dress or manner of speech. But she must try her cases in a manly fashion, by which I mean simply be thoroughly prepared and capable."[31] According to the reporter, Allen successfully navigated this seemingly impossible challenge: "An outstanding example is Florence Allen. Her success is a bright star before us. She has opened up avenues not only to herself, but to other women."[32] As an interesting addendum to the media discussion of Allen and her appearance, we learned that her romantic partner, Susan Rebhan, advised her to avoid looking too masculine during her campaigns for public office.

Expectations related to gender norms were something that many of the shortlisted women confronted throughout their lives. If Allen conformed, Joan Dempsey Klein rejected expectations about aspects of her appearance, casting them off as ridiculous. In one news story, Klein was interviewed about her thoughts on high heels, a fashion statement she refused to make. She exclaimed, "They're ridiculous. I absolutely will not wear them. I think they are not only unhealthy, but it's demeaning for a designer to suggest that women, to be stylish, should wear such a shoe."[33] Yet even when women did conform to expectations, they were sometimes criticized. One lawyer accused Carla Hills of being "arrogant," and he went on to further remark in an apparent joke that "I also can't stand her because she's so neat looking all the time."[34]

Allen's influence on others regarding appearance continued long after her death. Hall reflected in her oral history interview that she was inspired by Allen's advice about the benefits of "unconscious femininity."[35] She remembered, "When I was first trying cases I wore a black suit I had worn in New York. I wore that black suit for every argument in the court of claims until it fell apart and then I felt this is silly. I'm not a man I should wear whatever I want. First time I wore a red dress caused a sensation."[36] All of this attention to Hall's clothing was infuriating to her, and she captured the underlying problem quite succinctly, stating, "You don't want the judges to watch you, you want the judges to listen to your case."[37]

Relationships

The love of one is better than none / The love of two is plenty
/ The love of three, it can't agree / You'd better not love so
many.[38]
—A poem clipped by Susie Sharp and pasted into her
journal

As the shortlisted women came of age, they were shaped by friends and intimate partners and the families they formed; these individuals played significant roles in their lives. Often, especially in the case of their lovers or husbands, the professional blurred with the personal, and it was hard to discern where one started or ended. This section explores some of these professional relationships and intimate connections.

Professional Relationships

Despite legal education's hostility to women in the early years, several of the shortlisted women benefited from strong relationships with, or at least affirmative guidance from, the deans of these institutions. Sometimes mentorship is better described as sponsorship, where a senior attorney does more than just provide advice and takes affirmative steps to help facilitate another's success. Mildred Lillie was encouraged to pursue a law degree at the University of California, Berkeley, by Dean Edwin Dickinson: "He apparently saw some promise in my studies."[39] She was concerned about being able to afford a legal education, but he promised her work, and she helped him with grading while she was a student. Joan Dempsey Klein, as noted in chapter 3, credited Dean L. Dale Coffman of UCLA for helping define her path. Coffman offered her admission despite the paucity of women students at that time, and the fact that, as she herself conceded, her credentials did not place her at the top of the applicant pool. Carla Hills also received advice from a law dean. She did not come from a family that included other lawyers. Instead, she set herself along the path to the profession alone. When she sought guidance from Stanford Law Dean Carl B. Spaeth, he actually dissuaded her from attending his own institution, telling her instead to attend Yale, which she ultimately did. After law school, Mildred Lillie benefited from her relationships with male lawyers in practice, including Frank Belcher, who was a lawyer active in Republican politics and aided in her campaigns.

However, sometimes, guidance, advice, and mentorship were found not in the professional but rather the personal, intimate spaces of the shortlisted women's lives.

Intimate Relationships

Many of the shortlisted women navigated romantic lives as they endeavored to secure positions of power and leadership. Most intertwined the personal and professional in their romantic relationships, finding mentors in their partners, like Mentshikoff. Some of the women led seemingly dual lives, presenting publicly in one way but living quite differently in private life, like Allen and Sharp. Others pursued more traditional marriages with men, like Ginsburg, Hills, and O'Connor. A few of the women, like Hall, Klein, and Lillie, were married earlier in their lives and then later remarried. Sotomayor, by contrast, chose not to remarry after divorce. Others, including Kagan, Kearse, Rymer, and Sharp, never married and managed to keep any significant others out of the public light.

All of the women engaged in relationships that were relatively unique, at least insofar as their deviation from the pervasive and gendered narrative of the happily-ever-after marriage of a career man and his homemaker wife. We find these glimpses fascinating as we contemplate how some of their relationships, or the lack thereof, shaped the women's professional trajectories. Importantly, the wide-ranging differences in the women's intimate relationships further emphasize the importance of seeking more than just token representation of women.

Professional advice was uniformly dispensed by the women's intimate partners. Allen spent her life in two long-term, serious relationships with women, largely outside of the scrutiny of public attention, and both of her partners offered her advice behind the scenes as she navigated her judicial elections. Kennedy was married to a non-lawyer who worked in advertising. His background came in handy when she vied for judicial office and needed campaign ads. Hall was widowed during the time she was considered for the Court, and the internal White House memo evaluating her candidacy described her as the "head of household."[40] Hills had a more conventional marriage with a man whose career was high-powered just like hers, as did Hall, Ginsburg, and O'Connor, and all benefited from their partners' understanding of their careers. Miers was romantically linked to Texas Supreme Court Chief Justice Nathan Hecht, who spoke out publicly on her behalf during her brief nomination to the Supreme Court.

Lillie's husband was known to advise her decisions. He encouraged her to apply for a job as a municipal judge and later to put her name in for consideration with the California governor to be considered for a position on the Court of Appeals in that state. He also actively supported the decision for her to retain her last name, rather than change it to reflect her new marital status, recognizing that changing her name could be problematic when she ran for reelection.[41]

Mentschikoff and Llewellyn developed an intimate relationship after she was his student at Columbia. She served as his research assistant, working at a desk in his office, and their love affair developed while he was still married to another woman. The two eventually did marry, after much agony experienced by Mentschikoff; being the "other woman" was not a role she easily tolerated. Finally, she sent Llewellyn an ultimatum letter, emphasizing the consequences of failing to leave his wife. She wrote, "You are making a great mistake in not plucking for divorce. So long as I was around, it was barely a livable marriage. Now that I'm gone, it will be intolerable . . ."[42] He soon left his wife and married Mentschikoff.

We also found connections between Mentschikoff and Sharp related to their involvement with married men. It was not until Anna Hayes began researching Sharp's life for a biography that many of these details surfaced. At the time, Sharp's public persona might have read similarly to that of Allen or even Kearse, about whose personal life very little is known. News accounts described Sharp as a "lifelong spinster,"[43] an image she seemed to cultivate. Hayes poured through Sharp's journals (many of which were written in shorthand and had to be translated) and painstakingly pieced together fragments of love letters that were often cut into pieces to obscure the identity of the author and nature of the relationships. Hayes described cutout letters as a sort of "lace"— love lace. One of us also spent hours combing through overwhelmingly voluminous archives of Sharp's personal documents at the University of North Carolina, which contained what seemed to be every piece of paper she ever touched, including speeches, handwritten notes documenting the tip paid to a bellman, makeup application advice, her daily diet (with recipes!), and her exercise routine. As a result, we know that as much as she devoted her life to the practice of law and public service, Sharp poured the emotional part of herself into longstanding and complex relationships.

Sharp never married or had children, but romance nonetheless dominated her life. She was seriously involved with three different male lawyers, and these relationships sometimes overlapped. Two of Sharp's most serious relationships took place entirely in private, as these men were both married to other women. One of her lovers, John Kesler, was a man she dated in law school with whom she had reconnected later in life, and the other was a former law professor, Millard Breckenridge. She kept lists of hotel room numbers, documenting her romantic liaisons. Sharp did contemplate marrying Kesler for a brief time and "becoming an ordinary housewife."[44] Although she chose her career over marriage, she nonetheless always longed for deep, intimate connections. Her diaries reflect a certain torment surrounding her love affairs and their lack of legitimacy, but also a resignation to the choices she had made.

In her later years, Sharp continued this pattern of engaging in secret romantic relationships. She shared a strong professional connection with a fellow (more senior) judge on the North Carolina Supreme Court, Judge William Haywood Bobbitt. Their relationship reflected significant professional camaraderie and support and took place more in the public eye than her earlier ones, though not entirely. The two maintained incredible discretion in their interaction with each other, even though he was a widow, meaning they were free to carry on as a public couple if they chose to do so. The couple never did marry, ostensibly due to the potential professional complications that might arise. Though the connection between Bobbitt and Sharp was exceptionally strong, Sharp maintained contact with her married lovers throughout her life. Given the intensity of her relationships, it is difficult to imagine how she managed to keep her romantic life private. Today, public interest in the private lives of judges can be, for some, quite intense and unrelenting.[45]

Florence Allen faced critique based on her lack of a husband and the accompanying suspicion that she was in committed relationships with women. Some scholars speculate that Allen's sexual orientation was likely a factor that influenced the presidents who did not nominate her, but it was not something discussed explicitly in the public realm as it is today.[46] One of Allen's most ardent supporters, Eleanor Roosevelt, also lived a life hidden at least in part from public view; she carried on a serious, long-term, intimate relationship with journalist Lorena Hickok.[47] While we uncovered no direct evidence linking Allen and Roosevelt romantically, we speculate that the women found each other to be kindred spirits, navigating public lives amidst private desires.

Some considered Allen to be asexual and disinterested in pursuing romance as she was so clearly focused on her work; this asexual dimension was often ascribed to women who did not marry and instead pursued professional paths. (Kagan, recall, was similarly described as having books as companions rather than romantic partners.) But free from assumptions regarding homosexuality that surround lesbian women today, women like Allen hid their sexuality and consequently enjoyed a certain freedom to carry on relationships with other women outside of the public eye, often without scrutiny or judgment. In contrast to Susie Sharp, whose archives were overflowing with personal items, Allen intentionally organized and edited her papers before they were donated, to ensure that only public life was reflected in them. Her memoir also does not reference her intimate relationships, making just one offhand reference to a woman with whom she lived without naming or identifying her. We relied upon the work of historians to inform the discussion of her private life here.

These are just a handful of examples from the relationships that helped support the women throughout their careers.

Motherhood/Competing Careers

A career woman's chief handicap is that she doesn't have a wife.[48]
—Susie Sharp's prepared notes for a news interview with WLOS in Asheville, N.C.

The classic double bind surrounding motherhood calls into question women's ability to be simultaneously effective workers and mothers. The presumption is that women can excel at one but not both. Typically, women enter the workforce without one of the benefits men have long enjoyed: wives. Or, more accurately and appropriately described, without the benefit of someone to provide assistance with the personal aspects of their lives. It is as Sharp suggests, a "handicap" that women must deal with along with discrimination and other barriers as they enter the professional world.

Most male lawyers who ascend into significant leadership positions have enjoyed and at times exploited the benefits provided by their wives. The law is known to be an all-consuming profession, but any career pursuit inevitably demands long hours at inconvenient times for one's caregiving obligations to children and family. "[H]aving a wife" in these sorts of careers "might be bloody handy," observes one political commentator.[49] As she notes, "you can therefore see why women—who are so much less likely to have a wife, and much more likely to be one—do not wind up getting to the top" positions in equal numbers as men.[50] Susie Sharp felt much the same way.

Because women do not have partners performing the traditional role of a stay-at-home wife, they are forced to either forgo motherhood and homemaking roles (à la Allen, Mentschikoff, and Sharp) or to juggle not only child-rearing but often also support a spouse's competing career (like Hills and Hall). Some of the women rejected the rigidity of a separate sphere approach adhered to by their earlier shortlisted sisters and merged work and family in their lives, but often at significant cost. Klein is a perfect example. In the early years of her career, "I was trying to do my job, raise a couple kids, schlep back and forth, resolve one marriage, and start a new one. It was kind of a tough life."[51] Despite the challenges in juggling career and family, she seemed to manage the often competing demands, recalling, "I tried to do the mom thing as best as possible. I had good housekeepers and I did the PTA thing, the Little League thing, studied with the kids at night and made sure the homework was done and that they understood how to study. I always had a family dinner, we were all together and we talked about what happened during the day and who did what and so on. We always took family vacations."[52]

Hall also navigated a divorce and a subsequent remarriage. As a single mother, she left her three-year-old daughter in the care of her parents in Arizona for a year so she could live in the dorm at New York University Law School. (There were no accommodations suitable for a single mother.) She pursued her LLM in tax after a law firm partner told her specialization was the only chance of being hired. A man in her shoes would likely have had a wife to care for his child. As a single woman at the time, Hall turned to her family to provide this kind of support. Looking back on her choices, Hall, who later remarried, contemplated whether "women who give up a husband or a family to have a career or give up a career to have a family . . . get to a point when they realize they've missed something. I liked having a husband, I love my children, and I wouldn't give up my career for all the world, although I've worked hard to manage them all."[53] Hall outsourced many of the duties that men often expect their wives to perform. In addition to family, she had the help of a full-time nanny when her kids were young because, as she put it, she needed to know that her kids were taken care of when she was trying a case. Early on, Hall struggled financially as a single parent while she worked in government. She sewed clothes, curtains, and bedspreads because she could not afford to buy them. It is likely that a man in her position in that era would have had a wife at home to take care of such details. She explained, "It's a financial struggle. It's a time problem."[54] Carla Hills similarly benefited from full-time child care providers. Cornelia Kennedy, when asked about the challenges of juggling both a career and children, credited her husband for stepping in whenever she was not able to care for their son, as did Ruth Bader Ginsburg, whose husband was such a well-known family chef that the cookbook "Chef Supreme: Martin Ginsburg" was created by the spouses of the Supreme Court justices as a tribute after his death.

After the birth of her children, Sandra Day O'Connor reduced her law practice to part-time for four years, allowing her to devote time to their care as well as other civic activities. In fact, the *New York Times* reported that "[w]hile Judge O'Connor is most often described as a diligent, non-onsense [*sic*] woman, always ready to move up the next notch of success, close friends say that in private she talks frankly of working hard to be both a successful public figure and a successful wife and mother."[55] Today, work-life balance like this example forms a central part of our cultural conversation, and the search for this elusive goal pervades professional lives. Over the years during which many of the women in our study were developing their professional identities, such an idea was unheard of. The approach of Hall, Hills, Ginsburg, Klein, and O'Connor reflects the more contemporary notion that women can "have it all," and that having it all necessarily means combining and balancing traditional domestic and familial roles with that of professional ones. We are suspicious of whether this balance can be achieved. Instead, we appreciate the nuanced way that Hall describes her dual roles as mother/wife and professional; she depicts her efforts as an attempt to "manage" but not necessarily balance the various demands. We revisit this idea and propose some strategies in chapter eight.

Not all the women featured in this book had children, but even those who did not sometimes endured the burdens of being a primary caretaker. Mentschikoff "had strong feelings for New York and understandably considered New York the center of the commercial world," but was willing to move to Chicago as a way for her to "consolidate her family and her work."[56] She "convert[ed] the third floor of the house into an apartment for her mother and father; furthermore, because the house was so spacious, she was able to house her nieces, Sandy Levendahl and Jean Mentschikoff, for many years."[57] She raised them as her own daughters. Sharp similarly provided care for members of her extended family even though she had no children of her own.

Sharp was steadfast in her opinion that women belonged either at home or at work; she did not think it was possible or desirable to balance the multiple identities of professional and homemaker. Her perspective stands in stark contrast to women like Hall, Hills, Ginsburg, Klein, and O'Connor, who juggled careers with marriage and children. When interviewed about her appointment to the North Carolina Supreme Court, Sharp commented that she would support the right female candidate for governor or president, but that in her opinion, the average woman belonged in the home. For Sharp, it was an either-or proposition regarding work and family. In prepared answers to an interview with the press in response to a question about sacrifices she may have made, she wrote, "Career has been totally possessive. I could not have had the career I have had and done justice to a husband and children."[58] She continued, "As a special judge I held court all over the state and was at home only on weekends. A man judge leaves the wife and children at home. I would not have been willing to do that."[59] Allen similarly believed that while women were certainly welcome into the professional sphere, they could not simultaneously stand in the domestic one.

Mothers are often perceived to be less competent and committed than those women without children, or they are treated as novelties with superhuman capabilities that the "average" woman cannot replicate. Remnants of this specific kind of bias and discrimination against women in the workplace persist today. It has been described as the "maternal wall," i.e., a "bias against women not because they are women, but because they are mothers."[60] This bias extends to all women simply by virtue of having the *potential* to be mothers, regardless of their actual choice about the matter. Many women face career "gaps" and corresponding consequences such as lower pay and fewer promotions because they took time away for child-rearing. And as for women who do attempt to juggle a career and children, they are critiqued as sacrificing one at the expense of the other or held out as an exception that most women could never attain. A "mythical" depiction of Carla Hills appeared in the media shortly after her appointment to President Ford's cabinet:

> In the spacious living room of her boxlike 1930s house, a slim, pretty woman smiles while her 4-year-old daughter shows off objects d'art made from paper napkins and staples. Out in the yard, near the trampoline, lie a pair of crumpled children's socks. In and around the house, in various states of motion, are three dogs, two cats (one of whom ate the gerbil), seven goldfish, three other children all under 14, a Belgian maid and a husband. The husband wonders aloud if they are going to spend another winter without curtains on the living room windows. She thinks it over, indicates that the view of the woods is charming. "No," she adds softly, "we are not going to cover the windows." This cozy domestic scene recently took place in the home of one of America's newest Cabinet officials. The secretary, described by colleagues as "tough as nails," "strong willed" and "forceful," is 41-year-old Carla Hills. She is the fourth person to head the office of Housing and Urban Development and the third woman to sit in the Cabinet.[61]

The choice to become, or not become, a mother illustrates the classic no-win situation. Women today are held to higher standards of parenting than men and are often judged as "insufficiently committed, either as parents or professionals."[62] Similarly, non-mothers are critiqued or subject to similar double binds as those women who do have children, scrutinized like Kagan and Sotomayor over their single, childless status. However, the concern expressed about the paucity of mothers on the Court is self-contradictory, as the other side of the motherhood double bind presumes women are less committed to their jobs.

Juggling the demands of motherhood is a significant challenge faced by professional women, but certainly not the only one. Sometimes, competition experienced by the shortlisted sisters came from their intimate partners, many of whom had high-profile careers themselves.

Consider Soia Mentschikoff's relationship with Karl Llewellyn. Harvard hired her as a visiting professor but refused her a tenure-track position because the school's anti-nepotism policy prevented husbands and wives from being hired for the same department. Even so, it was well known that "[o]f the two, the Harvard faculty was most impressed with Soia."[63] Recall from part one that when the two were recruited to join the University of Chicago Law faculty by Dean Edward Levi, he found Soia's references preferable to Karl's.[64] But it was Karl who received a tenured position. He was also paid more than his wife (though she did command a high salary compared to other women faculty across the country). Once he passed away, however, the University of Chicago finally (and rightly) promoted Mentschikoff into a tenured role. Becoming Karl's wife, something significant to her personally, had professional consequences. Enduring this kind of professional sacrifice was, unfortunately, not something unique to Mentschikoff.

Carla Hills's husband, Roderick Hills, also occupied a position in public service as head of the Securities and Exchange Commission. Her appointment was technically more prestigious than his, though both clearly were exceedingly talented and successful lawyers. The *Washington Post* noted about Hall, "She not only has held public office longer than her husband but a cabinet member always outranks the head of an agency, no matter if it is the prestigious and important SEC."[65] The article commented on the potential social awkwardness at dinner parties given the reversed gender roles evidenced by the status of wife over husband, even a husband who was also a prominent figure.

When Cynthia Holcomb Hall was considered for the U.S. Tax Court in 1972, her husband's job as an attorney for a Los Angeles law firm created a challenge. Barbara Franklin, tasked at the time with recruiting more women to the federal judiciary, and who later took on the job of compiling extensive historical documentation of many of these women, discussed this dilemma: "What were we going to do with John Hall?

Well, you know, they both wanted to come to Washington. So I think it was the first case for this. We found a job for John Hall in the administration. He became deputy assistant secretary for tax policy at treasury."[66] Franklin noted how difficult it could be to leave one's family behind or move a family to a new location. For some women, these barriers keep them from taking leadership positions. The couple, as one of the first husband-and-wife teams to work in the executive government, helped reframe perceptions about anti-nepotism policies that historically held women back.

Age

We still live in a society where men are supposed to age into
power and women are supposed to age out of sight.[67]
—Sady Doyle, in a 2018 article

A classic and often unnavigable challenge faced by women who seek leadership positions involves their age: young women are seen as lacking experience, while older women are sometimes viewed as too grandmotherly. Men, by contrast, are characterized as "boy wonders" in their youth and "wise senior statesmen" as they age. Women in their middle years are often focused on child-rearing; lacking support traditionally provided to men by their wives, they are also effectively held back by familial demands. In 2012 and again in 2018, as part of the Democrats' battle to select its Speaker of the House of Representatives, a firestorm erupted surrounding Nancy Pelosi's pursuit of the position. Pelosi was criticized by both political parties as being too old, even though her age differs little from male politicians. Many of the leading (male) Democrats were in the same age range as Pelosi, who at the end of 2019 was seventy-eight. That same year, President Trump was seventy-three, and two of the leading contenders for the next presidential race, Joe Biden and Bernie Sanders, were respectively seventy-six and seventy-eight. This double standard is impossible to ignore: "Pelosi's age is cast as ugly and scary and freakish in a way her male colleagues' ages aren't; she is defined by being an old woman, whereas they are politicians who happen to be old men."[68]

Among the shortlisted women, several experienced outright denials of opportunities based on their age, for being either too young or too old. Allen, who was considered for multiple vacancies during several presidential administrations, achieved the pinnacle of success as a lawyer and jurist. But her advanced age during Truman's presidency was used against her. Allen was in her fifties when Roosevelt considered her, but approached her mid-sixties during Truman's presidency. One historian speculated that Allen's age "would certainly have been raised at confirmation hearings."[69] As a contemporary reporter noted, "'Women' and 'seniority' are not supposed to occur in the same sentence. The act of building a life over time, of working one's way up to leadership or securing a position as a respected elder, is denied to us. Age, experience, and authority are intrinsically connected for men; we've all grown up with images of sage, white-bearded elder statesmen."[70]

Hall was also discounted for being too old—in her mid-fifties—as part of the vetting process as a potential nominee. A glowing memorandum on her candidacy in President Reagan's papers concluded, "Indeed, it is tough to find any shortcomings in Judge Hall save that she is 56 instead of 46. . . ."[71] In 1971, during the time Nixon was searching for a nominee for the Court, his wife spoke openly about the importance of appointing a woman. But, Mrs. Nixon lamented, "The trouble is . . . the best qualified women are too old."[72] Bacon, on the other hand, only 39 when considered by Nixon for the Court, was critiqued for not being old enough.[73]

Age was a decisive factor in Reagan's decision-making as he combed through his shortlist for the Court. Kennedy herself suspected O'Connor's younger age gave her an advantage for the appointment, and this intuition turned out to be true. Kennedy received official phone calls from both Attorney General William French Smith and Senator Strom Thurmond (who was on the Senate Judiciary Committee at the time), informing her that she had not been selected. During the senator's call, he revealed that age had been a determinative factor; O'Connor was simply younger. We even found a memorandum in President Reagan's papers where ages of potential female nominees were handwritten into the margin, with "51" written next to O'Connor and "58" written next to Kennedy.[74] The author did not even bother calculating Sharp's age, even though her name also appeared. Born twenty-three years before O'Connor, the author wrote "age" with a notation, suggesting she was disqualified for that reason. Kearse's name appeared with "44" scratched in, apparently too young, even though Clarence Thomas was forty-three when confirmed. One commentator explains it this way: "As those women's careers kept tracking higher (like men's do), women increasingly began attaining their greatest power and influence just when our culture deemed they should become invisible. That visibility makes people deeply uncomfortable—and that discomfort, predictably, gets projected onto the women themselves, who are cast as monsters simply because they didn't crumble into dust the second they turned 50."[75] Age, as colored by our cultural biases, effectively functions as a form of sexism.

* * *

The challenges and binds that confront women across professional contexts impede their ascendance into leadership positions. We include the anecdotes and stories highlighted in this chapter to expose these tensions and, hopefully, help future women live more fully unified lives judged by their qualifications, not personal attributes or choices. We return to address these challenges in chapter eight, but next we examine why women make a difference on the Supreme Court and in other professional contexts.

7

No Longer Zero

It's been an amazing century for us . . . It was not that long
ago that the only relevant statistic regarding women in the
legal profession was zero percent—as in zero associates, zero
equity partners, and zero judges.[1]
—Sandra Day O'Connor, speech at Harvard University, 2009

That we are no longer at "zero" in the legal profession is surely
something to acknowledge, but it is not entirely cause for celebration. Glass ceilings remain unshattered for many positions of power
in law and elsewhere. In early 2020, zero remained the number of
women who have served as chief justice of the Supreme Court or as
president. Many states have never seen a female governor and most
Fortune 500 companies have not witnessed a female CEO. Women
keep putting cracks in the ceiling, "about 18 million" as Hillary
Clinton wryly noted after her unsuccessful bid for the Democratic
nomination in 2008.[2] Yet, even after Clinton finally snagged the
presidential nomination a decade later, the ceiling remains solidly
intact in many ways.

What might have happened had Hoover or Roosevelt placed Florence Allen on the Court in the 1930s? Would seeing a woman in this
role have changed the minds of law firm partners who refused to hire
women during the 1940s, '50s, '60s, and '70s? Surely the shortlisted
sisters would have had a few more legal employment options. Had
Allen been appointed and then remained on the Court until 1961, the
justices may have come to a different conclusion in the cases involving
female issues, such as whether women should be excluded from jury
service. Allen worked tirelessly to reverse this practice. But the nine

men on the Court upheld the exclusion in 1961 on the grounds that "woman is still regarded as the center of home and family life."[3]

O'Connor *could* have joined a Court made up of all women, or at least one that more accurately reflected the gender ratio of the nation. Allen retired from the Sixth Circuit before Mentschikoff made it onto the shortlist prepared by Attorney General Katzenbach for Presidents Kennedy and Johnson in 1962, and Allen passed away in 1966, so it is unlikely these women would have overlapped on the Court. But what if Mentschikoff had been confirmed and had then been joined by Sylvia Bacon and Mildred Lillie in 1971? Mentschikoff lived until 1984 and Lillie until 2002. These women jurists could have been joined by Carla Hills or Cornelia Kennedy in 1975, with Kennedy on the Court until she died in 2014. Bacon and Hills could have remained even longer. And there were plenty of opportunities to fill vacancies with other qualified women. The archives for Nixon, Ford, Carter, and Reagan contain files filled with numerous recommendations—there is no question that highly credentialed, competent women were available for the job.

Admittedly, the notion of an all-female Court, much less a majority-female Court, is merely a thought experiment at this point in time. Our objective here is to better understand the difference women make in leadership roles in any discipline or profession by speculating about how the appointment of one or more (or all!) of the shortlisted sisters might have changed the Supreme Court, its judicial opinions, the legal profession, and women's placement in positions of leadership. Would a Court with more women have expedited the nation's progress toward gender equality? Would a female chief justice or president already be part of our nation's history and seem less like a novelty? Would it have affected the types of cases selected by the Court for review and the opinions the justices subsequently rendered? Might we have already attained wage and hiring equality? How might more women prominently seated on the Court improve the numbers of women in leadership broadly? This chapter examines these questions by exploring the impact female judges have had both on case outcomes and the administration of justice generally. While the focus is on the judiciary, the conclusions drawn here apply across all fields.

The Impact of Women on Case Outcomes

Had one woman served on the Court from the 1930s, or two or three or four women from the 1970s, with O'Connor as a fifth in 1981, the cases selected for review on the nation's highest court surely would have been impacted. After all, only four justices are needed to approve a grant of certiorari to hear an appeal. Case outcomes also likely would have been impacted. As one woman wrote to President Ford in 1975 urging the appointment of a female nominee, "the male judges have consistently refused to give women equal rights under the fourteenth amendment. Thus, women have been forced to work for still another Equal Rights Amendment."[4] Without representation on the Court, women were left with only the legislative process, still unfinished in early 2020.

Being a woman alone does not necessarily mean that one champions women's causes like the ERA, as we revealed in chapter six. But even though all women did not unanimously support the ERA, we believe the sound of more female voices on the Court from the 1930s going forward would have resulted in more pro-woman outcomes. For example, a plurality of male justices indicated in 1973 that sex discrimination should be treated the same way as race discrimination under the Constitution, but the specific issue was not before them at the time.[5] When the issue finally did arise in 1976, the still all-male Court instead decided in a closely divided opinion that people who experience sex discrimination are entitled to less protection than those who experience racial discrimination.[6] We think it is a safe bet that an all-female Court would have reached the opposite result, even if also closely divided.

Numerous studies have considered the question of whether or not women decide cases differently than men. The results are mixed, as some scholars argue for and others argue against the proposition that gender makes a difference.[7] A rich and diverse literature explores the impact of gender on judging and questions whether women decide cases in a "different voice."[8] The theory of the "different voice" has been applied to Sandra Day O'Connor's opinions, finding that her decisions reflected a feminist jurisprudence of sorts, revealing concern for individual rights in the context of a wider community and not just as autonomous, independent persons.[9] And yet, O'Connor herself disagreed with this assessment. She eschewed notions that women judges decide cases differently because they are women. She challenged the academic theory that her opinions differed in a feminine way from that of the male justices, countering that this was just an example of "the old myths we have struggled to put behind us."[10] Even so, O'Connor's judging inevitably *was* informed by her life experiences, which included, of course, being a woman. Unlike the men she joined on the Court, she was offered a secretarial position after law school, not a legal job. She understood hiring and wage disparities in a personal way. Her voting while on the Court reflected a more liberal and nuanced understanding of women's issues than that of her male counterparts, in particular the other justices appointed by Reagan—Kennedy and Scalia.[11]

One notable study tested the hypothesis that female judges are different than male judges by focusing on "the relationship between the gender of judges and judicial quality," and considering "whether gender has a significant effect on judicial performance."[12] After examining all the state high court judges from 1998 to 2000 using three measures of "judicial output"—"opinion production, outside state citations, and copartisan disagreements"—the study failed to find meaningful evidence that gender affects the quality of judicial performance.[13]

Our focus, however, is not judicial performance—we are not surprised that women and men judges compare similarly on measures of judicial output—but on how the female experience and presence impacts deliberations, case outcomes, and other leadership decisions. Some empirical work finds a correlation between a judge's gender and the outcome of decisions at least in certain kinds of cases; empirical findings show that women state supreme court justices are more likely to decide pro-woman on women's issues,[14] search and seizure cases,[15] and death penalty and obscenity cases.[16] They also are more likely than their male colleagues to vote in "support of the female litigant's position in cases of divorce, child custody, child support, spousal maintenance, and property settlement,"[17] and "somewhat more likely to incarcerate defendants and impose somewhat longer prison sentences than [male] judges."[18] Female judges are more likely than male judges to determine that a law violates gay rights.[19] And even studies finding men and women judges "quite similar in their voting behavior" note "one exception: sex harassment cases."[20]

Not only do women sometimes reach different decisions, but their mere presence may impact the decision-making process of men sharing the bench. Studies show men vote more pro-plaintiff in anti-discrimination cases and sex discrimination cases if a woman is part of the three-judge appellate panel.[21] However, some legal commentators are critical of studies that suggest a correlation between an increase in female judges and an increase in results that will support feminist values.[22] For example, some contend that merely adding more women will not necessarily result in more judges who are "sympathetic to pro-feminist views."[23] We agree with the observation that men can advance a feminist agenda, and that, conversely, women might compromise that same agenda.[24] A study conducted by political scientists reveals that one's life experience (e.g., raising a daughter) is more likely to cultivate feminist values than one's gender.[25] Other research suggests that political party affiliation is the best predictor.[26]

One thing that empirical studies simply cannot evaluate is what happens in the closed-door deliberations among the nine justices of the Supreme Court as they debate and eventually develop a response to some of the most relevant and often controversial concerns of the day. We know that female perspectives matter (as do minority perspectives) because our female justices have spoken and written about it. For example, Lady Brenda Hale, the first female president of the Supreme Court of the

United Kingdom, observed that "the incorporation of difference on the bench subtly changes and, ultimately, improves the judicial product."[27] As another example, think back to our reference in part one to the case involving the strip-search of a thirteen-year-old girl accused of hiding ibuprofen to help with menstrual cramps. Justice Ginsburg observed, after her eight male colleagues indicated during oral argument they were not concerned by the search, that they themselves had never been in such a situation. Ginsburg explained in an interview with *USA Today*, "It's a very sensitive age for a girl. . . . I didn't think that my colleagues, some of them, quite understood."[28] It is hard to refute the evidence of a female Supreme Court justice pointing out that her perspective has had an impact on the men who are also involved in deciding a case. The strip-search case was decided 8–1 in favor of the teenage girl.[29] But would the outcome be the same had Ginsburg not been on the Court? Would any of the male justices have offered the same kind of perspective as did Ginsburg? Regardless of one's conservative or liberal views, women can understand the discomfort of having one's bra and underpants searched during early puberty.

Ginsburg's perspective has proved instrumental in many other cases, perhaps most notably in a dissent to Kennedy's opinion upholding the federal "partial-birth" abortion ban. Kennedy wrote about his concern that women might feel guilt over the decision. Ginsburg fired back, noting his opinion was based upon "ancient notions of women's place in the family and under the Constitution—ideas that have long since been discredited."[30] As another example, while on the D.C. Court of Appeals, Ginsburg authored an opinion imposing liability on a commercial landlord after a woman had been raped in a vacant portion of his office building.[31] The duty to exercise reasonable care to avoid a rape was triggered, according to Ginsburg, because the landlord had knowledge of prior thefts in the building and knew that the vacant areas could be accessed easily, and measures had been implemented after the rape to block access to these spaces.

In yet another example of the difference women make on the Court, but also the complexity of not always sharing the same view, consider the outcomes of three Supreme Court cases: *Gebser v. Lago Vista Independent School District* (1998),[32] *Davis v. Monroe County School Board* (1999),[33] and *Ledbetter v. Goodyear Tire & Rubber Company* (2007).[34] The question presented to the Court in *Gebser* was whether civil rights laws prohibit the sexual harassment of a student. A teenage girl had a longstanding relationship with her teacher, and once discovered, her parents sued the school district. O'Connor authored the 5–4 decision ruling that the school district *did not* have liability for the teacher's conduct unless the school had actual knowledge of the behavior and ignored it. Ginsburg dissented.

A year later in *Davis*, the Court faced another instance of sexual misconduct in schools. This case involved reports from a fifth-grade girl about unwanted sexual harassment and a school district accused of ignoring her repeated complaints. O'Connor authored the 5–4 decision again, this time with Ginsburg on her side, concluding that the school district *did* have liability.

By the time the Court heard Lilly Ledbetter's pay discrimination case, nearly a decade after *Davis*, O'Connor had been recently replaced by Samuel Alito and Ginsburg was the lone woman on the Court. Lilly Ledbetter had worked her entire career at Goodyear Tire, only to learn near her retirement that she had been paid seventy-one percent of what men at her level received. She sued, and a jury awarded her back pay plus more than $3 million in punitive damages. Goodyear appealed, arguing to the Supreme Court that her complaint was time-barred because she did not file a complaint within six months of the time the discrimination occurred. The Supreme Court agreed with the company in a 5–4 decision authored by Alito. Ginsburg took the highly unusual step of reading her scathing dissent from the bench: "In our view, the Court does not comprehend, or is indifferent to, the insidious way in which women can be victims of pay discrimination."[35] She further explained, "Pay disparities often occur, as they did in Ledbetter's case, in small increments; only over time is there strong cause to suspect that discrimination is at work. . . . An employee, like Ledbetter, trying to succeed in a male-dominated workplace, in a job filled only by men before she was hired, understandably may be anxious to avoid making waves."[36]

In 2009, Congress enacted the Lilly Ledbetter Fair Pay Act, the first bill President Obama signed into law during his presidency, which effectively restarted the time for filing a complaint about discriminatory pay each time the paycheck is issued. The legislation would help women in the future, but did nothing to remedy the injustice suffered by Ledbetter. We will never know whether the outcome for Ledbetter might have been different had Harriet Miers replaced O'Connor instead of Alito or if O'Connor had held off her retirement. But we are fairly certain that it would have been.

Factoring in the intersectionality of race and other facets of identity, it becomes even more difficult to assess the impact of gender from an empirical standpoint. The first black woman to serve on a federal court was Constance Baker Motley, appointed to the United States District Court for the Southern District of New York in 1966. Dorothy Comstock Riley became the first Latina elected to a state supreme court—the Michigan Supreme Court in 1982. The first black female state supreme court justice, Juanita Kidd Stout of the Pennsylvania Supreme Court, did not take her seat until 1988. Joyce Luther Kennard was the first Asian American/ Pacific Islander justice, joining the California Supreme Court in 1989. Virginia Linder of the Oregon Supreme Court was the first openly lesbian woman to sit on a state supreme court when she took office in 2007. Leah Ward Sears became the first black woman to serve as the chief justice of a state supreme court in 2005 on the Supreme Court of Georgia. The first openly LGBT female to serve in this role is Maite Oronoz Rodriguez, appointed as chief justice of the Supreme Court of Puerto Rico in 2016. A minority woman serving on any court remains a rarity, and thus it is impossible to statistically evaluate their impact.

Absent empirical evidence, however, we can look to the words of Justice Sotomayor to offer some insight into the difference a minority woman's presence makes in the judiciary. In a 2014 case concerning Michigan's ballot initiative on race-conscious admissions policies in higher education, Sotomayor wrote in her first oral dissent from the bench, "Race matters to a young woman's sense of self when she states her hometown, and then is pressed, 'No, where are you really from?' regardless of how many generations her family has been in the country."[37] She further explained, "This refusal to accept the stark reality that race matters is regrettable. The way to stop discrimination on the basis of race is to speak openly and candidly on the subject of race, and to apply the Constitution with eyes open to the unfortunate effects of centuries of racial discrimination."[38] She also infamously declared in a 2001 speech, "I would hope that a wise Latina woman with the richness of her experiences would more often than not reach a better conclusion than a white male who hasn't lived that life."[39] In response to questions from Jeff Sessions during her confirmation hearing more than fifteen years later, she qualified her statement as a "rhetorical flourish that fell flat" and explained, "I don't stand by the understanding of that statement that I will ignore other facts or other experiences because I haven't had them. I do believe that life experiences are important to the process of judging; they help you to understand and listen, but that the law requires a result, and it will command you to the facts that are relevant to the disposition of the case."[40] Sotomayor raised a similar concern about male justices after Obama nominated Merrick Garland instead of another woman: "A different perspective can permit you to more fully understand the arguments that are before you and help you articulate your position in a way that everyone will understand."[41]

It is not just the *female* justices who acknowledge the impact of their personal experience on their judicial decision-making. Justice Alito noted the influence of his own background as an Italian male in response to questions about immigration during his confirmation hearing: "I can't help but think of my own ancestors."[42] However, no one cited that as a basis to critique his credentials for the Supreme Court appointment. Media clung to the notion that Alito would adhere to Chief Justice John Roberts's model of the umpire calling balls and strikes. By contrast, Justice Sotomayor was chastised by media and politicians for acknowledging that her background as a Latina would inevitably inform her perspective in judicial decision-making. President Obama was also taken to task for selecting a nominee based upon qualities that included "empathy" when he named Sotomayor.[43] But he was not the first president to value empathy in his Supreme Court nominee. George H. W. Bush praised Clarence Thomas, describing him as "a warm, intelligent person who has great empathy."[44] Only *female* ancestry and *female* empathy were perceived to be problematic by commentators, the media, and politicians. Once again, qualities championed for men were liabilities for women.

The Impact of Women on the Administration of Justice

Female judges not only influence judicial decisions, but they also impact the administration of justice, that is, access to the courts and preservation of the rule of law. A court that reflects the population is an important component of institutional legitimacy. Women on the bench can impact the hiring of clerks, sexist behavior by lawyers and court employees, even the availability and location of bathrooms. Their presence has "inspired other women to aim for judicial appointments, they have raised the comfort level of women appearing in court and they have—through their extrajudicial volunteer commitments—worked to increase access to justice."[45] Seeing women in judicial roles is a powerful symbol of what is possible for young girls as they navigate their coming of age. The symbolic effect of women on the highest court of a nation also has implications for the rule of law in that it both emblemizes and enables access to justice for women and girls from all backgrounds.[46]

The United States lags behind on the international scene in placing women in judicial leadership. Some countries, including Angola, Australia, Canada, Ecuador, Rwanda, Serbia, and Slovenia have already attained gender parity, or near-parity, on their highest courts. As of late 2019, more than thirty nations have made a woman their chief or president of the highest court. Table 7.1 provides many examples of a growing list.

TABLE 7.1. Female Chief Justices or Presidents of International High Courts

1966	Ingrid Gärde Widemar, Sweden
1994	Sujata V. Manohar, India
1996	Joan Sawyer, Bahamas
	Désirée Bernard, Guyana
	Frances Johnson-Morris, Liberia
	Cecilia Sosa, Salvador
	Lombe P. Chibesakunda, Zambia
1997	Gloria Maya Musu-Scott, Liberia
1999	Sian Elias, New Zealand
2000	Beverley McLachlin, Canada
2001	Roseline Ukeje, Nigeria
2002	Mabel Agyemang, Gambia
2006	Ellen Gracie Northfleet, Brazil
	Dorit Beinisch, Israel
	Kaïta Kayentao Diallo, Mali
2007	Georgina Theodora Wood, Ghana
	Luisa Estella Morales, Venezuela
2008	Umu Hawa Tejan-Jalloh, Sierra Leone
2010	Marianne Lundius, Sweden
2011	Susan Denham, Ireland
	Hadiza Moussa Gros, Nigeria
	Shirani Bandaranayake, Sri Lanka
2012	Aloma Mariam Mukhtar, Nigeria
	Maria Lourdes Aranal Sereno, Philippines
2013	Zarela Villanueva Monge, Costa Rica
2014	Nthomeng Justina Majara, Lesotho
	Malgorzata Gersdorf, Poland
2015	Maria de Fátima Coronel, Cape Verde
	Miriam Naor, Israel
	Mathilda Twomey, Seychelles Isles
	Irene Mambilima, Zambia
2016	Cármen Lúcia, Brazil
	Sushila Karki, India
	Toril Marie Øie, Norway
	Julia Anna Przylebska, Poland
2017	Susan Kiefel, Australia
	Brenda Hale, United Kingdom
	Sophia Akuffo, Ghana
	Esther Hayut, Israel
	Mandisa Maya, South Africa
2018	Teresita Leonardo-De Castro, Philippines
2019	Tengku Maimun Tuan Mat, Malaysia

Women in these roles use their power to enable greater access to justice for other women. For example, Ghana's Chief Justice Georgina Wood focused on family justice issues impacting women and children, especially domestic violence. The vice president of the Supreme Court of Argentina, Justice Elena Inés Highton de Nolasco, implemented the inaugural Domestic Violence Office of the Supreme Court. Canada's Chief Justice Beverley McLachlin championed diversity on the bench, stating, "If we are to fully meet the challenges of judging in a diverse society, we must work toward a bench that better mirrors the people it judges."[47] Her call led to reform in the process for the high court's appointments, including increased transparency and other efforts to enhance accountability and diversity.[48]

That so many countries placed women into top leadership on their highest courts makes the United States's omission all the more stunning, particularly given that "[t]here is consistent agreement among scholars that diversity on the federal bench is a good thing."[49] We do note that state courts have a better record, with many making women the chief judge or justice as listed in Table 7.2.

Table 7.2 Female Chief Justices of State Supreme Courts

1965	Lorna E. Lockwood (AZ)	
1975	Susie M. Sharp (NC)	
1977	Rose Elizabeth Bird (CA)	
1979	Mary S. Coleman (MI)	
1984	Ellen Ash Peters (CT)	
1986	Rhoda B. Billings (NC)	
1992	Rosemary Barkett (FL)	
1993	Ann K. Covington (MO) Judith Kaye (NY) Margaret L. Workman (WV)	
1994	Annice M. Wagner (DC)	
1995	Kay McFarland (KS) Alma Wilson (OK) Barbara Durham (WA)	
1996	Deborah T. Poritz (NJ) Shirley S. Abrahamson (WI)	
1997	Linda Copple Trout (ID) Miriam Shearing (NV) Yvonne Kauger (OK)	
1998	Mary Mullarkey (CO) Kathleen A. Blatz (MN) Lenore Prather (MS) Robin Jean Davis (WV)	

1999	Margaret H. Marshall (MA) Elizabeth A. Weaver (MI) Pamela B. Mizner (NM)
2000	Dana A. Fabe (AK) Jean H. Toal (SC)
2001	Leigh Ingalls Saufley (ME) Maura Corrigan (MI) Karla M. Gray (MT) Beverly Lake (NC)
2002	Mary Ann McMorrow (IL) Christine M. Durham (UT)
2003	Deborah A. Agosti (NV) Petra Jimenez Maes (NM) Miriam Naveira Merly (PR)
2004	Betty C. Dickey (AR) Barbara J. Pariente (FL)
2005	Ruth V. McGregor (AZ) Leah Ward Sears (GA) Nancy A. Becker (NV)
2006	Marsha K. Ternus (IA) Sarah Parker (NC)
2007	Sue Bell Cobb (AL) Chase T. Rogers (CT) Laura Denvir Stith (MO)
2008	Peggy Quince (FL) Janice M. Holder (TN)
2009	Rebecca White Berch (AZ) Carol W. Hunstein (GA) Catherine D. Kimball (LA) Marilyn Kelly (MI)
2010	Tani Cantil-Sakauye (CA) Lorie Gildea (MN) Cornelia A. Clark (TN) Barbara Madsen (WA) Marylin S. Kite (WY)
2011	Linda S. Dalianis (NH) Maureen O'Connor (OH) Cynthia D. Kinser (VA)
2013	Rita B. Garman (IL) Mary Ellen Barbera (MD) Mary R. Russell (MO) Bernette J. Johnson (LA)
2014	Nancy E. Rice (CO) Loretta H. Rush (IN) Barbara J. Vigil (NM) Sharon G. Lee (TN)
2015	Patricia Breckenridge (MO) Patience D. Roggensack (WI)
2016	Lyn Stuart (AL) Janet DiFiore (NY)
2017	Mary Fairhurst (WA) Judith K. Nakamura (NM)

TABLE 7.2. (*Continued*)

2018	Martha Walters (OR)
2019	Anne M. Burke (IL)
	Marla J. Luckert (KS)
	Bridget Mary McCormack (MI)
	Cheri Beasley (NC)
	Noma Gurich (OK)
	Elizabeth Walker (WV)
2020	Debra L. Stephens (WA)

Cases involving equal pay, education rights, reproduction, same-sex benefits, transgender rights, violence against women, women's health, and similar issues will likely appear on the Supreme Court's docket in the coming years. These issues directly impact women's autonomy over their bodies, their roles as primary caretakers for children and aging parents, the persistent pay gap, and lack of opportunities for women to advance in the workplace as compared to men. Women make up the majority of the nation. Women should be the majority of decision makers on courts and in other leadership roles.

We acknowledge that not all women will necessarily share the same views on these issues. We do not believe that there is or even should be a monolithic "woman's voice." Nor do we assume that all female judges adjudicate from a feminist standpoint. We do not equate being a woman with being a feminist, and we make no distinction between feminist and non-feminist identities of lawyers or judges. Nevertheless, we do unequivocally believe that there should be a sufficient number of women on the Court to represent a wide array of conservative and liberal perspectives on issues involving women's bodies and lives, as well as issues involving our national life. Men have had a range of viewpoints represented since the founding of the nation. Why not women?

Moving beyond zero and toward overall gender parity is an important goal for the Supreme Court and all institutions. But how do we get there? Direction from the first woman on the Court may prove instructive. Justice O'Connor believed "the first step in getting power is to become visible to others."⁵⁰ What we see is what we believe we can become. It is nearly impossible to envision ourselves in a position of leadership or power if we do not see others with whom we can identify in that role. Madeleine Albright noted in more than one speech, "I never imagined that I would one day become secretary of state. It's not that I lacked ambition. It is just that I had never seen a secretary of state in a skirt."⁵¹ Albright's point highlights the fact that sometimes ascending into positions of power requires a vision of the possibility.

The historical absence of women in the legal profession makes the shortlisted women's accomplishments so very extraordinary. At the time they entered the profession, women did not yet hold the positions they would attain over the course of their careers. But each made herself visible in her own way so that others who would follow could see the opportunities as possible. Seeing Soia Mentschikoff in the halls of the University of Chicago as a law student is part of why Herma Kay Hill became a law professor and the first female dean of the University of California at Berkeley Law School.⁵² She reflected, "I never had any courses from her other than her participation in [Karl] Llewellyn's first-year course, where she came in and gave a lecture one day. But I had a sense, from seeing her and feeling her presence in the school, that this was something that could be done."⁵³ One of us similarly became a law professor in part because Mentschikoff's portrait hung on the wall in the echoing, concrete halls of the University of Chicago Law School. The other of us was left uninspired by the lack of portraits of female professors adorning the walls of the University of Iowa College of Law.

Being visible is necessary, but not alone sufficient, to attain equal representation in positions of leadership and power. Some countries have experimented with gender quotas to address this reality with questionable success: "In England and Wales as well as France, quotas are restricted to political elections and are not applicable to professional elections, recruitment and career advancement. . . . In Germany target quotas are laid down by law. To achieve gender parity, women have to be given preference in appointments and promotions in cases of equal qualifications. . . . However, in practice, in the judiciary these quotas hardly ever have any bearing on actual appointment decisions."[54] South Africa's constitution, adopted in 1996, contains a voluntary, aspirational provision noting that the judiciary should reflect the public it serves for both race and gender, although parity has not yet been achieved. As one scholar notes:

> In contrast to the assertions in the United States that judges function like baseball umpires [as claimed by Chief Justice John Roberts during his confirmation hearings], in South Africa a frequently expressed and undisputed justification for the appointment of those previously excluded by racism and sexism is precisely so that they would and should provide perspectives previously absent; that they would therefore be essential to advancing the Constitution's promises. African, Coloured, Asian and women judges were and are expected to add value—they were and are expected to make a difference in the decisions rendered; they were and are expected to make a difference in the development of the New Democracy's jurisprudence.[55]

Mandatory quotas seem more effective for achieving equal representation of women. Kenya's constitution, adopted in 2010, contains a mandatory quota that provides that "not more than two-thirds of members of elective or appointive bodies should be of the same gender."[56] There were no female judges in Kenya until 1983, and the second was not appointed until 1986, followed by a third in 1993.[57] By July 2011, however, forty-four percent of High Court judges were women.[58] Similarly, Ethiopia's first female head of its Supreme Court, Meaza Ashenafi, was sworn in November 2018, as part of the newly elected Prime Minister Abiy Ahmed's effort to bring gender parity to government leadership roles. Half of Ahmed's cabinet officials are women.

However successful mandatory quotas may be, they are an unlikely solution to gender disparity in the U.S., though that has not kept scholars and policy-makers from proposing them.[59] As of early 2020, however, only one state had adopted a gender quota in any professional context:

in 2018, California passed a law mandating the presence of women on corporate boards.[60] While well-intentioned, the law has done little to achieve equal representation. Corporate boards are obligated only to include one woman by the end of 2019, and at least two (for five-member boards) or three (for boards of six or more members) by the end of 2021. And, as Governor Jerry Brown conceded when signing the law into effect, it likely will be struck down in the courts as unconstitutional.[61] The Illinois legislature considered a similar measure in 2019 but declined to adopt it, instead passing legislation that only requires companies to report information about diversity, such as the gender and race/ethnicity of board members and demographic diversity efforts.

It is important that women are well represented in positions of power in the legal profession, regardless of their political ideology. But, given that legislative or constitutional quotas are an unlikely path to equal gender representation for the U.S., what else can be done? Chapter eight offers ideas about how to move more women from shortlisted to selected.

8

Surmounting the Shortlist

[M]y life's story touches people because it resonates with
their own circumstances. . . . The idea of my becoming a Supreme Court Justice—which, indeed, as a goal would inevitably elude the vast majority of aspirants—never occurred
to me except as the remotest of fantasies. But experience
has taught me that you cannot value dreams according to
the odds of their coming true. Their real value is in stirring
within us the will to aspire.[1]
—Sonia Sotomayor, *My Beloved World*, 2013

Shortlisting happens to many women in competitive professional contexts, even if they are unlikely to find themselves on a president's list for
a Supreme Court vacancy. Our mission is to move more women and
minorities from shortlisted to selected.

Shortlisting inevitably occurs with any pursuit of leadership or advancement, whether it's the judge in the courtroom, the CEO in the
corner office, or the coach on the playing field. Women, and especially
female minorities, regularly find themselves equally or more qualified
than the white men on the shortlist, but they are far less likely to be selected. Shortlists thus project a façade of diversity with their inclusion of
women and minorities but function to preserve the status quo.

Diverse shortlists are a prerequisite for producing diverse leaders, but
they are not sufficient in and of themselves to achieve this goal. Moreover, sometimes individuals self-shortlist by declining to be considered
among a pool of candidates, or forgoing a position even if offered because of other priorities, due to a lack of confidence, fear of an unwin-
nable situation, or the perception of being less than qualified despite

objective evidence to the contrary. Most often, however, shortlisting is in the hands of the decision maker and is attributable to bias, discrimination, prejudice, and the dominant group's desire to remain in control.

Diversity includes much more than gender or race or ability or religion or ethnicity or sexuality or socio-economic status. Individuals sharing the same facets of their identity commonly differ in their perspectives on politics, policy, and in many other respects. Our point is simply that the symbolism of diverse shortlists is unlikely to increase diversity in leadership unless additional efforts are implemented to shift diverse candidates from shortlisted to selected. Systemic shortlisting of women and minorities risks the hollow achievement of symbolic diversity at best, and at worst becomes a mechanism to actively hold back the underrepresented.

The fact that women even appear on shortlists is some measure of progress, given that this nation was founded by men who completely excluded women from all aspects of public life. During the first hundred years of our nation's existence, women could not hold property in their own name or vote or pursue an education at many institutions. While each wave of feminism pushed women's rights forward, the progress has proven insufficient for most and practically nonexistent for minority women. One might be tempted to think that the #MeToo movement has finally been a catalyst for real change. After all, record numbers of women ran for office during the 2018 midterms following President Trump's election—270 campaigned for Congress and governor, not to mention state and local offices—and many of them won. One hundred twenty-seven of them, to be exact, were sworn into Congress. For the first time in the nation's history, more than one hundred members of the United States House of Representatives were women, including the first Muslim women (Michigan's Rashida Tlaib and Minnesota's Ilhan Omar), the first Native American women (Kansas's Sharice Davids and New Mexico's Deb Haaland), and the first Latinas elected from Texas (Veronica Escobar and Sylvia Garcia). Some states saw their first female senator elected to Congress (Marsha Blackburn of Tennessee and Krysten Sinema of Arizona, also the first openly bisexual member of Congress). Others saw entire slates of women in leadership, like with Michigan, electing Governor Gretchen Whitmer, Attorney General Dana Nessel (also the first openly lesbian attorney general in the nation), and Secretary of State Jocelyn Benson; along with U.S. Senator Debbie Stabenow and U.S. Representatives Elissa Slotkin, Haley Stevens, and Rashida Tlaib; as well as Chief Justice Bridget Mary McCormack. Harris County, Texas, elected nineteen black, female judges, heralded as the "#Houston19" by *Cosmopolitan* magazine.[2] They campaigned with the slogan "Black Girl Magic" to change the face of the court system in the nation's fourth largest city, with a population bigger than twenty-four of its states.[3] A twenty-seven-year-old immigrant from Colombia, Lina Hidalgo, won the seat of Harris County's chief executive, essentially the governor of Houston. The state of Nevada will be the first in the nation to have a statehouse composed of more than fifty percent women, a body truly representing the gender diversity of the governed.

The 2018 election cycle marked the first time in American history where wins for women meant wins for women from a wide range of backgrounds, including diversity in ethnicity and sexual orientation. There is much to celebrate in this evolution, but history cautions that one year of positive advances for women may not lead to permanent change. We need strategies and structural reforms to ensure that 2018 does not go the way of 1992's "Year of the Woman"—a point we will return to at the end of this chapter.

Electing more women is surely part of the solution, but not everyone can turn to the public for a vote. Far more positions of leadership are filled in ways that more closely mirror the Supreme Court shortlisting process.

* * *

One might think that a president would take the lack of women on the Supreme Court into account when crafting a shortlist in the twenty-first century. It seemed Trump was doing so when he showcased his shortlist on the White House.gov website immediately after taking office in 2017.

He was the first president to offer his shortlist so publicly, affirmatively breaking with the tradition of keeping shortlists confidential until the ultimate nominee is announced. Trump originally shared eleven names during his campaign: eight men and three women, all of whom were white.[4] He expanded the list to twenty-five potential nominees shortly after his election.[5] Of the twenty-five names, six were women (all white): Amy Coney Barrett, Allison Eid, Britt Grant, Joan Larsen, Margaret Ryan, and Diane Sykes. All were more than qualified for the Court based on their education and career experience, though Trump's shortlisting process was criticized as being too heavily influenced (if not entirely orchestrated by) the Federalist Society.

Trump's first opportunity to nominate a justice occurred immediately upon his inauguration. Justice Scalia's seat went unfilled for nearly a year after his death in 2016 because Senate Republicans refused to hold confirmation hearings despite President Obama's nomination of Merrick Garland. Trump swiftly selected Neil Gorsuch, a Harvard-trained lawyer who had sat on the United States Court of Appeals for the Tenth Circuit since 2006. He was confirmed by a vote of 54–45. (It is worth noting just how politicized the process has become in recent years. The confirmation votes for Antonin Scalia were 98–0 in 1986, and Ruth Bader Ginsburg received votes of 96–3 in 1993. By contrast, President Obama's nominees received far more divided votes—68–31 for Sonia Sotomayor in 2009 and 63–37 for Elena Kagan in 2010—and his final nominee never even made it to a Senate confirmation hearing, let alone a vote.)

When Trump made his second nomination in 2018 after Justice Kennedy's retirement announcement, we penned an op-ed published by the *Houston Chronicle* proposing that Trump select one of the six women on his shortlist not simply because they were female, but because the Court's legitimacy and credibility are enhanced when its membership represents the general population. Alas, he did not heed our advice (even though we did tweet it to him). In hindsight, he might have regretted his choice, given what transpired with the nominee he did select, Brett Kavanaugh.

The Kavanaugh confirmation hearing gripped the country, vividly displaying the enduring misogyny in America. Women across the nation reeled from the stinging memories of their own sexual assaults as they watched Dr. Christine Blasey Ford painstakingly testify before the Senate Judiciary Committee about how a drunken Brett Kavanaugh forced himself upon her at a high school party. More than 20 million people watched her testimony live.[6]

The hearing also illustrated many of the gendered phenomena that impact women in the workplace. We saw this from the moment Senator Charles Grassley opened the hearing. Senators Kamala Harris and Mazie Hirono both attempted to raise objections to the form of the proceeding, but Grassley spoke over them and did not stop talking until one of his male colleagues, Senator Cory Booker, interrupted to raise the same objections. Only then did Grassley yield to listen to a man repeat the same arguments raised by the two women.

The hearing unfolded much like the confirmation of Clarence Thomas, where Anita Hill was inappropriately treated as if she were under investigation or on trial, even though Thomas (and his questionable behavior) was the actual target of the process. (In 2019, Senator Joseph Biden, Jr. publicly expressed regret for the role he played overseeing the Judiciary Committee's questioning of Hill, but he stopped short of formally issuing an apology to her.) This time around, however, in a purported effort toward objectivity and sensitivity, Republican senators hired a female sex crimes prosecutor to question Ford. Once the questions turned to Kavanaugh, however, they essentially "fired" her, cutting off her questions and taking over the process to address Kavanaugh directly.

Ford delivered highly credible testimony, showing deference to and respect for her questioners. Hundreds of women law professors signed a letter thanking her for her bravery. In return for her testimony, she faced death threats forcing her to flee her home with her family. Kavanaugh delivered evasive testimony, at times belligerent. He was especially disrespectful to Senator Amy Klobuchar, demanding to know whether she had an alcohol problem when she asked him reasonable questions about his own alcohol use. His responses were partisan, even prejudicial, threatening at one point that "what goes around comes around."[7] More than 2,400 law professors signed a letter to the Senate arguing against his confirmation based upon the partisan and prejudicial behavior he exhibited. Canon 2(1) of the Code of Judicial Conduct for U.S. Judges, which applied to him as a judge on the United States Court of Appeals for the D.C. Circuit at the time, requires, "A judge should respect and comply with the law and should act at all times in a manner that promotes public confidence in the integrity and impartiality of the judiciary." Anyone viewing his testimony would be hard-pressed to argue that he followed the letter or the spirit of this provision, though he did later publicly apologize to Senator Klobuchar. The Senate voted to confirm him 50–48, one of the slimmest margins in history.[8] Kavanaugh went on to hire an all-female group of law clerks, though it remains to be seen whether his judicial decisions will support or compromise women's rights.

As this book went to press, Trump had yet to select a woman from his shortlist. Instead, his shortlist functioned precisely in the same way as most shortlists: lending the auspices of diversity and equality to the nomination process but ultimately preserving the status quo. We recognize that each individual's journey from shortlisted to selected is nuanced and unique. Yet for some, especially for white men from privileged backgrounds, there are clear-cut, well-trodden pathways. Just ask Neil Gorsuch and Brett Kavanaugh where they went to high school. (Spoiler alert: they both attended the exclusive Georgetown Preparatory School, followed by similar paths to elite colleges, law schools, clerkships, and practice.) In contrast, pursuing positions of leadership and power is often messy for women, and especially minority women. It typically involves detours and cul-de-sacs and back roads and toll roads.

The first, second, and third waves of feminism failed to accomplish what its founding mothers hoped and its followers championed. Sadly, even in the midst of fourth-wave feminism, the treatment of women appears increasingly misogynistic, especially for women who seek positions of power or challenge the men who hold those positions. This nation's president has publicly boasted of perpetrating acts of sexual violence, and one-third of the current male Supreme Court justices have been credibly accused of sexual misconduct.[9]

We are not here to assign blame in the wake of feminism's failures from Seneca Falls to the #MeToo era. We note, however, a common omission in each wave of women's rights since that early gathering. White women frequently fail to include minorities in their pursuit of equality or in more subtle efforts to expose misogyny. The fact that only two women in our study here represent minority groups, one shortlisted (Judge Kearse) and one selected (Justice Sotomayor), evidences the greater hardships and barriers faced by female minorities. Until the feminist and women's rights movements account for intersectional experiences of ability, ethnicity, race, religion, sexuality, and more, meaningful equality in leadership positions will remain elusive.

Our call for intersectional inclusion is in the spirit of the efforts that opened the world to each of our shortlisted women. Common "solutions" offered for modern women who aspire to achieve positions of leadership largely revolve around preserving the status quo for men in power, unfortunately. Law firms and corporations tout "benefits" like flexible hours and on-site child care to help with work-life balance, but reforms like these still assume the primary responsibility of child-rearing and family care rests with female employees. Some experts blame women for not sitting at the table and leaning in.[10] These sorts of recommendations burden women. They are also not entirely relevant or helpful for women living in countries where child marriage is legal or where women do not enjoy basic freedoms like the ability to hold a job without their husband's permission.[11] Addressing these inequities is beyond the scope of this book, but we acknowledge that, even in the midst of our critique of the experience for women living in the United States, there is relative privilege compared to the lives of women elsewhere in the world.

Countless conferences have been held and even more articles, books, essays, and op-eds have been authored to offer solutions. We held our own event at the Book Cadillac Hotel in downtown Detroit, Michigan in 2012, a symposium for the *Michigan State Law Review* titled "The Legal Profession's Pipeline to Power," keynoted by *New York Times* op-ed contributor and former Supreme Court reporter Linda Greenhouse and federal judge Nancy Gertner, among a dozen other speakers (including at least three law professors who have since become law school deans: Theresa Beiner, Angela Onwuachi-Willig, and Carla Pratt).[12] One of us also organized the inaugural Women's Power Summit on Law and Leadership, an event that brought together the nation's most prominent and accomplished leaders in law, including Justice Sandra Day O'Connor, and resulted in the production of a manifesto to guide efforts toward gender parity in the legal profession. Despite efforts like these, much work remains to finally eradicate gender inequality in the upper echelons of power.

Shortlisted to Selected

One might question whether yet another book on gender equality can actually make a difference. We think the answer is yes, a conclusion we did not come to lightly, and only after researching the women profiled here for more than a decade. Themes drawn from their lived experiences reveal a set of strategies for counteracting the biases and prejudices that endure. They went after elite roles when no women held the positions they sought and men actively worked to keep them at bay. Each went from shortlisted to selected, repeatedly, during her ascendance to positions of power, whether or not she ultimately made it off the shortlist for the Supreme Court. Their guidance can help more women move from shortlisted to selected.

We offer a list of "strategies" with some hesitation and trepidation, because we do not mean to suggest that if these items are accomplished, all gender inequality in leadership roles will immediately be eradicated. Nor do we suggest in any way that following these "strategies" means one will find herself under consideration for the Supreme Court or any particular leadership position. Instead, our intention here is to set out ideas for moving forward drawn from the collective experiences of our shortlisted sisters.

Strategy 1. Leverage Legal Education

One common experience among all of the women profiled in this book is their pursuit of legal education. A law degree offers legitimacy and credibility. The practice of law is not just the training ground for developing one's legal and analytical skills; it is also a place to practice the survival skills necessary to endure and move beyond prejudice and bias. "Law represented capability to me," Carla Hills explained when asked about why she went to law school.[13] She had read a biography about Alexander Hamilton as a young girl: "You look at people like Hamilton, great contributors to our history, and many of them have been trained in the law."[14]

Consider a contemporary example. When Rachel Denhollander had concerns about sexual abuse suffered at the hands of now-convicted Michigan State University and U.S. Women's Olympic Gymnastics team physician Larry Nassar, she pursued a *law degree*.[15] That education equipped her with knowledge *and* confidence. Denhollander credited her legal training with the ability to bring her perpetrator to justice, and after she came forward, more than five hundred women did so as well to document his abuse. He will likely remain in prison for the rest of his life. In the wake of the Nassar scandal, in 2018 the voters of Michigan elected an all-female slate of candidates to lead their state, all of whom also happen to be—that's right—*lawyers*. Michigan's governor, secretary of state, attorney general, and chief of the supreme court hold law degrees. In fact, of the more than one hundred women elected to Congress during the 2018 midterms, thirty-eight hold law degrees from twenty-nine different law schools.[16]

Though some may question the value of a law degree, it can be an important first step for women toward credentialing themselves for positions of leadership and power. It is not the only route, but it is one that can be leveraged to forge the path toward selected-status. For many of our shortlisted sisters, their time in law school also provided an opportunity to cultivate key relationships that served them well in their rise through the legal profession.

Strategy 2. Partner with Friends and Lovers Who Value Women's Professional Lives

Choose personal partners—whether in friendship or in romance— who value one's professional life and allow for the possibility of non-traditional relationships. The women featured here entered into relationships with those who not only saw them as equals, but supported and celebrated their professional success even if it meant the women might ultimately outperform or overshadow them. In some instances men took on the role of "wife" to support the women's careers. In other cases, the couples blended traditional roles.

Allen never married, but lived a quiet life with two very supportive women, albeit outside of the public eye. Susie Sharp was deeply in love with three men, often simultaneously, at different stages in her life. Two of these relationships were established in law school—a fellow student and a professor—and the third relationship began with another justice on the North Carolina Supreme Court. These relationships gave her the freedom to pursue her professional dreams even as she went on to surpass her lovers' own accomplishments. Soia Mentschikoff fell in love with her law professor/mentor who became her husband as the two taught at Harvard and the University of Chicago. Mildred Lillie's husband urged her to keep her own last name to increase her odds of reelection. Hills relied upon her husband, Rod, in her early years of practice to introduce her to male lawyers who would put her on prestigious bar committees, but she would later outrank him, serving as secretary of housing and urban development for President Ford while her husband was chair of the Securities and Exchange Commission. Joan Dempsey

Klein's first husband helped her make connections to secure a job out of law school in the California State Attorney General's Office; while there, she would have two children with him before they divorced, and she later married another attorney in the Attorney General's Office.

William Rehnquist, who proposed marriage to O'Connor after dating her in law school, lobbied to have her join him on the Court. (One wonders what her fate might have been had she accepted his proposal rather than marry John O'Connor, who steadfastly supported her career and was comfortable with her surpassing him professionally.) Their friendship persevered, with O'Connor attending Rehnquist's swearing-in ceremony at the Court and Rehnquist later supporting her nomination. A close relationship with Rehnquist seems to be a common thread between more than one of the shortlisted sisters' lives. It was rumored in the Washington, D.C., political circles that he and Hall were romantically involved after her husband's death.[17] As one reporter put it, "Chief Justice William Rehnquist . . . has a new love interest—and some say a new bounce to his step. Rehnquist, 69, is romantically involved with Cynthia Holcomb Hall, 65, a judge on the 9th US Court of Appeals in San Francisco. When she's in town, she's been seen in the Supreme Court's guest seats."[18] Mentschikoff and Rehnquist exchanged letters and visits as well.

After kindling friendships while at Stanford, the Rehnquists, O'Connors, and Cynthia Holcomb Hall remained close, socializing in Phoenix where they all lived during their first years of practice after law school. Looking back, Hall acknowledged that "John was terrific" about "Sandra's going to Washington."[19] "He did it with a smile," eventually spending half the year in Arizona and half in Washington, D.C.[20] She noted how Marty Ginsburg similarly "gave up his whole life in New York City" practicing law and "took a professorship at Georgetown to be in D.C."[21] As noted earlier in the book, Marty also took responsibility for homemaking activities, like cooking, and was instrumental in lobbying behind the scenes to secure his wife's seat on the Court. Hall's husband similarly gave up a job he loved practicing law in California when she received the offer from President Nixon to join the United States Tax Court in Washington, D.C. We could continue this list of anecdotes from the women's lives for many, many more pages, but the point is clear. These women all chose relationships with individuals who supported, valued, and even facilitated their professional goals.

Strategy 3. Collaborate to Compete

The concept of going from shortlisted to selected necessarily assumes some amount of competition—after all, only one individual will "win" a particular position. The stories profiled here, however, reveal how collaboration among women can make them more competitive, collectively, for positions of power. Success gives those in power access to structures and systems. Some women leverage this access by participating in political and social movements, or speaking out publicly about issues that are important to them. Others offer mentorship to women, which can function as a sort of professional activism, by providing guidance and counsel to those in the pipeline.

Klein, herself a contender for the Supreme Court, testified before the Senate Judiciary Committee on behalf of O'Connor during her confirmation hearings. Women close to presidents—including their advisers, wives, and daughters—also spoke to them on behalf of other women.[22] As one reporter observed, "While she has not invaded the Oval Office, Mrs. Ford gets her views across when she and the President are alone: she called it 'pillow talk.'"[23] Barbara Hackman Franklin, who led Nixon's initiatives to bring more women into government leadership, stated in her oral history that Pat Nixon spoke "a little more sharply" to her husband when he did not appoint a woman, after Mrs. Nixon and her daughters had advocated for one.[24] As Julie Nixon Eisenhower, one of Nixon's daughters, put it when describing her mother: "I remember she was very strong about a woman on the court. This was one instance where she really spoke up. I remember a family dinner where she didn't tell him off, but she said I think there should have been a woman and

I'm very disappointed, etc."[25] Leaders from nonprofit, political, and women's rights organizations flooded presidents' offices with letters and telegrams offering names of possible female Supreme Court nominees. We read dozens of these letters and were struck by how many of the authors, women themselves successful in their own right, championed other women for selection.

Collaboration also means reaching beyond political or other divides. Several of the shortlisted sisters embodied this strategy, finding themselves nominated by presidents from both parties for various judgeships. Cornelia Kennedy was nominated to the bench first by a Republican (Nixon), then elevated to a higher court by a Democrat (Carter), and shortlisted for the Supreme Court by a Republican (Reagan). Amalya Kearse, initially placed on the Second Circuit by Carter, was considered for the high court by Reagan and Clinton. Lillie, a Democrat, was shortlisted by Nixon. Similarly, Sotomayor was nominated by George H. W. Bush and confirmed to the United States District Court for the Southern District of New York in 1992, then elevated to the Second Circuit in 1998 on a nomination from Clinton before Obama placed her on the Supreme Court. Allen campaigned as an independent against Democratic and Republican opponents to win her seat on the Ohio State Supreme Court in 1922, the first woman ever elected to a state supreme court. Her victory was the product of women coming together across party lines. As women compete for leadership and power, these examples show how collaboration can help secure those roles.

Mildred Lillie shared in her oral history a perspective on how women should support each other: "I have encouraged women lawyers to advance in the profession and those who are about to enter law school or who are already studying law . . . I have had a number of young women serve with me as externs, and I have done everything I could to encourage them to branch out and use their legal education to their fullest advantage. I am proud that some of these young women are now successful practitioners and are serving in judicial capacities."[26] Joan Dempsey Klein also took seriously the obligation to mentor and support women lawyers. She accomplished this through work with professional organizations for women lawyers and judges, as a founder of both the National Association of Women Judges (NAWJ) and California Women Lawyers. Likewise, Cornelia Kennedy was involved with the creation of NAWJ in its early days; she found the camaraderie among female judges from across the country quite inspiring, especially in light of the fact that many of the judges were the solitary woman in their jurisdiction. Additionally, Kennedy was part of a group of judges who worked to create the National Conference of Federal Trial Judges (NCFTJ). In the formative stages, Kennedy was elected secretary of the organization, but unlike the other executive positions, it did not carry with it an automatic rotation into the role of president. Without the potential to become the NCFTJ president, Kennedy initially declined the appointment. The protocol was subsequently changed, and Kennedy eventually rotated into the organization's top leadership position.

Mentschikoff's presidency of the Association of American Law Schools exemplified a different kind of collaboration distinct from formal organizing around women's issues. Historically, female professors were less likely than their male colleagues to attend the meetings of this organization. Herma Hill Kay, who later also assumed the presidency, credited Mentschikoff with creating significant policy changes, including the timing of the meeting, which used to take place between the Christmas and New Year holidays: "It was always my view that the men wanted to get out of the house between Christmas and New Year to get away from all the visiting family and kids, [laughs] so they went off to Chicago and had this wonderful meeting for themselves. Then, when women started joining the faculties, it became pretty obvious that this was not a great time to leave home and have professional meetings. I think Soia had that in mind when she got the date changed."[27] Sometimes, as illustrated by this example, a woman's presence in a leadership role allows for implementing structural change that might appear to be minor but significantly enhances the participation of women. In this case, the meeting date change allowed for increased involvement of women law professors (including both of us—we spoke at many AALS annual meetings, even winning a paper competition there together in 2012, at the same time we were raising infants, toddlers, and teens, which would have been impossible had the meeting remained in the midst of the holidays).

Strategy 4. Create Meaningful Opportunity, Don't Wait for It

One experience shared by all of the women in this book is a conscious decision to create and actively pursue opportunities, rather than wait for them. Reflecting on her success, Allen explained, "One valuable lesson I learned in the woman suffrage movement was to take advantage of every circumstance which would get me a hearing."[28] Most of the women struggled to find work practicing law despite graduating with high grades from top schools. Nearly all of the shortlisted sisters heard refrains from interviewers wishing that they were men. Contrast Allen's experience transferring law schools with her early efforts to find a job. As noted in chapter one, she felt a sense of purpose and solidarity when transferring from the University of Chicago, where she was the only woman, to New York University to finish her legal education, where she felt women "were in the Law School on equal terms with men."[29] But when she returned home to Ohio, she found no employers willing to hire a woman to practice law, so she created her own practice in legal aid.

Other women turned to government in the face of rejection from private practice, working as assistant attorneys general or U.S. attorneys. Hills interviewed with New York firms after graduating in the top ten percent of her class from Yale Law School, but she was told, "What we believe is the appropriate specialty for women is trust and estates or marital law."[30] Those areas were not for her, so she became an assistant U.S. attorney in Los Angeles. At one point, Susie Sharp even stopped practicing altogether and left the firm with her father to work as a secretary at her alma mater because she felt it would offer different opportunities for both her professional and personal life. Klein worked to support herself in law school as a playground director even though UCLA prohibited students from being employed. She regularly visited her husband, who had graduated ahead of her and taken a position with the California Attorney General's Office, and, after meeting "a lot of folks in the office . . . was offered a position" herself.[31] The new job came at a cost, however, as she had to accept a pay cut to practice law—she made $370 a month with the Department of Parks and Recreation but only $260 a month as a lawyer in the Attorney General's Office![32] When Kennedy learned of vacancies that arose on the United States Court of Appeals for the Sixth Circuit, she affirmatively applied for consideration. With each of these decisions, the women created opportunities for the next, repeatedly moving from shortlisted to selected as they rose through positions of increasing power and prestige.

Strategy 5. Implement Structural Changes That Do Not Burden Women

When Cornelia Kennedy observed that the honorific "Justice" need not be prefaced with "Mr.," leading to its removal from the doors of the justices' chambers and the pages of Supreme Court decision reporters, she prompted a structural change that imposed no burden on women but instead set the stage for equality—the same title for male and female justices.

Others from our shortlisted cohort demanded structural equality in more formal ways. Sylvia Bacon advocated for rape reforms in the late 1970s, because she recognized the humiliation survivors often faced, feeling as if they were on trial themselves when testifying against their perpetrators in the courtroom. (Her concern was prescient in foreshadowing the treatment of Anita Hill and Christine Blasey Ford decades later when they confronted their perpetrators about sexual misconduct.) Sharp worked to include women on juries after observing the contradiction that while she could practice law, women could not participate in the decision-making in the same legal system. Allen marched for women's right to vote. Klein experienced "an epiphany" during her time working in the California State Attorney General's Office that she recounted in her oral history:

There was a point in my life when I recognized discrimination against women for what it was. . . . It just hit me, and that was when I was in the State Attorney General's office. I was supposed to be getting an elevation, yet when I was talking to the head of the office, it became clear to me from this man, that I wasn't going to do much of anything there because I was a woman. At that point in time I made a commitment to myself that I would devote a certain portion of my every day to try and to eliminate discrimination against women.[33]

She became "supersensitive" in demanding equality, and would go on to found several women's legal organizations and take on other significant leadership roles to advocate for women's rights. Some women demanded equality by declining certain requests, as we saw when Mentschikoff declined to write an article about women lawyers as estate planners or when Allen refused to handle the divorce docket.

These structural reforms do not require women alone to be agents of change. Although President Carter never had the opportunity to short-list let alone nominate a woman for the Supreme Court, he implemented a plan for diversifying the federal bench that was more successful than any other president. Carter understood that one of the most powerful roles of a president is the appointment of judges, who remain in office long beyond a presidential term. In February 1977, Carter issued an Executive Order to establish the United States Circuit Judge Nominating Commission with the explicit goal to document efforts for diversity. Thirteen panels were created representing regions across the country, with a specific mandate that each include men, women, and minorities. The panels were charged with nominating appropriate candidates for the federal judiciary. Panel members included Amalya Kearse, who at the time was still practicing law at Hughes, Hubbard & Reed in New York. (She would, of course, soon find herself on the U.S. Court of Appeals for the Second Circuit two years later, in June 1979.) To formalize the diversity efforts, the Nominating Commission members and senators were specifically asked, when considering appointments, what steps were taken to give public notice to minorities and women, including the names of organizations and groups receiving notice, as well as lists of all women and minorities who responded. Of the individuals considered, the Commission and senators were required to specify how many were women and minorities.

The Carter administration also asked targeted questions of judicial candidates to determine their commitment to equality for women and minorities. These questions included: "How have you worked to further civil rights, women's rights, or the rights of other disadvantaged groups on a national, state or local level?" "How many women attorneys and minority attorneys does your office or law firm include?" "How many women partners?" "Minority partners?" "What do you think the most crucial legal problems of women and minorities will be over the next few years? How should these problems be remedied?"[34]

During Kearse's confirmation hearing, Senator Patrick Leahy asked her whether she believed the Carter process aided "in the selection of minorities and women."[35] Her initial response was diplomatic: "It may or it may not depending on the makeup of the panel and the instructions given to the panel and perhaps to the group of candidates who come before the panel."[36] Leahy pressed her further about the experience: "Were there any women on the panel?" Kearse replied: "There were 5 women out of a total panel of 11 in the Second Circuit."[37] We can never know for sure if an all-male panel would have reached the same result on Kearse's candidacy, but we do know that Carter's diversification of the decision makers led to five times the number of women in federal judgeships by the end of his presidency. Let that sink in. As Carter said in a speech to the National Association of Women Judges in 1980, "When I became President, only 10 women had ever been appointed to the Federal bench in more than 200 years. I've appointed 40 more. And if the process was not so complicated, involving the United States Senators who represent a particular State—[laughter]—there would have been more still."[38]

Leaders in all professions should demand structural reforms that increase diversity. In law, judges and those in positions of power such as general counsels should require equality from those who appear before them and from those they hire. They should also impose consequences for non-compliance. Judge Jack B. Weinstein, a senior judge in the Federal District of Brooklyn, implemented a court rule to encourage the participation of young women and minorities, expanding upon an effort implemented by a small number of other judges to offer junior attorneys more experience.[39] Australian bar associations have implemented an equitable briefing policy, which establishes aspirational gender-based quotas for brief-writing assignments, so that when senior lawyers consider whether to involve a junior lawyer in a matter, the senior lawyer will consider an appropriately qualified woman to do the work. Initiatives like these should be implemented widely.

Another measure toward structural changes that promote equality involves transparency. Sunlight is needed on the shortlists, as well as on the process surrounding how individuals are ultimately selected. One challenge while researching this book was how difficult it can be to locate an official presidential shortlist. We spent many hours combing through archives and we built upon the work of other scholars who spent a great deal of time uncovering internal memos with handwritten notes or newspaper reporting of speculations and official announcements. We need accurate data and transparency about who is shortlisted, not just for the Supreme Court, but across professions and in all positions of leadership and power. We were surprised to learn that no uniform, official records are maintained about presidential shortlists (except for President Trump). We were surprised to learn that the Supreme Court maintains no official data on hiring judicial clerks, a role which is a natural pipeline to positions of power in the legal profession. The *National Law Journal* had to piece together information from phone calls and emails to former clerks and others to assess hiring, finding in 2017 that white men continue to dominate the Supreme Court clerk pool.[40] We speculate that had hiring data been compiled and made publicly available years ago, this reality might be different.

Statistics on gender and minority hiring should be documented and disclosed, inclusive of both who is shortlisted and who is selected for positions of leadership and power in the profession, equivalent to disclosures required by the ABA for legal education. Klein credited the disclosure of "factual data [that] indicated the paucity of women accepted into law school" with opening law school doors to women.[41] She explained, "In the late fifties and through the sixties, and seventies, it was women lawyers who began to perceive discrimination and to go about fighting it by gathering facts to dispel myths about women."[42] Klein predicted in 1981 that it might take a couple of decades, but that "the law will probably be the first fully integrated profession."[43] Her prediction was overly optimistic, but her observations about the power of transparent data documenting inequality to remedy it are well taken.

Salaries are another area where sunlight is required. The pay discrepancy between Soia Mentschikoff and Karl Llewellyn when hired by the University of Chicago in the 1950s, and Hills's salary compared to her husband's in the early years of their law partnership in the 1960s, still exists today. As just one example, in 2015, the Equal Employment Opportunity Commission sued the University of Denver Sturm College of Law for its consistent practice of underpaying female faculty dating back to at least 1973. The university knew about this persistent wage disparity at its law college since at least 2012, but failed to take corrective steps to address the problem. The school settled the litigation with seven female faculty members for $2.66 million in 2018 and agreed to undergo regular monitoring and evaluation of its pay practices moving forward.[44]

The responsibility for structural reforms and transparency rests on the shoulders of institutions. Women and minorities should not bear this burden.

Strategy 6. Provide Early Child Care as a Public Good

When Cynthia Holcomb Hall was asked what she believed was the single greatest challenge to true equality, she replied, "child care."[45] Some of our shortlisted women, like Allen and Sharp, believed they had to make a choice between raising children and rising in a career. These two, plus Kagan, Kearse, Sotomayor, and Rymer, never had children. Others navigated both while regularly enduring the burden of being the primary caregiver, even with the most supportive of spouses, and all relied on outside help from extended family and/or paid caregivers.

Stories like that of Edith Jones becoming the first female partner at Andrews Kurth while on maternity leave are the rare exception, but they should be the norm. Many third- and fourth-wave feminist proposals include recommendations such as flex-time schedules or on-site daycare, but these are imperfect solutions. Women are still more likely than men to be the ones juggling child care responsibilities while working part-time or from home, and they are still more likely than men to handle household chores and administrative tasks like filling out school forms, planning playdates, and navigating doctors' appointments.

Solutions to "help" women balance the burdens of this "second shift,"[46] especially in the early years of infancy and preschool, are piecemeal at best and remain unavailable for many women, especially in the United States. (Early child care in Europe, by contrast, is typically funded by the government.) No one in our society would expect an individual to pave their own road in order to drive from home to school or work. Instead, taxpayer dollars fund resources that we all benefit from, like roads, police, and K–12 education. Why is early child care any different? Everyone benefits when infants and toddlers have quality care. Government-funded, high-quality, early child care and paid family leave should be available as a public good.

Employers are also well positioned to create both formal and informal policies to minimize child care (and related burdens) for employees. Much like the changes Soia Mentschikoff implemented in scheduling

AALS meetings at a time that allowed for greater participation by female law professors, employers should consider changing their workplace cultures to support working parents. One simple, preliminary suggestion would be to refrain from scheduling meetings during early evening hours when working parents are typically sharing meals and navigating bedtimes. Another proposal is mandatory paternity leave, which would remove the stigma associated with taking time to provide care for infants.

Strategy 7. Use Caution in Self-Shortlisting

Sometimes women self-shortlist by declining a leadership role even if offered to them. A number of the shortlisted sisters made this decision at various points in their careers. Kearse declined to be considered for a federal district court seat, opting instead to hold out for a court of appeals appointment because she viewed the work of that court as more desirable. Hills told President Ford that "she liked her job at H.U.D." when he asked her whether she wanted to become a Supreme Court justice.[47] O'Connor declined to run for governor of Arizona when approached by the Arizona Republican Party. And Rymer removed herself from consideration for a seat on the California Supreme Court, preferring to wait and see what possibilities might emerge on the U.S. Court of Appeals for the Ninth Circuit. We recognize that there are sometimes good reasons for turning down promotions or positions of increased power. One simply may not enjoy or desire that sort of work, or other demands such as family or personal interests may take priority. The role may also be perceived to be a "glass cliff," a term coined by researchers who document that women are more often than men selected to fill risky leadership positions where failure is likely.[48]

We also know, however, that women forgo opportunities because they do not view themselves as qualified.[49] This is also a form of imposter syndrome, or the sense that one is not actually as qualified or competent as others might think, a condition that plagues women more than men.[50] Married women are also more likely to defer or abandon leadership roles because of a spouse's career, often related to their child care obligations. We urge women to resist self-shortlisting and instead embrace leadership opportunities.

Strategy 8. Find Mentors in "Her"story

Women are frequently counseled to seek a mentor as they ascend to power. Doing so is not always easy, however, in part because it can be difficult to find someone willing to reveal the complexities of navigating personal and professional challenges in a vulnerable and honest way. This is not surprising given that in order to advance in professional settings, women often suppress the desire to speak out about disadvantages due to fear of retaliation, and sometimes they fail to recognize injustice because "it's just the way things are." Remembering the stories of women who made themselves visible at a time when women were not seen can inspire a world led by individuals who reflect the public we serve.

Their stories also encourage women to stand in their own truth, or "to know my own mind," as Sharp wrote in her high school yearbook's prompt for future hope and plans.[51] The white mainstream feminism of the 1970s and 1980s suggested it was time for women to "have it all," that is, a career, a husband, and children, thus demeaning and excluding those who do not fit stereotypical roles. For example, Kagan, Miers, and Sotomayor were all repeatedly taken to task by the media for their single, childless status during their time on the shortlist. One message we uncovered in researching the archives and personal histories of the women covered in this book is that it is actually ok not to have it all. Most women declined to engage in stereotypical female tasks like sewing (Allen) and cooking (Ginsburg), while at least one (Hall) was forced to sew in the early years of her career because as a single parent she could not afford to buy ready-made drapes or clothes. Some women never married and some married more than once. Some women had children, some did not, some raised the children of others. All of the women, however, seemed to find true satisfaction in the pursuit of their careers.

Another truth we discovered in our research was that the short-listed sisters were not perfect, and sometimes women who attain power through assimilation into the male hierarchy are not necessarily supportive of women who refuse to similarly conform. We marveled at ways in which Sharp sometimes felt like a kindred spirit and were simultaneously horrified to learn of her racist ideologies that informed her affection for North Carolina's constitutional ban on interracial marriage, among other vestiges of slavery. Reconciling Sharp's racist ideas with our admiration for her accomplishments proves challenging, but her leadership successes ought not be dismissed simply because of her flaws. Rather, this offers yet another reason for cultivating a strong cohort of talented women reflecting many backgrounds, paths, and viewpoints.

The women's experiences explored in this book represent just a sampling of the possibilities for finding guidance and inspiration. A long list of autobiographies and biographies about transformative women leaders in the law follows at the end of this book. We encourage you to select a few "her"stories to mentor, inspire, and guide you in your own professional pursuits.

* * *

Whether one is in the role of being on the shortlist, or creating the shortlist, these strategies can help move more women and minorities from shortlisted to selected.

Conclusion

Even after multiple waves of feminism, misogyny remains pervasive in the twenty-first century.[1] We are reminded of this each morning when we tune into our local public radio stations or glance through the headlines, only to be confronted by more news about the mistreatment of women. As we finished writing this book, the latest news featured Republican Senator Charles Grassley claiming women refused to serve on the Judiciary Committee because it involved "too much work"[2] and President Trump tweeting about his "horse-face" former lover, the porn star Stephanie Clifford, aka Stormy Daniels.[3]

Visceral and sometimes violent prejudice is a common experience for women. Women still walk at night, vigilant and guarded, carrying mace cans or car keys spread between their fingers, and avoid traveling alone on public transportation or along dark streets. Women are cat-called, groped, slut-shamed. Women are vulnerable to sexual assault, discrimination, and harassment. Women are conditioned to be grateful for their professional accomplishments, whereas men are believed to be deserving or entitled. Many of the women in this book were chided about their law school admissions because they had taken seats that could have gone to men. While the presence of women in professional education is common today, to the extent they make it to the corner office, the head of the organization, or highest court, it is commonly chalked up to "luck" or the need for a token. It is no wonder that women do not attain—or retain—positions of leadership and power in numbers equal to men.

We ourselves were just in the early years of college during *Time* magazine's Year of the Woman in 1992, believing that equality had been ushered in and we could simply ride the wave. We were wrong. Instead, our own professional paths involved aspects of shortlisting. We were counseled to avoid career advancements because they might cause too much stress or because our partners had jobs that could support us. One of us was considered for a leadership role that ultimately went to a man who condescendingly kissed her hand upon meeting her. That same one of us was later offered a similar position at a rival institution and self-shortlisted, declining to accept, wary of a glass cliff. One of us made it off the shortlist to lead an elite women's organization only to abandon the role to follow a then-spouse's career. Both of us were paid less doing the same work as men holding the same positions—and this was in the 2000s. One of us was called the "Norma Rae"[4] of her colleagues for pointing out the discrepancy and securing fair pay for herself and others.

Stories of the shortlisted sisters in the preceding pages gave us courage to speak up, and to pursue our careers, and it is our hope they will do the same for others. This is why we wrote the book. At a time when women still have not achieved parity with men in attaining leadership roles, it is worthwhile to explore not just the successes or the ends, but to examine the spaces in between. The history of the United States Supreme Court is incomplete, missing the stories of how women came to be considered, even if they were ultimately never nominated. There is power in the collective stories of these women seen not in isolation, but as a whole. No one story is the same; however, when recounted together they offer a path forward. Our goal is to inspire women from all backgrounds as they navigate their own professional advancement into positions of power and leadership. We seek to shift the discourse away from our strange token status or what we look like to who we are and who we might eventually become.

There is not one magic answer to these longstanding problems, but one thing we know for sure is that it is not sufficient or even accurate to argue we should simply exercise patience. Women have been qualified for a century or more. The strategies identified in this book have the potential to move more women from shortlisted to selected, but there is no static, one-size-fits-all solution. When President Obama greeted Justice Ginsburg at Justice Kagan's swearing in, he asked, "Are you happy that I brought you two women?"[5] She replied, "Yes, but I'll be happier when you bring me five more."[6] We will be happier too, seeing more and more women selected for the Supreme Court and positions of power across all professions.

ACKNOWLEDGMENTS

The evolution of this book project spanned more than a decade. During this time, we relied on family, children, friends, students, colleagues, institutions, archivists, scholars, librarians, and others for help with various aspects of the process, including research, inspiration, ideas, critique, support, humor, and love. This book would never have made it out of our heads and into print without the guidance and wisdom of the good people at NYU Press, especially our editor Clara Platter and the anonymous reviewers who provided helpful feedback.

The list is long of those we individually and collectively owe an incredible debt of gratitude for their professional support generally and helpful suggestions for this project specifically as it has evolved over the past years. As a truly collaborative endeavor, we find it impossible to separate our appreciation and so we offer it together. We thank Ben Barton, Terri Baxter, Len Baynes, Josh Blackman, Emily Boynton, Susan Carle, Elizabeth Chambliss, Barb Cox, Bridget Crawford, Michele DeStefano, Joanne and Larry Doherty, Ben Edwards, Nancy Gertner, Bruce Green, Linda Greenhouse, Joan Howarth, Becky Jacobs, Elly Jordan, Corinna Lain, Peter Lederer, Ellen Marrus, Judy Perry Martinez, Kcasey McLoughlin, Melissa Mortazavi, Lumen Mulligan, Carol Needham, Laura Oren, Russ Pearce, Meg Penrose, Carla Pratt, Deborah Rhode, Jesse Rutledge, Paula Schaefer, Niels Schaumann, Laurel Terry, Tracy Thomas, Steven Vaughan, Greg Vetter, Gina Warren, Janet Welch, and Daniel Yeager. We learned much from students in our seminars, including participants in Renee's "Gender, Power, Law, and Leadership" seminars (2018–2020) at the University of Houston Law Center; Hannah's "Gender, Power, Law, and Leadership" and "Global Perspectives on Women in Law" seminars (2010–2018) at both Michigan State Uni-

versity and California Western School of Law; and our jointly taught
Honors Research Seminar at Michigan State University (2014–2015).

Our work benefited substantially from research assistance at vari-
ous stages of this project provided by Katy Badeaux, Barbara Bean,
Eric Clarkson, Kathleen Darcy, Michael Dearman, Sierra Denny, Brent
Doman, Janesha Freelove-Sewell, Ana Hernandez-Pace, Limayli Hueget,
Chris Iannuzzi, Sasha Jamshidi-Nezhad, Heather Johnson, Jane Meland,
Victoria Rickard, Abigail Rury, Anne Stieg, Kirby Swartz, and Amanda
Watson. The reference librarians at California Western School of Law,
Michigan State University College of Law, and University of Houston
Law Center provided invaluable help to both of us.

Much of this book is drawn from primary source research, and we
could not have written this book without help from the reference librarians, archivists, historians, and staff at many institutions for their patience
as we rolled up our sleeves and dug through their archives. Renee thanks
those who assisted her research at the George H. W. Bush Presidential
Library Center, the Gerald L. Ford Presidential Library, the Jimmy Carter
Presidential Library, the Joseph Regenstein Library at the University of
Chicago, the Library of Congress, the Louis Round Wilson Special Collections Library at the University of North Carolina–Chapel Hill, the LBJ
Presidential Library, the National Archives, the Richard Nixon Presiden-
tial Library, and the Ronald Reagan Presidential Library. She is especially
grateful for the University of Houston Small Research Grant Award, which
funded many of her visits to those archives. Hannah thanks those who assisted her research at the Bentley Historical Library at the University of
Michigan and the Western Reserve Historical Society. We also thank the
Federal Judicial Center, the Franklin D. Roosevelt Presidential Library, the
Harry Truman Presidential Library, the Herbert Hoover Presidential Library, and the Library of the U.S. Court of Appeals for the Sixth Circuit for
making materials available online and by mail. The Women Trailblazers
Project, a collection spearheaded by Brooksley Born with support from
the American Bar Association and American Bar Foundation and hosted
at Stanford University's Robert Crown Law Library, provided a treasure

trove of oral histories. The National Center for State Courts assisted us in verifying our list of state court female chief justices.

Talking about this project helped it evolve, and we are incredibly appreciative of the feedback we received from participants and audiences at various speaking engagements. We co-presented aspects of the book at the Law and Society Annual Meeting in 2011; the 2012 Association of American Law Schools New Voices in Gender Paper Competition; the *Michigan State Law Review* Gender and the Legal Profession's Pipeline to Power Symposium in 2012; the Annual Meeting of Law, Culture and Humanities at the University of Virginia in 2014; and the Southeast Association of Law Schools Annual Meetings in 2018 and 2019. Renee presented about the book at the Fordham Law Legal Ethics Schmooze in 2014; the American Bar Foundation in 2015; the University of Kansas Law Faculty Workshop in 2017; the University of Houston Law Center Annual Yale Rosenberg Lecture in 2017; the University of Houston National Women's Law Conference in 2017; the South Texas College of Law Faculty Workshop in 2018; the Law and Society Annual Meeting in 2018; the International Legal Ethics Conference Bi-Annual Meeting in 2018; Australian National University in 2019; the Law College of Victoria in 2019; the Queensland Law Society and Women's Law Association in 2019; the Sydney Legal Innovation Festival in 2019; the Texas Women Rainmakers Annual Conference in 2019; the U.S. Fifth Circuit Court of Appeals Appellate Lawyers Annual Conference in 2019; the University of Tasmania Law School in 2019; and Washburn University School of Law in 2020. Hannah presented at the Feminist Judgments Conference in 2016; the San Diego Lawyer's Club Bench Bar Luncheon in 2019; and the Osher Lifelong Learning Institute at the University of California San Diego in 2019.

We received generous support in the form of research grants from California Western School of Law, Michigan State University College of Law, the Michigan State University Honors Research Program, and the University of Houston Law Center. The American Bar Foundation and Stanford Law School's Center on the Legal Profession provided respite for Renee to think and write during her 2015 sabbatical.

We are grateful to the University of California Los Angeles Women's Law Journal, and The Regents of the University of California, for publishing portions of the book in its earliest iteration in "Shortlisted," 24 *UCLA Women's Law Journal* 67 (2017). We also thank the *Temple Law Review* for publishing "Rethinking Gender Equality in the Legal Profession: A Study on Media Coverage of Supreme Court Nominees," 84 *Temple Law Review* 325 (2012), the article from which ideas for this book were first sparked and excerpts of the book were also originally published.

Finally, we have many personal thanks to give.

FROM RENEE:

I'm blessed to share life with Wallace B. Jefferson, who is a partner in the truest sense of the word. He has listened to me talk about this book for countless hours, patiently and enthusiastically embracing each discovery, sometimes questioning and always encouraging as I wrote and re-wrote the next sentence or needed to visit just one more archive. Writing can be a lonely enterprise, but our love completes me and is the fuel needed to tackle the next chapter, again and again. Thank you, Wallace, for finding me and living with me. I love you.

Seeds were planted for this project when I was shortlisted—well, technically waitlisted—for a seat in the class of 1999 at the University of Chicago Law School. Had I not been selected for one of the last spots, I might never have pursued an academic career and I surely wouldn't have been introduced to Professor Soia Mentschikoff via her portrait hanging in the law school hallway. I'm grateful for that start.

Friendships with strong, powerful women shaped my thoughts over the years. I thank each one of you for embracing me and inspiring me to take the next step, whether we were navigating careers or children or both: Elizabeth Anker, Shelley Davis Boyd, Colette Evangelista, Caroline Heintzelman, Lenore Knight Johnson, Sara Kiefer, Jen Nelson, Rebecca Purdom, Gina Warren, Gretchen Whitmer, and Amy Wilson. I look forward to more adventures with all of you.

Writing a book often feels like having a child, which means my children Grace Renee Knake and James Cannon Knake each have another sibling, as they literally grew up with this book over the past decade. I hope knowledge about who sits on our Supreme Court and in other positions of power serves them well and inspires them as much as they do me every day. I am especially appreciative of their understanding as I spent many weekends writing and traveling the country researching in archives. There are no words to convey how much I love and appreciate them, so I will just say this: you are my beginning and my end and everything in between. I love you both so much. It's been my greatest life project to help you grow into the amazing individuals you are and I can't wait to see how you each go on to make your own mark in the world. I also thank Ron and Susan Newman for lots of child care, especially in those early years as I navigated the academic tenure-track with infants and toddlers. This book would still be a work in progress if you all had not made time in our lives to let it grow up too.

Last, but certainly not least, if I hadn't written this book with Hannah Brenner Johnson, it would be dedicated to her, the ultimate kindred spirit! Thank you, Hannah, for writing this book with me and for everything else we encountered and conquered together along the way.

FROM HANNAH:

There are no words big, bright, or bold enough to express the overwhelming gratitude and love I have for my life partner and best friend, Mark Johnson. He has shown me that there is always a path—in life or in the rainforest—even when it appears otherwise. It is easy to lose perspective at any time, but especially when writing a book, and he helped me find my way on more occasions that I can count. Mark, I love you. I cannot imagine life without you and our beautiful, wondrous, endless conversation.

I will always be grateful for the patience and love extended by my children—Isaac Louis, Aidan Fischer, and Willow Elayna—while I worked on this project, and always. These three inspire me every single day to fight injustice and inequality so that the world might be a better place for them and the generations that follow. Willow always makes sure I am well fed, preparing extraordinary culinary delights for me while I write. I am so proud of her fiery passion for social justice, the brilliant advice she routinely dispenses, and the kindness she extends to everyone she encounters. Aidan has taught me so much about persevering through adversity, the importance of forgiveness, and starting each day with a clean slate. I will always be grateful for his unwavering support. Isaac offers up a constant supply of humor that helps me keep things in perspective, and has provided more hours of child care for his siblings than I can possibly count or ever afford to repay. You all mean the world to me.

My parents, Phyllis and Lou, unknowingly at the time, ignited what has become a lifelong passion by encouraging me to pay attention to women in positions of leadership and power, like Geraldine Ferraro, who ran for vice president during the years I was coming of age, and Susan B. Anthony, whose image graced the one-dollar coins I was given as a child. My father used to implore me to "do the law" in the years before his untimely death just as I began law school. It is largely for him, and for my mom, that I have done just that. I love you both so much.

Many individuals have offered me inspiration, mentorship, advice, and friendship as I navigated my often complex personal and professional path over the past several decades. I am especially grateful to Ruth Briscoe, Carolyn Combs, Floralynn Einesman, Sarah (Burge) Grunner, Catherine Hardee, Betty Harris, Greg Johnson, Heather Johnson, Marie and Neal Johnson, Danette Kiessel, Regina and Richard Kuhl, the dear Laurie McReynolds (who passed away much too early in 2018), Cindy Simon Rosenthal, Kellen Scanlon, Sarah (Blaney) Seide, Kyle Stock, Mark and Barb Weinstein, and Zipporah Wiseman.

Finally, I owe so very much to my most brilliant friend and co-author, Renee Knake Jefferson. There is no one else in the world with whom I could imagine embarking on this project and I look forward to all of our adventures that are yet to come.

APPENDIX 1

Our Methodology for Determining Supreme Court Shortlists

Determining what constitutes an official presidential shortlist presents somewhat of a conundrum. The United States Constitution is silent on the qualifications required to serve as a justice on the Supreme Court, mandating only that justices be appointed by the president and confirmed by the Senate. Great deference is therefore extended to and great discretion is exercised by presidents as they consider potential nominees, since there is no standardized or uniform shortlisting process.

The fact that there is no universally agreed-upon method for selecting nominees to the Court in part explains why "the most difficult problem in empirically [or otherwise] studying presidential selection politics is to determine presidents' shortlists of candidates for nomination."[1] Typically, the shortlisting process happens in quiet discussions among a president's most senior advisers. Only with President Donald Trump was a shortlist aired publicly long before a vacancy was actually filled. As a starting place, we based our collection of shortlisted women primarily upon research conducted by Christine Nemacheck. Her book *Strategic Selection: Presidential Nominations of Supreme Court Justices from Herbert Hoover through George W. Bush*[2] appears to offer the most comprehensive examination to date of primary sources and other materials used to determine the presidential shortlists.[3] Nemacheck researched presidential archives to compile her lists, relying upon a single list if located in the papers and expanding her sources to correspondence, diaries, and internal memoranda as necessary.

We, too, spent many hours combing through the presidential papers of Presidents Hoover, Roosevelt, Kennedy, Johnson, Nixon, Ford, Carter,

Reagan, and H. W. Bush to verify her research and learn more about the women appearing on the shortlists. We adopted Nemacheck's presidential shortlists as the foundation for this project, with a few exceptions—we added judges Florence Allen and Sylvia Bacon. Allen does not appear in Nemacheck's findings, but there is historic evidence to suggest that Allen was in fact considered by numerous presidents long before Soia Mentschikoff. Nemacheck identifies Mentschikoff as the first woman shortlisted, crediting Johnson (we found additional evidence to also credit Kennedy).[4] Nevertheless, an abundance of documentation, including White House memoranda and news accounts, exists to justify Allen's inclusion as the first woman considered for the Court. Sylvia Bacon likewise does not appear on Nemacheck's list, and we debated if the news media and other historical sources documenting her consideration for the Court justified her inclusion here. Ultimately, we determined that Bacon belongs in the shortlisted group because her name appeared on the official list of nominees under consideration by President Nixon as reported by numerous media sources, including the *New York Times*,[5] and she was also included by President Nixon on the list he officially submitted to the American Bar Association for potential vetting.[6] Our list of women formally shortlisted by presidents for the Supreme Court pre-O'Connor therefore begins with Florence Allen and includes Soia Mentschikoff, Sylvia Bacon, Mildred Lillie, Carla Hills, Cornelia Kennedy, Amalya Lyle Kearse, Joan Dempsey Klein, and Susie Sharp.

We also note that there are numerous other women who were considered *informally* over the years. Many female contenders received strong support from various organizations, politicians, and others reported by the media, but their names never officially appeared on presidential shortlists.[7] We engaged in extensive conversations about who to include in this study, and at times this list was much longer. Ninth Circuit U.S. Court of Appeals Judge Shirley Hufstedler, for example, was frequently mentioned for the Court during the Carter administration, but a vacancy never occurred. District of Columbia Circuit U.S. Court of Appeals Chief Judge Patricia Wald was another to accomplish many firsts "as the one of fewer than a dozen women in her Yale Law School class, the first woman to serve on her important court, the first to be its chief judge."[8] But she was also omitted from official shortlists for the Supreme Court and so we do not include her here.

For every woman included in this book, there are dozens if not hundreds whose stories deserve telling, and we hope others will do so.

APPENDIX 2

A Note on Historical Research

Conducting historical research occasionally reveals factual inconsistencies among sources, and we encountered this in our work here. For example, some historians maintain that President Kennedy[1] or Johnson[2] was the first to include women on his Supreme Court shortlists. In our research for this book, we found evidence to suggest that Presidents Hoover, Roosevelt, and Truman all considered Florence Allen as a possible nominee. As another example, Sandra Day O'Connor took credit for the removal of the honorific "Mr." before "Justice" on the bronze nameplates adorning the justices' chambers, according to an article appearing in the *New York Times*,[3] as did political scientist Beverly Blair Cook, who claimed Chief Justice Burger removed the "Mr." after he encountered Cook leading through the Supreme Court a tour of women from her National Association of Women Judges, which she founded with Joan Dempsey Klein.[4] But, as we document in chapter three, it was actually Cornelia Kennedy who ushered in that change through her influence on Justice Stevens (at least according to Justice Stevens!).

Sometimes the inconsistencies are actually errors.[5] Sometimes the inconsistencies exist because history has not been accurately or completely preserved. Sometimes the inconsistencies occur because the human experience necessarily means that we each perceive the same set of circumstances through our own world view. People may recollect the same moment differently and their memories may evolve or fade over time. Barbara Hackman Franklin's oral history offers an example of these dynamics when she explains the failed nomination of Mildred Lillie:

The one that was surfaced . . . was Mildred Lillie from Los Angeles from around this area, and she was some kind of a state—I can't remember now, but either a state or local judge. She really was not, according to the American Bar Association, qualified to sit on the highest court in the land, although she looked like a very good woman, a lot of community activity and whatever. So she got shot down pretty much because the ABA just didn't approve. But the bottom line was that at least there was a search for women, and one had been named. The cynical among us thought that some of the men had put her forward just so she'd get shot down as not qualified, and that would be the end of that. I looked at it differently. I really thought there was now more emphasis on the idea of women out here.[6]

Franklin could not remember some details—like the judgeship Lillie held in California—and she offered multiple perspectives on the motive of Nixon's shortlisting. There may be several plausible explanations or views for many circumstances, and it is up to the scholar or reporter to decide which explanation/s is/are documented or discounted. We have tried to fill in the gaps, piece together the stories, and offer the reader a more complete picture of the Supreme Court and women's history. As another example of how the same facts may yield varying conclusions, while we find that the statistics on women in the judiciary are just as abysmal as those for women in other positions of leadership and power, others argue that "[d]espite the disappointing numbers of women at the top of law firms, the bench appears to be a more welcoming place for women, who make up one-third of the justices on the U.S. Supreme Court and 25 percent of judges on the U.S. district courts and courts of appeal."[7] We hope this book allows all readers to reach their own conclusions more fully informed about the past and the future for women in leadership on the Court and beyond.

Even with these sorts of errors or inconsistencies or even missing historical evidence, one thing we know for sure is that the women profiled in this book moved from shortlisted to selected repeatedly in extraordinary ways as they ascended into positions of leadership and power in the legal profession, whether making it to the Supreme Court or not. To the extent we found discrepancies when doing research, we tried to seek additional sources to confirm the information or note the differences, recognizing that inevitably others may find errors or inconsistencies in our own work. We were surprised to find that no official lists of female chief justices exist, so we endeavored to create our own (see Tables 7.1 and 7.2 in Chapter 7). We worked hard to avoid omissions, and are grateful to the National Center for State Courts in helping us in this effort. Any errors are our own. We believe that uncovering, documenting, and revising forgotten histories like those of our shortlisted women should be an ongoing process. We hope that this work encourages others to engage in further research as a collective effort toward accurately preserving this important and inspiring history.

NOTES

PREFACE

1 "For the second time in a year, a childless, unmarried woman in her 50s has been nominated to be a justice on the Supreme Court and the critics have come out swinging." Laura M. Holson, "Then Comes the Marriage Question," *New York Times*, May 16, 2010.

2 Ann Gerhart, "The Supreme Court Needs More Mothers," *Washington Post*, May 16, 2010.

3 "Solicitor General Kagan decided to wear the same outfit that then-Judge Sonia Sotomayor wore to day one of her confirmation hearings: an electric blue blazer over a black blouse." David Lat, "Elena Kagan v. Sonia Sotomayor: Who Wore it Better?," *Above the Law*, June 28, 2010, www.abovethelaw.com.

4 Peter Beinert, "Put a Mom on the Court," *Daily Beast*, April 25, 2010, www.thedailybeast.com.

5 Paul Campos, "Fat Judge Need Not Apply," *Daily Beast*, May 4, 2009, www.thedailybeast.com.

6 Brenner and Knake, "Rethinking Gender Equality in the Legal Profession's Pipeline to Power," 364–75.

INTRODUCTION

1 "Potential High Court Nominees," *New York Times*, October 14, 1971.

2 Barbara B. Martin, "Sketch of Judge Lillie," *New York Times*, October 23, 1971.

3 Bradwell v. Illinois, 83 U.S. 130, 141 (1873).

4 Dean, *The Rehnquist Choice*, 155.

5 Destiny Peery, *2018 NAWL Survey on Retention and Promotion of Women in Law Firms* (Chicago: National Association of Women Lawyers, 2018), 1.

6 Ibid., 5. Other studies reach a similar conclusion. For example, Julie Triedman reports that "the absolute number of women non-equity partners reported by The Am Law 200 surged by 9.5 percent between 2011 and 2014, while the number of female equity partners remained flat," and that "in 2014, 26 percent of non-equity partners were female, compared with 16.8 percent in the equity tier." Julie Triedman, "A Few Good Women," *American Lawyer* (June 2015), 41.

7 Peery, *2018 NAWL Survey*, 5.

8 American Bar Association Commission on Women in the Profession, "A Current Glance at Women in the Law" (Chicago: American Bar Association, 2018), 3, www.americanbar.org.

9 Ibid., 4; Padilla, "Women Law Deans, Gender Sidelining and Presumptions of Incompetence." Women of color make up a smaller percentage of law deans (less than eight percent at ABA-accredited law schools).

10 Of 5,398 tenured faculty members in 2013, only 1,766 were women. American Bar Association, "Data from the 2013 Annual Questionnaire, ABA Approved Law School Staff and Faculty Members, Gender and Ethnicity: Fall 2013" (Chicago: American Bar Association, 2013), www.americanbar.org.

11 "2012–2013 Law Review Diversity Report," 3. "In 2012–2013, women continued to lag behind their male counterparts in the Top 50 Sample, as women held 46% of leadership positions, and only 38% of EIC positions." Ibid. The number does reflect parity, however, when considering all law schools in the United States. Ibid.

12 Center for American Women in Politics, *Women in Elective Office*, 2018, www.cawp.rutgers.edu.

13 Horne, *Capitol Research*. As of 2018, only six states had female governors and in twenty-three states no woman had ever held the position. Center for American Women in Politics, *Women in Elective Office*, 2018, www.cawp.rutgers.edu. Also notable was the 2010 North Carolina Supreme Court election, which resulted in a majority of women on the court for the first time in the state's history. "With a Majority of Women, State's Top Court Hits Milestone," *News & Record*, November 10, 2010. In January 2015, Associate Justices Rhonda Wood and Karen Baker were sworn in for eight-year terms on the Arkansas Supreme Court, marking the first time in the state's history that women have outnumbered men on the state's highest court. Spencer Williams, "3 Sworn in on State's High Court," *Arkansas Democrat Gazette*, January 7, 2015.

14 Center for American Women in Politics, *Women in Elective Office*, 2018, www.cawp.rutgers.edu.

15 Horne, *Capitol Research*, 1. "A 2014 survey found that 5,049 women were serving as state court judges, representing 29 percent of the total 17,156 positions. . . . Currently, 120 women serve on a state final appellate jurisdiction court (Supreme Court or equivalent)." Ibid.

16 "Gender Diversity Survey," *The American Bench: Judges of the Nation*, ed. Amanda Long (Frisco, TX: Forster Long, 2015), 25. The states with a majority of women serving on the highest court are Massachusetts, New York, Ohio, Washington, and Wisconsin. Idaho, Iowa, and Maryland had no women on any of the states' highest appellate court in 2015. Ibid.

17 Tony Mauro, "Supreme Court Specialists, Mostly Male, Dominated Arguments This Term," *Supreme Court Brief*, May 11, 2016.

18 Although the first woman was elected to the Ohio Supreme Court in 1922, followed by a second woman elected to the Arizona Supreme Court in 1960, it

was not until 2003 that a Latina became the chief justice of the New Mexico Supreme Court and not until 2005 that the first African American woman "preside[d] over a state court of last resort." Carroll, "Women in State Government," 442–43. For a comprehensive analysis addressing why "blacks have had little success breaking into the upper echelons of the elite bar," see Wilkins and Gulati, "Why Are There So Few Black Lawyers in Corporate Law Firms?," 497. In addition, the median salaries for black lawyers are generally lower than those of other groups. Ronit Dinovitzer et al., *After the JD: First Results of a National Study on Legal Careers* (Overland Park, KS: NALP Foundation for Law Career Research and Education and the American Bar Foundation, 2004), 64. The ABA Commission on Women in the Profession provides specific strategies for law firms and lawyers to improve diversity based on research conducted with twenty-eight women of color partners in national law firms. Arin N. Reeves, "From Visibly Invisible to Visibly Successful: Success Strategies for Law Firms and Women of Color in Law Firms" (Chicago: American Bar Association Commission on Women in the Profession, 2008). Additionally, the ABA Commission on Women in the Profession identifies specific barriers and obstacles facing women of color lawyers. "Among all employers listed in the 2015–2016 NALP Directory of Legal Employers, just 7.52% of partners were minorities and 2.55% of partners were minority women;" "almost one in five offices reported no minority partners and almost 47% reported no minority women partners." ABA Commission on Women in the Profession, *Visible Invisibility: Women of Color in Law Firms* (Chicago: American Bar Association, 2006); "Women and Minorities at Law Firms by Race and Ethnicity—New Findings for 2015," NALP Bulletin (January 2016), www.nalp.org. "The typical firm has 105 white male equity partners and seven minority male partners, and 20 white female equity partners and two minority female equity partners." Lauren Still Rikleen, *Report of the Ninth Annual NAWL National Survey on Retention and Promotion of Women in Law Firms,* (National Association of Women Lawyers, 2015), 6. "Although people of color make up roughly one-third of the nation's population, 25 states currently have all-white Supreme Court benches." Maida Malone, "States' High Courts Sorely Lacking in Diversity," *National Law Journal,* June 2016.

19 "Studies on presidents' nominees to the U.S. Supreme Court have traditionally focused on those individuals officially nominated and most often confirmed to seats on the Court." Nemacheck, *Strategic Selection,* 13.

20 "In short, the pipeline leaks, and if we wait for the time to correct the problem, we will be waiting a very long time." Rhode, "The Difference 'Difference' Makes," 7.

21 Meghan Tribe, "Mansfield Rule 2.0 Aims to Boost Diversity Efforts," *American Lawyer,* June 22, 2018.

22 "41 Law Firms Announced as Mansfield Rule Certified: 'Mansfield Rule'—the Next Generation of the Rooney Rule—Certifies that Law Firms Consider at Least

30% Diverse Lawyers for all Governance and Leadership Roles," *Diversity Lab*, August 20, 2018.

23 Elizabeth Olson, "New Paper Finds Fuzzy Definitions for Board Diversity," *New York Times*, October 20, 2014, https://dealbook.nytimes.com; Molly Petrilla, "The SEC Wants New Rules for Board Diversity—Here's Why That Matters," *Fortune*, January 29, 2016, http://fortune.com.

24 Root, "Combating Silence in the Profession," 809.

25 Hayes, *Without Precedent*; Tuve, *First Lady of the Law*. Only two of the shortlisted women in this study are the subject of biographies: Susie Sharp and Florence Allen. Others have been the focus of academic articles or given interviews for oral histories. But some have had little written about them other than passing mentions in news articles. None have been considered collectively, as we do here.

PART I. THE SHORTLISTED SISTERS

1 Myra Bradwell, "Admission of Women to the Bar," *Chicago Legal News*, February 15, 1879.

2 We note this authorship mindful of the critique that early feminists primarily emphasized the plight of white women, often at the expense of rights for other minorities. This is also why we do not assume that using the word "feminism" necessarily includes a concern for *all* women's rights.

3 Declaration of Sentiments, Seneca Falls, New York, 1848.

4 Brent Staples, "How the Suffrage Movement Betrayed Black Women," *New York Times*, July 28, 2018.

5 Bradwell v. Illinois, 83 U.S. 130, 142 (1873).

6 Kaiser v. Stickney, 102 U.S. 176 (1880).

7 United States v. Cherokee Nation, 202 U.S. 101 (1906).

8 Collins, *When Everything Changed*, 79.

9 Ibid.

10 Hope B. Daus, "Equal Representation: A Study of Gendered Voting Patterns on the ERA, FMLA, and VAWA," University of Houston Law Center, November 30, 2018 (unpublished paper).

11 Illinois House of Representatives Congressional Record debate on the Equal Rights Amendment, May 30, 2018 (unpublished audio record).

12 Ibid.

13 Some argue the ERA had to be ratified within seven years because of language Congress included when the amendment was first proposed; others argue that a prior Congress cannot bind a future Congress from extending or eliminating the time limit.

14 Betty Friedan famously wrote about these issues, which characterized the second wave of feminism. Friedan, *The Feminine Mystique*.

15 Several of those same women commemorated the event at the University of Houston in 2017, including Gloria Steinem.

16 Meritor Savings Bank v. Vinson, 477 U.S. 57 (1986) (holding that a plaintiff could prove violations of Title VII "by proving that discrimination based on sex has created a hostile or abusive working environment").

17 "From Anita Hill to Capitol Hill: A Flurry of Fresh Female Faces Vindicates 'The Year of the Woman,'" *Time*, November 16, 1992.

18 Ibid.

19 Jon Blistein, "Watch Carly Fiorina Respond to Trump's 'Look at That Face' Insult," *Rolling Stone*, September 10, 2015 ("Trump saw Fiorina on TV and remarked 'Look at that face! Would anyone vote for that? Can you imagine that, the face of our next president?! I mean, she's a woman, and I'm not s'posedta say bad things, but really, folks, come on. Are we serious?'").

20 Alastair Jamieson, "2016 Presidential Debate: Trump Accused of 'Stalking' Clinton on Stage," *NBC News*, October 10, 2016.

21 "Transcript: Donald Trump's Taped Comments About Women," *New York Times*, October 8, 2016.

22 Philip Rucker, "Trump Says Fox's Megyn Kelly Had 'Blood Coming Out of Her Wherever,'" *Washington Post*, August 8, 2015.

23 Alex Wayne, "Trump Insults ABC Reporter, Saying She 'Never' Thinks," *Bloomberg*, October 1, 2018.

24 Martha S. Jones, "When Black Women Journalists Fight Back," *Washington Post*, November 12, 2018.

25 Jeva Lange, "61 Things Donald Trump Has Said About Women," *The Week*, October 16, 2018, https://theweek.com; "Donald Trump Sexism Tracker: Every Offensive Comment in One Place," *Telegraph*, July 14, 2017.

26 Matt Broomfield, "Women's March Against Donald Trump is the Largest Day of Protests in US History, Say Political Scientists," *Independent*, January 23, 2017.

27 Nadja Sayej, "Alyssa Milano on the #MeToo Movement: 'We're Not Going to Stand for It Any More,'" *Guardian*, December 1, 2017.

28 Connie Chung, "Dear Christine Blasey Ford: I, Too, Was Sexually Assaulted–and It's Seared Into My Memory Forever," *Washington Post*, October 3, 2018.

29 "How Saying #MeToo Changed Their Lives," *New York Times*, June 28, 2018.

30 Audrey Carlsen et al., "#MeToo Brought Down 201 Powerful Men. Nearly Half of Their Replacements Are Women.," *New York Times*, October 29, 2018.

31 "If there is not the intentional and action-based inclusion of women of color, then feminism is simply white supremacy in heels . . . Racism is as American as pie. In order for the feminist movement to truly be progressive and intersectional, white women must face this fact and begin to take on their load of work." Rachel Elizabeth Cargle, "When Feminism Is White Supremacy in Heels," *Harper's Bazaar*, August 16, 2018.

32 Adichie, *We Should All Be Feminists*, 48.

33 Gillian Tan and Katia Porzencanski, "Wall Street Rule for the #MeToo Era: Avoid Women at All Costs," *Bloomberg Business*, December 3, 2018.

CHAPTER 1. THE FIRST SHORTLISTED WOMAN

1 Allen, *To Do Justly*, 150.
2 "Few know that [Florence Allen], not Sandra Day O'Connor, could have been, and arguably should have been, the first woman to become a Supreme Court Justice." Organ, "Sexuality as a Category of Historical Analysis," 6. Cook, "Florence Ellinwood Allen," 11–13.
3 Herbert Hoover Presidential Library, Presidential Papers—Subject File, Judiciary—Supreme Court of the U.S., Notes.
4 Ibid. It is unclear whether the application was filled out by Allen herself, or by someone in Hoover's administration.
5 Perry, *A "Representative" Supreme Court?*, 113.
6 Tuve, *First Lady of the Law*, 110.
7 "A Woman on the Supreme Bench?," *Christian Science Monitor*, March 12, 1930.
8 E. L. Kenyon, Letter to President Calvin Coolidge on December 27, 1924. Letter held in the National Archives.
9 Ibid.
10 "Women Candidates for Harlan's Seat on Supreme Bench," *Day Book*, February 12, 1913, Library of Congress.
11 Ibid.
12 Allen, *To Do Justly*; Tuve, *First Lady of the Law*.
13 Allen, *To Do Justly*, 9.
14 Ibid., 21.
15 Ibid., 24.
16 Ibid.
17 Ibid., 28.
18 Allen's own biography is silent on the issue of opportunities in New York being foreclosed to her, but other sources suggest this to be the case. www.supremecourt.ohio.gov.
19 Tuve, *First Lady of the Law*, 40.
20 Ibid.
21 Ibid., 27.
22 Ibid., 32.
23 Ibid., 37.
24 Allen, *To Do Justly*, 38.
25 Ibid., 43.
26 Ibid., 68.
27 "2000 Nominate Woman Judge," *New York Times*, September 4, 1920.
28 Allen, *To Do Justly*, 65.
29 "Ohio Woman Judge Was News Writer," *Washington Post*, November 11, 1922.
30 Allen, *To Do Justly*, 48. "One could see here the influence of the women voters. The women's interest was keenly aroused because for the first time they were serving on the jury and also because they saw a member of their sex sitting on the

bench. They had elected me and in a way that made them feel a special ownership in the Court of Common Pleas. This is a real reason for having competent and upright women serve as judges. When women of intelligence recognize their share in and their responsibility for the courts, a powerful moral backing is secured for the administration of justice." Ibid.

31 "The Trend of Events," *Herald of Gospel Liberty*, May 3, 1923, 115, 118.

32 We use the term "first lady" to refer to the women married to United States presidents because of its widely accepted use. However, we recognize that the term "lady" is a somewhat sexist and gendered term.

33 Roosevelt, "What Ten Million Women Want," *Home Magazine*, 5 (March 1932).

34 "The Trend of Events," 115.

35 Ibid.

36 Ibid., 116.

37 Pierce took a sabbatical in order to accompany her to Chattanooga for the infamous *Tennessee Valley Authority* hearing.

38 Cook, "Women as Supreme Court Candidates," 323–25.

39 Cook, "The First Woman Candidate for the Supreme Court," 22.

40 Allen, *To Do Justly*, 112, 115, 122.

41 One such case was Tennessee Valley Authority v. Tennessee Electric Power Company, 21 F. Supp. 947 (6th Cir. 1938).

42 Marshall, "Judge Allen," 5.

43 "Memorandum in Re Supreme Court," August 3, 1937. PSF: Supreme Court File, Box 165, Franklin Delano Roosevelt Presidential Library.

44 Turner Catledge, "A New Deal Foe: Conservative Writes to President He Will Quit June 2, End of Term," *New York Times*, May 19, 1937.

45 Korematsu v. United States, 323 U.S. 214 (1944).

46 Griswold v. Connecticut, 381 U.S. 479 (1965).

47 In a twist of irony, years earlier Justice Sutherland had actually campaigned on the same ticket as Florence Allen's father for Congress in Utah. Allen, *To Do Justly*, 111.

48 Ibid., 110.

49 Cook, "The First Woman Candidate for the Supreme Court," 19–35.

50 Eleanor Roosevelt, *My Day*, November 17, 1948.

51 Florence Ellinwood Allen Papers, Western Reserve Historical Society, Cleveland, Ohio [Container 6, Folder 6] MS 3287. One of the letters written by Allen was intended to clear up an untrue news report that she had failed to pay income tax while on the bench. Her tone was deeply apologetic; Eleanor Roosevelt's reply was brief and indicated that she had shared the letter with the president. Another of Allen's letters had more of an embarrassing tone; she acknowledged that several women's groups had selected her as their first choice for president of the United States, but she was unable to give a full public response to the media because of her role as a judge.

52 Tuve, *First Lady of the Law*, 126.
53 Edwards, "Oral History Interview with India Edwards," interview by Jerry N. Hess, 84.
54 Goldman, *Picking Federal Judges*, 93.
55 A recess appointment occurs when the Senate is not in session. This constitutional provision, enumerated in the Appointments Clause, requires that the appointment must be confirmed by the end of the next Congressional session.
56 Bert Wissman, "President Nominates Woman, Two Men for District Bench: First of Her Sex to Be Appointed," undated article, Harry Truman Presidential Library.
57 Linda Greenhouse, "Burnita S. Matthews Dies at 93; First Woman on U.S. Trial Courts," *New York Times*, April 28, 1988.
58 Yalof, *Pursuit of Justices*, 215, citing "Memorandum on 'Supreme Court Judgeships,'" July 23, 1945, Supreme Court folder, Clark papers, Harry Truman Presidential Library.
59 Edwards, "Oral History Interview with India Edwards," interview by Jerry N. Hess, 84.
60 Ibid., 85.
61 Ginsburg, "The Supreme Court," 196.
62 Yalof, *Pursuit of Justices*, 38.
63 Brown v. Board of Education of Topeka, 347 U.S. 483 (1954).
64 Goldman, *Picking Federal Judges*, 124.
65 Ibid., 143.
66 Ibid.
67 Faderman, *To Believe in Women*, 322.
68 The story on Judge Donlon, "Miss Donlon Wins Gallant Backing," appeared adjacent to an article entitled "The Fall Fashion Trends From Abroad." *New York Times*, July 29, 1955.
69 Cook, "Women as Supreme Court Candidates," 318.
70 Organ, "Sexuality as a Category of Historical Analysis," 129.
71 Ibid., 109.

CHAPTER 2. THE SHORTLISTS BEFORE THE FIRST NOMINEE
1 Ford, *A Time to Heal*, 335.
2 Walker, *Presidents and Civil Liberties from Wilson to Obama*, 237.
3 Ibid., 235.
4 Katzenbach, *Some of It was Fun*, 37.
5 Belknap, *The Supreme Court Under Earl Warren, 1953–1969*, 107.
6 Laura Kalman, "A Crony on the Court: ABE FORTAS," *Los Angeles Times*, November 18, 1990.
7 Califano Jr., *The Triumph & Tragedy of Lyndon Johnson*, 208.
8 Lynum v. The State of Illinois, 368 U.S. 908 (1963).

9 Blackmun would go on to author *Roe v. Wade* in 1973, furthering women's control over their bodies by finding a constitutional right to privacy for women with respect to the decision to have an abortion. This right was significantly constrained two decades later by *Planned Parenthood v. Casey*, and, as this book went to press, is becoming an increasingly vulnerable right, with multiple states passing restrictive laws designed to further weaken *Roe*.

10 Adam Clymer, "Book Says Nixon Considered a Woman for Supreme Court," *New York Times*, September 27, 2001.

11 Ibid.

12 Dean, *The Rehnquist Choice*, 201. "We think it would be very bad, in the event they don't approve the woman. I'm just saying this, it looks to me like it's a stacked jury, no women on the jury." Ibid.

13 John Dean, "Musing on a Belated Visit with California Justice Mildred Lillie," *Verdict*, January 9, 2015. John Dean, President Nixon's general counsel, reflected years later that Lillie was "every bit as qualified as Sandra Day O'Connor." Ibid.

14 Robert B. Semple, "Court Nominees Termed Nixon's Stand-By Choices," *New York Times*, October 23, 1971.

15 Dean, *The Rehnquist Choice*, 193.

16 Fred P. Graham, "Nixon Ends Prior Checks with Bar on Nominations," *New York Times*, October 21, 1971. President Reagan later ignored the ABA entirely when he nominated Sandra Day O'Connor.

17 Eileen Shanahan, "President Bypasses Women for Court; Talent Pool Small," *New York Times*, October 21, 1971.

18 James Warren, "Rehnquist Far From Nixon's Favorite Choice for Court," *Chicago Tribune*, December 24, 2000.

19 Ibid.

20 Dorothy McCardle, "GOP Women: Resigned," *Washington Post*, October 22, 1971.

21 Shanahan, "President Bypasses Women for Court."

22 Nixon, "Remarks at the Convention of the National Federation of Republican Women," *The Public Papers of the Presidents of the United States*, October 22, 1971.

23 Eileen Shanahan, "Women Seek a Bigger Role in Phase 2," *New York Times*, October 25, 1971.

24 McCardle, "GOP Women."

25 Ibid.

26 Shanahan, "President Bypasses Women for Court."

27 Ibid.

28 Ibid.

29 Dean, *The Rehnquist Choice*, 155.

30 Ibid.

31 Stout, *A Matter of Simple Justice*, 41 (citing an interview).

32 Ford, *A Time to Heal*, 335.

33 Ibid.

34 Letter from Charles Rangel to President Gerald Ford, November 18, 1975, Box 137, File FG 51, Supreme Court of the United States 11/20/75–11/25/75, Gerald R. Ford Library.

35 Letter from Ralph Regula (U.S. Rep. Ohio-R) to President Ford, November 19, 1975, Box 137, File FG 51, Supreme Court of the United States 11/20/75–11/25/75, Gerald R. Ford Library.

36 Ibid.

37 Letter from Vernon C. Loen, Deputy Assistant to President Ford, to Ralph Regula, November 20, 1975, Box 137, File FG 51, Supreme Court of the United States 11/20/75–11/25/75, Gerald R. Ford Library.

38 Letter from President Gerald Ford to Audrey Colom, July 11, 1975, Box 646, File Audrey Rowe Colom, Gerald R. Ford Library.

39 Telegram from Audrey Colom to President Gerald Ford, November 13, 1975, Box 646, File Audrey Rowe Colom, Gerald R. Ford Library.

40 Letter from Audrey Colom to President Gerald Ford, November 14, 1975, Box 646, File Audrey Rowe Colom, Gerald R. Ford Library.

41 Letter from Philip Buchen, Counsel to the President, to Audrey Colom, November 26, 1975, Box 646, File Audrey Rowe Colom, Gerald R. Ford Library.

42 Memo from Pat Lindh to Doug Bennett, November 13, 1975, Box 136, File FG 51, Supreme Court of the United States 8/9/74–11/19/75, Gerald R. Ford Library. The other women listed were: Mary Coleman, Judge, Supreme Court of Michigan; Julia Cooper, Judge, D.C. Court of Appeals; Martha Griffiths, attorney and former congresswoman from Michigan; Rita Hauser, attorney from New York; Margaret Haywood, Judge, Superior Court of D.C.; Shirley Hufstedler, Judge, U.S. Court of Appeals for the Ninth Circuit; Normalie Holloway Johnson, Judge, Superior Court of D.C.; Florence Kelley, Judge, New York City; Elizabeth Kovachevich, Judge, Judicial Circuit Court of Florida; Betty Southard Murphy, Chair of the National Labor Relations Board; Dorothy Nelson, Dean of the Law School, USC; and Harriet Robb, Professor of Law, Columbia.

43 Memo from Pat Lindh to Doug Bennett on Candidates for Supreme Court, November 14, 1975, Box 136, File FG 51, Supreme Court of the United States 8/9/74–11/19/75, Gerald R. Ford Library.

44 Memo from Pat Lindh to President Gerald Ford on the Attorney General's List of Candidates for the Supreme Court, November 17, 1975, Box 136, File FG 51, Supreme Court of the United States 8/9/74–11/19/75, Gerald R. Ford Library.

45 Ibid.

46 Ibid.

47 Linda Matthews, "Justice Department Gives ABA List of Court Nominees: Acts Quickly to Replace Douglas; Rep. Wiggins, Carla Hills, and Sen. Griffin Reportedly Included," *Los Angeles Times*, November 14, 1975.

48 James Kidney, "New Justice," UPI, Box 48, Sheila Weidenfeld Files, Folder Women—Supreme Court, Gerald R. Ford Library.

49 Letter from Audrey Colom to President Gerald Ford, December 5, 1975, Box 646, File Audrey Rowe Colom, Gerald R. Ford Library.

50 Telegram from Audrey Rowe Colom to President Gerald Ford, December 10, 1975, Box 646, File Audrey Rowe Colom, Gerald R. Ford Library.

51 Letter from Roland L. Elliot, Director of Correspondence, to Audrey Rowe Colom, December 11, 1975, Box 646, File Audrey Rowe Colom, Gerald R. Ford Library.

52 "Betty With Justice," UPI, November 28, 1975, Box 137, FG 51/A, File Supreme Court of the United States, Gerald R. Ford Library.

53 "Stevens Reaction," Associated Press, November 28, 1975, Box 137, FG 51/A, File Supreme Court of the United States, Gerald R. Ford Library.

54 "Betty With Justice."

55 *Roe v. Wade*, 410 U.S. 113 (1973).

56 *Safford United School District v. Redding*, 557 U.S 634 (2009).

57 George Volsky, "Soia Mentschikoff, Professor and Ex-Law Dean, Dies at 69," *New York Times*, June 19, 1984.

58 "University of Miami Names Soia Mentschikoff Law Dean," *Columbia Law School Alumni Association Observer* no. 12, 3.

59 Whitman, "Soia Mentschikoff and Karl Llewellyn," 1126–27.

60 Marion Bussang, "Dates, Clothes and Play Relevant, Not Material," *New York Post*, April 22, 1940; Soia Mentschikoff, Papers, Special Collections Research Center, Joseph Regenstein Library, University of Chicago.

61 "The announcement of Soia Mentschikoff's appointment at the Law School" in the *Harvard Alumni Bulletin* was titled *Non Sub Homine*." Basile, "False Starts," 149.

62 Whitman, "Soia Mentschikoff and Karl Llewellyn," 1126–27.

63 Ibid., 1124, 1126.

64 Ibid., 1126–27.

65 C. D. Rogers, "Soia Mentschikoff: The Legend and the Legacy," *Barrister: The University of Miami School of Law Alumni Magazine* (May 1981), 3.

66 It should be noted that while Mentschikoff holds the reputation as having been Miami's first official female dean, that distinction arguably belongs to the late Minette Massey, who served as "acting dean" for three years in the 1960s. Howard Cohen, "First Female Dean at UM Law School, Minnette Massey, Dies at 89," *Miami Herald*, November 16, 2016. The "acting" designation has been speculated as being a result of gender discrimination against Massey. Peter Lederer, correspondence to authors, February 5, 2017. We are grateful to Peter Lederer, an adjunct faculty member at the University of Miami School of Law and former research assistant to Karl Llwellyn, for bringing this history to our attention.

67 Ilene Barth, "If a Seat Opens: Will Nixon Choose a Woman for the Supreme Court?," *Lincoln Star*, January 7, 1973.

68 Conversation between Richard Nixon and John Mitchell, "Nixon Tapes: Judge Isn't Frigid 'B*tch,'" YouTube video, posted by rmm413c, 1:36–1:40, Aug 22, 2008, www.youtube.com/watch?v=MtOpG8msgMo.
69 Ibid.
70 Lillie, "Justice Mildred L. Lillie," 119.
71 Ibid., 26.
72 Ibid., 27–28.
73 Ibid., 30. It was in this same professor's class that Lillie did poorly her first semester. Her uncle, with whom she was very close, passed away and his death had a profound effect on her. In a rather compassionate move, Professor Kidd allowed Lillie to retake her exam in the subsequent semester and she passed the exam with high marks.
74 Memorandum from John Dean and David Young to Attorney General John Mitchell and John Erlichman, October 16, 1971, White House Central Files, Alphabetical Name Files, Lillie, Mildred, Judge [1 of 4], Richard Nixon Presidential Library.
75 Ibid.
76 Ibid. This dynamic of ignoring women endures as documented in a 2017 study showing that female Supreme Court justices are more likely than their male colleagues to be interrupted by other justices and lawyers during oral arguments. Jacobi and Schweers, "Justice, Interrupted."
77 Letter to President Richard M. Nixon from Burton W. Chance, October 14, 1971, White House Central Files, Alphabetical Name Files, Lillie, Mildred, Judge [1 of 4], Richard Nixon Presidential Library.
78 Memorandum written by John Dean and David Young for Attorney General John Mitchell and John Ehrlichman, October 16, 1971, White House Central Files, Alphabetical Name Files, Lillie, Mildred, Judge [1 of 4], Richard Nixon Presidential Library.
79 Ibid.
80 Ibid.
81 Letter to President Richard M. Nixon from U.C.L.A. law professors, October 19, 1971, White House Central Files, Alphabetical Name Files, Lillie, Mildred, Judge [1 of 4], Richard Nixon Presidential Library.
82 Nemacheck, *Strategic Selection*, 22.
83 Ibid., 23. The use of the ABA in rating judicial nominees has undergone significant transformation over the past decades. Today, its role is relegated to providing "after the fact" commentary once the nominee's name is revealed. For an in-depth look at the role of the ABA in judicial appointments, see Hall, "The Role of the ABA Standing Committee on the Federal Judiciary," 980–82; Tartt, "The Participation of the Organized Bar in Judicial Selection," 125–40; Totenberg, "Will Judges be Chosen Rationally?," 92–99.

84 John Dean, "Richard M. Nixon: Choosing Rehnquist," interview by Kate Ellis, American Radio Works, American Public Media.
85 Ibid.
86 John Dean, "Musing on a Belated Visit with California Justice Mildred Lillie," *Justia*, January 9, 2015, www.verdict.justia.com.
87 Dean, *The Rehnquist Choice*, 111.
88 Letter to the President from Dwight D. Miller, Former Superintendent of the Watertown Public Schools, October 15, 1971, White House Central Files, Alphabetical Name Files, Box 11, Folder Bacon, S. [1 of 2], Richard Nixon Presidential Library.
89 Ibid.
90 Ibid.
91 Dean, *The Rehnquist Choice*, 111.
92 Wade, "Burnita Shelton Matthews."
93 John P. MacKenzie, "List for Supreme Court Narrows to Six Names: 4 Judges Include 2 Women," *Washington Post*, October 14, 1971.
94 Memorandum from Stephen Hess to Jon Rose, July 29, 1969, White House Central Files, Alphabetical Name Files, Box 11, Folder Bacon, S. [1 of 2], Richard Nixon Presidential Library. ("In connection with our conversation today about the pressure on the Administration to appoint women to high positions, I am attaching the resume of Sylvia Bacon, a highly qualified lawyer, a Republican, and the daughter of a respected South Dakota newspaper publisher, who might be ideal for a District judgeship.")
95 "Miss Sylvia A. Bacon For Nomination to Federal Judiciary," White House Central Files, Alphabetical Name Files, Box 11, Folder Bacon, S. [1 of 2], Richard Nixon Presidential Library.
96 Ibid.
97 *Privacy of Rape Victims: Hearing on H.R. 14666 and Other Bills Before the Subcommittee on Criminal Justice of the H. Comm. on the Judiciary*, 94th Cong. 23, 28 (1976) (statement of J. Sylvia Bacon on behalf of the A.B.A.).
98 "A Gay Rights Victory at Georgetown," *New York Times*, April 2, 1988.
99 Elsa Walsh, "D.C. Judge Is Treated for Alcohol Abuse," *Washington Post*, July 30, 1986.
100 Ibid.
101 "Potential High Court Nominees," *New York Times*, October 14, 1971; Fred P. Graham, "President Asks Bar Unit to Check 6 for High Court," *New York Times*, October 14, 1971; "2 Women Are on the List and 4 Men From Border States or the South," *New York Times*, October 14, 1971.
102 "Potential High Court Nominees"; MacKenzie, "List for Supreme Court Narrows to Six Names."
103 Fred P. Graham, "Nixon Reported Unlikely to Pick Woman Justice," *New York Times*, September 30, 1971.

104 Letter from Marjorie Longwell to President Richard Nixon, October 19, 1971, Nixon Move 2010 Box SFSM PPF 069, Nominations to Supreme Court File 23, Richard Nixon Presidential Library.

105 Letter to Attorney General John Mitchell from United States Senator Bob Dole, June 15, 1969, White House Central Files, Alphabetical Name Files, Box 11, Folder Bacon, S. [1 of 2], Richard Nixon Presidential Library.

106 Letter from President Richard Nixon to Judge Bacon, December 15, 1971, White House Central Files, Alphabetical Name Files, Box 11, Folder Bacon, S. [1 of 2], Richard Nixon Presidential Library.

107 Letter from John Mitchell to President Richard Nixon, September 18, 1970, White House Central Files, Alphabetical Name Files, Box 11, Folder Bacon, S. [1 of 2], Richard Nixon Presidential Library.

108 Ibid.

109 Memorandum from Douglas P. Bennett to the President re Candidates for the Supreme Court, Box 11, Folder Supreme Court Nomination-Background on Recommended Candidates, Richard B. Cheney Files, Gerald R. Ford Presidential Library.

110 Memorandum listing preliminary Supreme Court candidates, June 15, 1981, Folder Judicial Selection Process, Classified Files of F. Henry "Hank" Habicht, II, 1981–82, Box 2 RG 60 Department of Justice, Ronald Reagan Presidential Library.

111 Saundra Torry, "Female Lawyers Face Persistent Bias, ABA Told; Delegates to be Asked to Confront and Remedy Discrimination," *Washington Post*, August 9, 1981.

112 John Betz, "The Washington Scene: 'Can Bring Something to Job'- Carla Hills," *Los Angeles Times*, March 9, 1975.

113 "Carla Anderson Hills," *Encyclopedia of World Biography* (2004).

114 Hills, "Oral History of Carla A. Hills," interview by Janet McDavid, 2.

115 "Carla Anderson Hills," *Encyclopedia of World Biography* (2004).

116 Hills, "Oral History of Carla A. Hills," interview by Janet McDavid, 5.

117 Marlene Cimons, "An Historic Third: Carla Hills' Day on the Hill," *Los Angeles Times*, March 10, 1975.

118 Hills, "Oral History of Carla A. Hills," interview by Richard Norton Smith.

119 Ibid.

120 Ibid.

121 William Gildea, "Reflecting on One of Their Own," *Washington Post*, March 11, 1975.

122 Ibid.

123 Ibid.

124 "'A Good Job': Personalities Prize Chess Honored," *Washington Post*, May 7, 1975.

125 Dorothy McCardle, "Who's King of the Hills?," *Washington Post*, October 26, 1975.

126 Louis Uchitelle, "A Crowbar for Carla Hills," *New York Times*, June 10, 1990.

127 Ibid.

128 George F. Will, "Who Will 'Represent' Quality?," *Washington Post*, November 17, 1975.

129 "Carla Hills: She's Getting Respect," *Washington Post*, December 6, 1975.

130 Joseph Kraft, "Mr. Ford's Choice," *Washington Post*, August 8, 1976.
131 "Women Justices?," *Washington Post*, December 2, 1970.
132 Derek J. Sarafa, "Michigan Lawyers in History—Judge Cornelia G. Kennedy: First Lady of the Michigan Judiciary," *Michigan Bar Journal* 79 (July 2000).
133 Ibid. Judge Schaeffer was elected to the 47th District Court in Farmington Hills, Michigan.
134 Address to the Women Law Students Association, October 21, 1978, Cornelia Kennedy Papers: 1932–2012, 1970–1999, Box 1, Bentley Historical Library, University of Michigan.
135 Sarafa, "Michigan Lawyers in History."
136 Cornelia G. Kennedy Papers: 1932–2012, Bentley Historical Library, www.quod. lib.umich.edu/b/bhlead/umich-bhl-2014163?view=text
137 Julie Titone, "Raised to Love the Law: A Conversation With Judge Cornelia Kennedy," 2003, unpublished manuscript, Library of the U.S. Court of Appeals for the Sixth Circuit, 13.
138 Kate Vloet, "Sisters in Law," *Michigan Today*, November 26, 2012, www. michigantoday.umich.edu.
139 Titone, "Raised to Love the Law," 12.
140 Ibid.
141 Ibid.
142 Batchelder, "In Memoriam of Judge Kennedy," 1016.
143 Ibid.
144 Sarafa, "Michigan Lawyers in History."
145 Stevens, "Fond Memory," 118.
146 Barth, "If a Seat Opens."
147 Kennedy, "Oral History of Cornelia Groefsema Kennedy," 122.
148 Ibid., 121.
149 Letter from Cornelia Kennedy to Warren Christopher, Chair, ABA Federal Judiciary Committee, December 23, 1975, Cornelia G. Kennedy Papers: 1932–2012, 1970–1999, Box 19, Bentley Historical Library, University of Michigan.
150 Hall, *The Supreme Court in American Society.*
151 Stevens, "Fond Memory," 1009.
152 Ibid. Stevens stated that the event occurred at Notre Dame. Kennedy recalled this same event and mentioned it in a number of speeches she delivered over the years. Her recollection, however, places the moot court event at Harvard, not Notre Dame.
153 Ibid.
154 Ibid.

CHAPTER 3. FROM SHORTLISTED TO SELECTED

1 Ted Vollmer, "Hufstedler Assails Reagan Promise on Supreme Court," *Los Angeles Times*, October 17, 1980.

2 "Carter Says Hufstedler Will Get Cabinet Post," *Wall Street Journal*, October 31, 1979.

3 Vollmer, "Hufstedler Assails Reagan Promise on Supreme Court."

4 "Amalya Kearse," *Academy of Achievement*, podcast audio, July 7, 1984, https://itunes.apple.com/us/podcast/amalya-kearse/id474596633?mt=2.

5 Tom Goldstein, "Amalya Lyle Kearse," *New York Times*, June 25, 1979.

6 Lee Katterman, "Amalya Lyle Kearse: Judge's Robe Cloaks an Individual of Many Talents," *University Record*, April 26, 1999, www.ur.umich.edu.

7 Professor Kimberlee Crenshaw is credited with defining the concept of intersectionality years later. Crenshaw, "Demarginalizing the Intersection of Race and Sex;" Crenshaw, "Mapping the Margins."

8 Jacqueline Bell, "The Best Firms for Minority Attorneys," *Law360*, June 17, 2018.

9 Broadcast Music Inc. v. Columbia Broadcasting System, Inc., 441 U.S. 1 (1979).

10 *Confirmation Hearing of Amalya L. Kearse, Senate Judiciary Committee*, 96th Congress (1979) (statement of Senator Jacob Javits), 115.

11 Johnathan M. Moses, "Judge Kearse Is Colleagues' Pick as Next Supreme Court Justice," *Wall Street Journal*, June 14, 1993.

12 Ibid.

13 Obama's presidential papers were not yet available at the time this book was written, so we relied on the media reporting of his shortlists.

14 Lou Cannon, "White House Counselor, Attorney General Pull Out of Running for Supreme Court," *Washington Post*, June 23, 1981.

15 "Special to the New York Times, Carter's Appointees Examined for Clues on Supreme Court Possibilities," *New York Times*, October 3, 1980.

16 George F. Will, "Who Will 'Represent' Quality?," *Washington Post*, November 17, 1975.

17 Hayes, *Without Precedent*, 313.

18 Ibid., 26.

19 State v. Black, 60 N.C. (Win.) 262, 263 (1864).

20 Phillip Elliott, "Men to Hillary: 'Iron My Shirt,'" *Sydney Morning Herald*, January 8, 2008.

21 "Father and Daughter Practice Law as Firm," *New York Times*, February 18, 1929.

22 Hayes, *Without Precedent*, 50.

23 Ibid., 47.

24 Ibid., 153.

25 Ibid.

26 Ibid., 2.

27 Jay Jenkins Shar, "Lady Jurist Named to N.C. Supreme Court," *Charlotte Observer*, March 10, 1962.

28 Ibid.

29 Aulica Rutland, "Courting Fame: Sharp Set Precedents for Women in Law," *Greensboro News & Record*, March 21, 1999.

30 Susie Sharp's personal notes in preparation for interview with WLOS Asheville, 4898 Subseries 1.1, General Subject Files, Autobiographical Materials, "Susie Sharp Papers," The Southern Historical Collection, Louis Round Wilson Special Collections Library, University of North Carolina, Chapel Hill, North Carolina.

31 Nemacheck, *Strategic Selection*, 153.

32 Hayes, *Without Precedent*, 308.

33 Ibid., 313.

34 "First Woman Justice," *Boca Raton News*, December 23, 1974.

35 Pat B. Anderson, "Fighting Prejudice Still: Bias Lingers for Women Lawyers," *Los Angeles Times*, September 14, 1975.

36 Michael Kernan, "For Her Honors; Sisterhood on the Bench; Joan Dempsey Klein & The Judges' Network," *Washington Post*, October 4, 1980.

37 Ibid.

38 Klein, "Oral History of Joan Dempsey Klein," 44.

39 Ibid., 7.

40 Ibid., 11–12.

41 Ibid., 14.

42 Mabel C. McKinney-Browning, "'Don't Call Me Madam!': The Personal Side of the Law, From Women Who've Made it to the Top," *Update on Law Related Education* 5, no. 3 (1981), 52.

43 Ibid., 53.

44 Ibid., 52.

45 Ibid., 53.

46 Klein, "Oral History of Joan Dempsey Klein," 27.

47 David Margolick, "Women on the Bench: A Sharing of Insights," *New York Times*, October 11, 1982.

48 *Confirmation Hearing of Sandra Day O'Connor: Testimony before the Senate Judiciary Committee*, 97th Congress 1 (1981) (testimony of Joan Dempsey Klein), 409.

49 Ibid.

50 Ibid.

51 Ibid.

52 "A Person for the Court," *New York Times*, July 8, 1981.

53 Kennedy, "Oral History of Cornelia Groefsema Kennedy," 124.

54 Ibid., 123.

55 Letter sent to President Ronald Reagan by President Gerald Ford, dated June 25, 1981. Ronald Reagan Presidential Archives, 0180000-019999, WHORM Subject File.

56 Letter sent to President Gerald Ford from President Ronald Reagan, dated July 11, 1981. Ronald Reagan Presidential Archives, 0180000-019999, WHORM Subject File.

57 Thornton, "'Otherness' on the Bench," 413.

58 Laura Berman, "1ˢᵗ Woman for Supreme Court," *Detroit Free Press*, July 8, 1981.
59 "Arizona Judge Sandra O'Connor, First Woman for Supreme Court, Many Here Wish It Were Kennedy," *Detroit Free Press*, July 8, 1981.
60 Ibid.
61 Ibid.
62 Kennedy, "Oral History of Cornelia Groefsema Kennedy," 121.
63 Francis X. Clines, "Baker Vows Support for Nominee," *New York Times*, July 8, 1981.
64 Yalof, *Pursuit of Justices*, 135.
65 Ibid.
66 Lou Cannon, "Chance to Name Woman; Reagan Given Opportunity to Name Woman Justice; Jockeying Could Be 'Real Headache,'" *Washington Post*, June 19, 1981.
67 July 16, 1981 to Helene Von Damn from Anne Higgins. [Mail Sample] 07/16/1981 / nomination of Sandra Day O'Connor (3) Box 70, Anne Higgins Files, Ronald Reagan Presidential Library.
68 Planned Parenthood of Southeastern Pennsylvania v. Casey, 505 U.S. 833 (1992).
69 Roe v. Wade, 410 U.S. 113 (1973).
70 Greenburg, *Supreme Conflict*, 11.
71 Ronald Reagan, "Remarks Announcing the Intention to Nominate Sandra Day O'Connor To Be an Associate Justice of the Supreme Court of the United States," *Public Papers of the Presidents of the United States*, July 7, 1981.
72 Editorial, "The Nomination of Mrs. O'Connor," *Washington Post*, July 8, 1981.
73 Lynn Rosellini, Jr., "Judge O'Connor Makes Courtesy Call at Capitol; Attorney General William French Smith," *New York Times*, July 15, 1981.
74 *Confirmation Hearing of Sandra Day O'Connor* (testimony of Joan Dempsey Klein), 409.
75 Bush v. Gore, 531 U.S. 98 (2000).
76 Memo from Diana Lozano, Special Assistant to the President for Public Liaison, to Elizabeth Dole, Director of the White House Office of Public Liaison, The White House, August 11, 1981.
77 Ibid.
78 Ibid.

CHAPTER 4. THE SHORTLISTS FOLLOWING O'CONNOR

1 Matt Essert, "How Many Women Should Sit on the Supreme Court? Ruth Bader Ginsburg's Answer is Badass," *Mic*, February 9, 2015.
2 "'Out of Order' at the Court: O'Connor on Being the First Female Justice," *Fresh Air: National Public Radio*, March 5, 2013.
3 Sandra D. O'Connor, "High Court's '9 Men' Were a Surprise to One," *New York Times*, October 5, 1983.
4 Nemacheck, *Strategic Selection*, 153.

5   Steven V. Roberts, "Washington Talk: The White House; Picking Another Nominee: Lessons from Bork," *New York Times*, October 28, 1987.

6   *The Performance of the Reagan Administration in Nominating Women and Minorities to the Federal Bench: Hearings Before the Senate Judiciary Committee*, 100th Congress (1988) (testimony of Senator Edward M. Kennedy), 4.

7   Ibid.

8   Ibid., 38 (statement of Patrick J. Leahy).

9   Ibid., 9 (statement of Senator Alan K. Simpson).

10 Ibid., 18 (testimony of Stephen J. Markman).

11 Judith Resnik, "This Question Changed the Face of the Supreme Court," *CNN Opinion*, September 25, 2018.

12 "As a long-time admirer of Judge Bork and a former colleague of his at the Justice Department, I suggest that the strong and inquiring mind that he displayed as a professor, together with the quality and restraint evidenced in his judgeship, hold the promise of new distinction for the Court." Carla Hills, "Take the Trouble to Understand," Patricia Mack Files Folder: [Robert Bork] Carla Hills Group Analysis of Bork (1) OA19247, Ronald Reagan Presidential Library.

13 Lee Liberman, "Memorandum on Cynthia Holcomb Hall," OA/ID 45303–005, Box 7, Hall, Cynthia Holcomb, George H. W. Bush Presidential Archives. The same memorandum is also located at "Memorandum on Cynthia Holcomb Hall," OA 19247, Box 14, Patricia Mack Bryan Supreme Court Files, Ronald Reagan Presidential Library.

14 Stout, *A Matter of Simple Justice*, 112.

15 Hall, "Diversifying the Judiciary."

16 Ibid.

17 Ibid.

18 Ibid.

19 Ibid.

20 Stout, *A Matter of Simple Justice*, 144.

21 Liberman, "Memorandum on Cynthia Holcomb Hall."

22 Roberts, "Washington Talk."

23 Dennis McLellan, "Rymer Dies at 70: Judge on the U.S. 9th Circuit Court of Appeals," *Los Angeles Times*, September 24, 2011, http://articles.latimes.com.

24 Planned Parenthood v. American Coalition of Life Activists, 290 F.3d 1058 (9th Cir. 2002).

25 "Hotties in the Holding Pen: Untimely SFJ Nominations," *Underneath Their Robes Blog*, July 17, 2004, http://underneaththeirrobesblog.com.

26 Melanie Kirkpatrick, "Chick List," *Wall Street Journal*, September 24, 2005.

27 "Young Judges See Bias in ABA Ratings Criteria," *Legal Times*, January 6, 1986.

28 Roe v. Wade, 410 U.S. 113 (1973).

29 Marc Kaufman, "Appellate Judge Bristled at Criticism of Nominees," *Washington Post*, July 2, 2005.

30 Ibid.

31 Lee Liberman, "Memorandum on Edith Jones," OA/ID 45303–029, Box 8, Jones, Edith, George H. W. Bush Presidential Library Center.

32 Ibid., speech of President George H. W. Bush.

33 Ibid., letter from Edith Jones to George H. W. Bush.

34 Michael Briggs, "Bush's Judges are Rich White Men," *Chicago Sun-Times*, January 1, 1992.

35 Ibid.

36 Ibid.

37 Memorandum from C. Boyden Gray to the Chief of Staff re Statistics on Federal Judges, March 10, 1992, OA/ID 45323–027, Judicial Selection–Women/Minorities, George H. W. Bush Presidential Library Center.

38 *The Performance of the Reagan Administration in Nominating Women and Minorities to the Federal Bench*, 38 (statement of Senator Patrick C. Leahy)

39 Catherine Pearson, "23 Ruth Bader Ginsburg Quotes That Will Make You Love Her Even More," *Huffington Post*, August 10, 2016, www.huffingtonpost.com.

40 "Ruth Bader Ginsburg: A Reading List," The Library at Washington and Lee University School of Law, last accessed December 27, 2018, https://libguides.wlu.edu.

41 Kathleen Quinn, "Treat Judge Ginsburg Like a Man," *New York Times*, June 20, 1993.

42 "Mr. Clinton Picks a Justice," *New York Times*, June 15, 1993 (stating that Ginsburg's career and gender stand for the principle of accepting or rejecting people and ideas on their merits, rather than prejudice or stereotypes).

43 Stephen Labaton, "The Man Behind the High Court Nominee," *New York Times*, June 17, 1993.

44 Jay Mathews, "The Spouse of Ruth: Marty Ginsburg, the Pre-Feminism Feminist," *Washington Post*, June 19, 1993.

45 Ibid.

46 "The Supreme Court: Transcript of President's Announcement and Judge Ginsburg's Remarks," *New York Times*, June 5, 1993.

47 Mary McGrory, "Clinton Unbridled," *Washington Post*, June 17, 1993. Ginsburg was also called "daughterly about her own mother, and sisterly enough to delight all but fanatical feminists." Ibid.

48 Brenner and Knake, "Rethinking Gender Equality in the Legal Profession's Pipeline to Power."

49 David Brooks, "In Her Own Words," *New York Times*, October 13, 2005.

50 Todd S. Purdum and Neil A. Lewis, "Hard-Working Advocate for the President," *New York Times*, October 4, 2005.

51 Elisabeth Bumiller, "A Place at the Table for Miers and High-Level Friends," *New York Times*, October 10, 2005.

52 Michael Grunwald et al., "A Deep Dedication to the President, and to Her Work," *Washington Post*, October 4, 2005.

53 Ibid.

54 Ibid.

55 Robert H. Bork, "Editorial: Slouching Towards Miers," *Wall Street Journal*, October 19, 2005.

56 "Nixon: 'I Should Like to Share With You . . . My Reasons,'" *Washington Post*, October 22, 1971.

57 Roe v. Wade, 410 U.S. 113 (1973).

58 Janny Scott, "Court Choice Conservative by Nature, Not Ideology," *New York Times*, November 7, 2005.

59 Laura M. Holson, "Then Comes the Marriage Question," *New York Times*, May 16, 2010.

60 President Obama's 2009 shortlist reportedly included Federal Court of Appeals Judges Sonia Sotomayor and Diane Wood, Solicitor General Elena Kagan, Homeland Security Secretary Janet Napolitano, Michigan Governor Jennifer Granholm, and California Supreme Court Justice Carlos Moreno. Bill Mears, "Sources: High Court Selection Process Down to Finalists," CNN Politics, May 13, 2009, www.cnn.com. His 2010 shortlist reportedly included Federal Court of Appeals Judges Merrick Garland, Diane Wood, and Sidney Thomas; Solicitor General Elena Kagan; Judge Merrick Garland of the U.S. Court of Appeals, D.C. Circuit; Judge Diane Wood of the Seventh Circuit Appeals Court in Chicago; Homeland Security Secretary Janet Napolitano; Michigan Governor Jennifer Granholm; Georgia Supreme Court Justice Leah Ward Sears; Harvard Law Dean Martha Minow; law professor Cass Sunstein; and Senator Sheldon Whitehouse. Jake Tapper, "Obama's Supreme Court Short List Includes Six Women," ABC News, April 13, 2010, https://abcnews.go.com.

61 Paul Campos, "Fat Judge Need Not Apply," *Daily Beast*, May 4, 2009, www.thedailybeast.com.

62 Amy Argetsinger and Roseanne Roberts, "Sotomayor: A Single Supreme?," *Washington Post*, May 27, 2009.

63 Ibid.

64 Ibid.

65 Sheryl Gay Stolberg, "A Trailblazer and a Dreamer," *New York Times*, May 27, 2009.

66 Keith B. Richburg, "Friends Provide Glimpse into Nominee's 'Very Full Life,'" *Washington Post*, May 31, 2009.

67 Ibid.

68 Ibid.

69 Holson, "Then Comes the Marriage Question."

70 Ibid.

71 Ann Gerhart, "The Supreme Court Needs More Mothers," *Washington Post*, May 16, 2010.

72 Ibid.

73 Lisa Belkin, "Judging Women," *New York Times*, May 23, 2010.

74 Amy Goldstein et al., "A History of Pragmatism Over Partisanship," *Washington Post*, May 11, 2010.

75 Ibid.

76 Frank Rich, "A Heaven-Sent Rent Boy," *New York Times*, May 16, 2010.

77 Ruth Marcus, "Smart Women, Fewer Choices," *Washington Post*, May 14, 2010.

78 The shortlist reportedly included Ketanji Brown Jackson, U.S. District Court for D.C.; Jane Kelly, U.S. Court of Appeals for the Eighth Circuit; Patricia Millett, U.S. Court of Appeals for the D.C. Circuit; Sri Srinivasan, U.S. Court of Appeals for the D.C. Circuit; and Paul Watford, U.S. Court of Appeals for the Ninth Circuit. Dylan Matthews, "Obama's Supreme Court Shortlist Has Leaked. Here are the 6 Contenders," *Vox*, March 12, 2016.

PART II. THEIR STORIES ARE OUR STORIES

1 Ginsburg, "The Supreme Court," 190.

2 Allen, *This Constitution of Ours*.

3 Allen, *To Do Justly*.

4 Ginsburg et al., *My Own Words*; O'Connor, *Out of Order*; Sotomayor, *My Beloved World*.

CHAPTER 5. AFTER SHORTLISTED, TOKENISM

1 Address to the Women Law Students Association, October 21, 1978, Cornelia G. Kennedy Papers: 1932–2012, 1970–1999, Box 1: 19, Bentley Historical Library, University of Michigan.

2 Jan Crawford Greenburg, "O'Connor Voices Hope For Day Affirmative Action Not Needed," *Chicago Tribune*, June 25, 2003.

3 *Oxford English Dictionary*, s.v. "Tokenism," accessed January 6, 2019, www.oed.com.

4 Kanter, *Men and Women of the Corporation*.

5 "Amalya Kearse," *Academy of Achievement*, podcast audio, July 7, 1984, https://itunes.apple.com/us/podcast/amalya-kearse/id474596633?mt=2.

6 Lillie, "Justice Mildred L. Lillie," 68.

7 Interview with Cornelia Kennedy and Margaret Schaeffer, Cornelia G. Kennedy Papers: 1932–2012, 1970–1999, Box 1: 19, Bentley Historical Library, University of Michigan.

8 Karin Klenke, professor of organizational leadership and head of the Leadership Development Institute International, explains that "[w]omen in leadership roles share many of the structural characteristics of tokens: they are highly visible, public individuals who attract attention with anything they do; as such, they are stand-ins for all women, symbols of how women behave and perform as leaders." Klenke, *Women and Leadership*, 176.

9 Memorandum from Elizabeth Dole to Diana Lozano, "Judicial Appointments—Status of Women," August 21, 1981, The White House, 2.

10 Solberg, "Court Size and Diversity on the Bench," 264, Table 2D.
11 Tom Goldstein, "Amalya Lyle Kearse," *New York Times*, June 25, 1979.
12 Elizabeth Bumiller, "A Place at the Table for Miers and High-Level Friends," *New York Times*, October 10, 2005.
13 Amy Argetsinger and Roxanne Roberts, "Sotomayor: A Single Supreme?," *Washington Post*, May 27, 2009.
14 Cruz and Molina, "Hispanic National Bar Association National Study on the Status of Latinas in the Legal Profession—Few and Far Between," 3.
15 Stefanie K. Johnson, David R. Hekman, and Elsa T. Chan, "If There's Only One Woman in Your Candidate Pool, There's Statistically No Chance She'll Be Hired," *Harvard Business Review*, April 26, 2016, https://hbr.org.
16 Lopez and Johnson, *Presumed Incompetent*, 392.
17 *Nomination of Sandra Day O'Connor: Hearings Before the Committee on the Judiciary United States Senate*, 97th Congress (1981) (statement of Joan Dempsey Klein, Presiding Justice, California Court of Appeals, and President, National Association of Women Judges), 410.
18 Rhode, *The Beauty Bias*.
19 Martin and Jurik, *Doing Justice, Doing Gender*, 127. In one study, the authors noted how "a judge allow[ed] the opposing attorney to label a woman attorney's appearance a 'distraction,' [thus] signal[ing] to others that it is acceptable to use a woman's looks as the basis for objecting against other woman attorneys." Ibid.
20 Ibid.
21 Marion Bussang, "Dates, Clothes and Play Relevant, Not Material," *New York Post*, April 22, 1940; Soia Mentschikoff Papers, Special Collections Research Center, Joseph Regenstein Library, University of Chicago.
22 "She Wore Fancy Hats to Labor Meetings," *Express*, June 19, 1974.
23 John Betz, "HUD Chief Opts for Saving Existing Stock," *Los Angeles Times*, August 8, 1976.
24 Ibid.
25 Rhitu Chatterjee, "A New Survey Finds 81 Percent of Women Have Experienced Sexual Harassment," February 21, 2018.
26 Lillie, "Justice Mildred L. Lillie," 31.
27 "Amalya Kearse," *Academy of Achievement*.
28 Dianne Curtis, "At 87, Forever Young Joan Dempsey Klein Wins Another Honor and Might Consider Retirement," *California Bar Journal*, November 2011.
29 Cynthia Hall, "A Few Good Women: Advancing the Cause of Women in Government, 1969–74," Pennsylvania State University Oral History Collection (1998), 30.
30 Ibid.
31 MacKinnon, *Sexual Harassment of Working Women*, 1.
32 Michael Kernan, "For Her Honors; Sisterhood on the Bench; Joan Dempsey Klein & The Judges' Network," *Washington Post*, October 4, 1980.
33 American Bar Association Model Rule of Professional Conduct 8.4(g).

34 Niraj Chokshi, "Federal Judge Alex Kozinski Retires Abruptly After Sexual Harassment Allegations," *New York Times*, December 18, 2017.

35 Joan Biskupic, "Judicial Council Takes No Action Against Former Judge Alex Kozinski," February 5, 2018, www.wral.com.

36 Testimony of Professor Renee Newman Knake before the Federal Judicial Conference, October 30, 2018, www.c-span.org.

37 For a discussion of gender sidelining, or the "many ways in which women across a wide range of employment settings face obstacles that inhibit their advancement at work through policies and practices not reached by traditional antidiscrimination laws," see Fink, "Gender Sidelining and the Problem of Unactionable Discrimination."

38 Eileen Shanahan, "President Bypasses Women for Court; Talent Pool Small," *New York Times*, October 21, 1971.

CHAPTER 6. CHALLENGING DOUBLE BINDS AND UNIFYING
DOUBLE LIVES

1 Hall, "Diversifying the Judiciary."

2 Frye, *The Politics of Reality*, 2.

3 Jamieson, *Beyond the Double Bind*, 120–45.

4 Mona Harrington et al, "Advancing Women in the Profession: Action Plans for Women's Bar Associations," MIT Workplace Center (2007), 8.

5 Brent Staples, "How the Suffrage Movement Betrayed Black Women," *New York Times*, July 28, 2018.

6 Allen, *To Do Justly*, 9.

7 Jacobi and Schweers, "Justice, Interrupted."

8 Joan Biskupic, "Ginsburg: Court Needs Another Woman," *USA Today*, May 5, 2009.

9 Ibid.

10 Our contemporary ideas surrounding which political groups might support the Equal Rights Amendment is at odds with the historical reality that progressives initially opposed the amendment. Their opposition stemmed from their fear that the legislation would be used by conservative courts in the 1920s through 1950s to strike down protective labor legislation ensuring minimum wage and maximum hours for women.

11 Robert Sherrill, "That Equal-Rights Amendment—What, Exactly, Does It Mean?," *New York Times*, September 20, 1970.

12 Susanna Dokupil, "Portrait of a Modern Feminist: Hon. Edith H. Jones, Independent Women's Forum," July 2, 2012, www.iwf.org.

13 Memorandum from John W. Dean and David R. Young to Attorney General John N. Mitchell and John D. Erlichman, "Interview with Justice Mildred L. Lillie October 14, 1971–3:30–8:00 P.M.," October 16, 1971, White House Central Files, Alphabetical Name Files, Lillie, Mildred, Judge [1 of 4].

14 Hayes, *Without Precedent*, 447–48, citing Elizabeth Shelton, "Are the Scales Weighted against Women Judges?," *Washington Post*, September 19, 1965.
15 Hall, "Diversifying the Judiciary."
16 Norgren, *Stories From Trailblazing Women Lawyers*, 66–67.
17 Epstein, *Women in Law*, 50.
18 Letter from Soia Mentschikoff to Frank Brenner, February 9, 1951, Soia Mentschikoff Papers 1913–1987, Special Collections Research Center, Joseph Regenstein Library, University of Chicago.
19 Emily Bazelon, "A Judge Who Didn't See Discrimination," *New York Times Magazine*, December 23, 2014.
20 Tom Goldstein, "Amalya Lyle Kearse," *New York Times*, June 25, 1979.
21 Testimony of Dennis W. Archer, President, Wolverine Bar Association, Before the Judiciary Committee of the United States Senate Concerning the Nomination of Judge Cornelia Kennedy to the United States Court of Appeals for the Sixth Circuit, 6–7.
22 Hayes, *Without Precedent*, 2.
23 Ibid., 197, citing Susie Marshall Sharp to Millard Sheridan Breckenridge, December 11, 1965.
24 Cook, "The First Woman Candidate for the Supreme Court," 21.
25 State ex rel Weaver v. Board of Trustees of Ohio State University, 126 O.S. 290 (1933).
26 Cook, "The First Woman Candidate for the Supreme Court," 21.
27 Allen, *To Do Justly*, 92.
28 Goldstein, "Amalya Lyle Kearse."
29 Marion Bussang, "Dates, Clothes and Play Relevant, Not Material," *New York Post*, April 22, 1940; Soia Mentschikoff Papers, Special Collections Research Center, Joseph Regenstein Library, University of Chicago.
30 "Law as a Career for Women Urged: Magistrate Kross and Justice Craig See Them Rapidly Gaining Recognition," *New York Times*, November 10, 1935.
31 Ibid.
32 Ibid.
33 Dorothy Harrington, "The Return of the 4 ½ Inch Heel," *Los Angeles Times*, March 24, 1977.
34 Marlene Cimons, "Carla Hills' Day on the Hill," *Los Angeles Times*, March 10, 1975.
35 Hall, "Diversifying the Judiciary."
36 Ibid., Part 1.
37 Ibid.
38 "Susie Sharp Papers," The Southern Historical Collection.
39 Lillie, "Justice Mildred L. Lillie," 25.
40 Lee Liberman, "Memorandum on Cynthia Holcomb Hall," OA/ID 45303–005, Box 7, Hall, Cynthia Holcomb, George H. W. Bush Presidential Archives. The same memorandum is also located at "Memorandum on Cynthia Holcomb Hall,"

OA 19247, Box 14, Patricia Mack Bryan Supreme Court Files, Ronald Reagan Presidential Library.

41 Lillie, "Justice Mildred L. Lillie," 7.

42 Twining, "'Looking Back Will Still Keep Us Looking Forward.'"

43 Hayes, *Without Precedent*, 2.

44 Ibid., 47.

45 Brenner and Knake, "Rethinking Gender Equality in the Legal Profession's Pipeline to Power," 143. Indeed, the media heavily scrutinized the personal lives of Justices Sonia Sotomayor and Elena Kagan following their nomination to the Court. David Souter also received scrutiny as an unmarried man, suggesting the issue is broader than gender and more related to a departure from traditional heterosexual marital norms.

46 Kenney, "Choosing Judges," 1499. Kenney states, "Men from President Roosevelt to President Reagan may have preferred their women trailblazers to have impeccable heterosexual credentials." "Because Allen's primary relationship was not with a man, her private life—in particular her relationships with other women—has been ignored in Cleveland history, legal history, and social policy history. All are impoverished by this consistent refusal to deal with the significance of women's relationships." Organ, "Sexuality as a Category of Historical Analysis," 12.

47 Quinn, *Eleanor and Hick.*

48 Susie Sharp, notes in preparation for radio interview with WLOS in Asheville, NC, "Susie Sharp Papers," The Southern Historical Collection.

49 Crabb, *The Wife Drought*, 250–51.

50 Ibid., 251.

51 Klein, "Oral History of Joan Dempsey Klein," 13.

52 Ibid., 50.

53 Liberman, Lee S., Judicial Candidate Files, Box Number 7, Hall, Cynthia Holcomb [OA/ID 45303–005], George H. W. Bush Presidential Library.

54 Hall, "Diversifying the Judiciary."

55 B. Drummond Ayres, Jr., "Woman in the News; 'A Reputation for Excelling,'" *New York Times*, July 8, 1981.

56 Whitman, "Soia Mentschikoff and Karl Llewellyn."

57 Ibid.

58 Susie Sharp, notes in preparation for radio interview with WLOS in Asheville, NC.

59 Ibid.

60 Williams, "Litigating the Glass Ceiling and the Maternal Wall," 288.

61 "Carla Hills Manages H.U.D., Hubby and Home," *People Magazine*, March 31, 1975.

62 Rhode, "The Difference 'Difference' Makes," 10.

63 Whitman, "Soia Mentschikoff and Karl Llewellyn," 1126.

64 Ibid.

65 Dorothy McCardle, "Who's King of the Hills?," *Washington Post*, October 26, 1975.

66 Barbara Franklin, "Barbara Franklin," interview by Timothy Naftali and Paul Musgrave, Yorba Linda, California, March 7, 2007. (Former Secretary of Commerce Barbara Franklin talked about her work as a staff assistant to President Nixon from 1971 to 1973).

67 Sady Doyle, "Nancy Pelosi Is Old. Good," *Medium*, November 20, 2018.

68 Ibid.

69 Cook, "The First Woman Candidate for the Supreme Court," 31.

70 Doyle, "Nancy Pelosi Is Old."

71 Liberman, "Memorandum on Cynthia Holcomb Hall."

72 "Pat Believes Age Is a Factor in Putting Woman on Court," *Chicago Tribune*, September 25, 1971.

73 Dean, *The Rehnquist Choice*, 111.

74 Box 37F, Fred Fielding Files, Supreme Court [Mostly Sandra Day O'Connor Nomination] (1 of 4), Ronald Reagan Presidential Library.

75 Doyle, "Nancy Pelosi Is Old."

CHAPTER 7. NO LONGER ZERO

1 Corydon Ireland, "O'Connor Marks Women's Progress in Legal Profession, but Warns in Radcliffe Talk of 'Victorian Echos,'" *Harvard Gazette Online*, June 11, 2009, https://news.harvard.edu.

2 Peter Baker and Jim Rutenberg, "The Long Road to a Clinton Exit," *New York Times*, June 8, 2008.

3 Hoyt v. Florida, 368 U.S. 57, 62 (1961).

4 Letter to President Ford from Beatrice Stegeman, November 15, 1975, File 20141215 140215, Gerald L. Ford Presidential Library.

5 Frontiero v. Richardson, 411 U.S. 677 (1973).

6 Craig v. Boren, 429 U.S. 190 (1976).

7 Collins et al., "Gender, Critical Mass, and Judicial Decision Making," 263 (reflecting that "[c]onsidered collectively, the result of research subjecting gender effects to empirical scrutiny in the judicial arena has been decidedly mixed," leading to a failure to "uncover systematic differences between male and female jurists"); Kenney, "Critical Perspectives on Gender and Judging," 436 (noting that political scientists have found that gender does not affect judicial decision-making, with the occasional exception of some sex discrimination and divorce cases); Deborah Rhode, "In a 'Different' Voice: What Does the Research About How Gender Influences Judging Actually Say?," *Slate* (June 2009), (discussing the "cottage industry of empirical work [that] has tried to disentangle the influence of gender on judging" and observing that the "[r]esults vary" on whether gender makes a difference).

8 Carol Gilligan's influential work *In a Different Voice: Psychological Theory and Women's Development* has been applied by many scholars and commentators to assess decisions by women judges. Gilligan theorized that men and women approach moral reasoning differently. Though her work has been critiqued as essentialist and based upon empirical studies that could not be replicated, she sparked a debate that continues even today about the difference women make in decision-making. Other scholars examining the impact of being a female or being a feminist as a judge include Dixon, "Female Justices, Feminism, and the Politics of Judicial Appointment," 304 (providing a list of scholars who suggest that "Justices O'Connor and Ginsburg have adopted a distinctively 'feminine' jurisprudential approach simply by reason of being female") and Hill, "What Difference Will Women Judges Make?," 185–86 (concluding that female judges "make a difference" on the bench because the contribution of their alternative perspective "reaffirms the promise of equality under the law" and may "influence . . . the overall direction the law takes").

9 Sherry, "Civic Virtue and the Feminine Voice in Constitutional Adjudication."

10 O'Connor, "Madison Lecture," 1553.

11 Hirshman, *Sisters in Law*, 300. "With the richness of her experiences as a woman lawyer coming up when society was arrayed against her, O'Connor's record on women's issues is by far the most liberal of all the bodies of law she created in her long career and much more liberal than the other Reagan appointees, Scalia and Kennedy." Ibid.

12 Choi et al., "Judging Women," 504, 505.

13 Ibid, 504. But see Barondes, "Federal District Judge Gender and Reversals" (arguing that the results in Choi et al., "Judging Women," are "not informative" because the authors do not consider that a relationship may already exist between gender and their selected measures of judicial performance, and therefore choosing a different methodology).

14 Allen and Wall, "Role Orientations and Women State Supreme Court Justices."

15 McCall and McCall, "How Far Does the Gender Gap Extend?," 67–82.

16 Songer and Crews-Meyer, "Does Judge Gender Matter?"

17 Martin and Pyle, "State High Courts and Divorce," 940–41.

18 Steffensmeier and Hebert, "Women and Men Policymakers," 1186.

19 Smith, Jr., "Gendered Justice," 2123.

20 Haire and Moyer, *Diversity Matters*, 53. ("[O]verall the empirical analyses support the findings reported by other studies that have tested for gender differences in judicial decision-making from earlier eras. Men and women on the bench are quite similar in their voting behavior, with one exception: cases involving sex discrimination.")

21 Farhand and Wawro, "Institutional Dynamics on the U.S. Court of Appeals"; Boyd et al., "Untangling the Causal Effects of Sex on Judging," 389.

22 Dixon, "Female Justices, Feminism, and the Politics of Judicial Appointment," 311–19.

23 Ibid., 338 (suggesting that the focus on gender parity is misguided, arguing instead for the addition of judges who have a feminist ideology). Dixon acknowledges feminists' desire for equal numbers of women in the judiciary, but concludes that "feminists must also weigh these benefits associated with the mere *presence* of a female justice on the Court against the importance of a justice's substantive approach to issues of central concern to feminists, such as abortion, pay equity, sex discrimination, sexual harassment, and an ongoing dialogue about the meaning of gender equality under the Equal Protection Clause." Ibid., 336.

24 Ibid., 338 (noting that a president might "exploit [feminists' focus on gender parity] in order to appoint an actively *anti-feminist* female judge" and that, in such an instance, feminists "should choose the feminist who is male").

25 Glynn and Sen, "Identifying Judicial Empathy" ("Looking at data from the U.S. Courts of Appeals, we find that . . . conditional on the number of children, judges with daughters consistently vote in a more liberal fashion on gender issues than judges without daughters").

26 Rhode and Kellerman, *Women and Leadership* (noting extensive research on U.S. legislatures finds that "party affiliation is more important than gender in predicting votes on women's issues, and that ideology is more important in predicting sponsorship of legislation on these issues" [citations omitted]).

27 Schultz and Shaw, *Gender and Judging*, 27.

28 Joan Biskupic, "Ginsburg: Court Needs Another Woman," *USA Today*, May 5, 2009.

29 Safford Unified School District v. Redding, 557 U.S. 364 (2009).

30 Gonzales v. Carhart, 550 U.S. 124, 185 (2007).

31 Doe v. Dominion Bank of Washington N.A., 963 F.2d 1552, 1554 (D.C. Cir 1992).

32 Gebser v. Lago Vista Independent School District, 524 U.S. 274 (1998).

33 Davis v. Monroe County School Board, 526 U.S. 629 (1999).

34 Ledbetter v. Goodyear Tire and Rubber Co., 550 U.S. 618 (2007).

35 Robert Barnes, "Over Ginsburg's Dissent, Court Limits Bias Suits," *Washington Post*, May 30, 2007.

36 Ledbetter, 550 U.S. 645.

37 Schuette v. Coalition to End Affirmative Action, 572 U.S. 291, 381 (2014).

38 Ibid.

39 Neil A. Lewis, "Debate on Whether Female Judges Decide Differently Arises Anew," *New York Times*, June 4, 2009.

40 Derek Hawkins, "'Wise Latina Woman': Jeff Sessions, Race and His Grilling of Sonia Sotomayor," *Washington Post*, January 13, 2017.

41 "Sotomayor Wants More Diversity on Court, After Obama Picks Garland, A White Ivy Male," *Fox News*, April 9, 2016.

42 Frank Rich, "A Heaven-Sent Rent Boy," *New York Times*, May 16, 2010.

43 Ibid.

44 Sheryl Gay Stolberg, "Say It with Feeling? Not This Time Around," *New York Times*, May 29, 2009.

45 Cowan, "Do Women on South Africa's Courts Make a Difference?," 328.

46 O'Connor and Azzarelli, "Sustainable Development, Rule of Law and the Impact of Women Judges," 3.

47 Justin Trudeau, "Why Canada Has a New Way to Choose Supreme Court Judges," *Globe and Mail*, August 2, 2016.

48 Ibid.

49 Beiner, "Is There Really a Diversity Conundrum?," 285.

50 O'Connor, *The Majesty of the Law*, 201.

51 Madeline Albright, "Madeleine Albright to Grads: The World Needs You," *Time* video, May 18, 2015, http://time.com/collection-post/3882439/madeleine-albright-tufts-graduation-speech/.

52 Kay, "Herma Hill Kay," 26.

53 Ibid.

54 Schultz and Shaw, *Gender and Judging*, 22.

55 Cowan, "Do Women on South Africa's Courts Make a Difference?," 320–321.

56 Kanau, "Women Judges and Magistrates in Kenya," 171.

57 Ibid., 180.

58 Ibid., 182. The High Court is the third level, below the Supreme Court and the Court of Appeal.

59 Monopoli, "Gender Parity and the United States Supreme Court"; Suk, "Gender Quotas After the End of Men."

60 "California Becomes First State to Require Women on Corporate Boards," *NBC News*, September 30, 2018. As this book went to press, the Illinois legislature was considering a similar measure to require at least one female and one African American director on boards. The Illinois House passed the legislation on March 29, 2019, with a vote of 61–27.

61 Emily Stewart, "California Just Passed a Law Requiring More Women on Boards. It Matters, Even if it Fails," *Vox*, October 3, 2018.

CHAPTER 8. SURMOUNTING THE SHORTLIST

1 Sotomayor, *My Beloved World*, ii–iii.

2 Hannah Smothers, "All 19 Black Women Running for Judge in a Texas Race Won Tuesday Night," *Cosmopolitan*, November 7, 2018.

3 Tom Dart, "'Black Girl Magic': 19 Black Women Ran for Judge in Texas County—and All 19 Won," *Guardian*, November 8, 2018.

4 Ginger Gibson, "Trump Identifies 11 Potential Supreme Court Nominees," *Reuters*, May 18, 2016.

5 "President Donald J. Trump's Supreme Court List," The White House, accessed January 6, 2019, www.whitehouse.gov.

6 "More Than 20 Million People Watched Brett Kavanaugh Hearing," *CBS News*, September 29, 2018.

7 Louis Jacobson, "In Context: Brett Kavanaugh and 'What Goes Around Comes Around,'" *Politifact*, October 4, 2018.

8 The only confirmation with a narrower vote was Justice Stanley Matthews, nominated by President James Garfield, who received a vote of 24–23.

9 This phenomenon is not limited to the United States. Former Israeli President Moshe Katsav served prison time for rape and other forms of sexual violence committed against women who worked for him. Similarly, the former head of the International Monetary Fund, Dominique Strauss-Kahn, has repeatedly been accused of harassment and sexual violence by multiple women spanning the globe, though he has never been convicted for these crimes in any country.

10 Sandberg, *Lean In*. While at first well received by women who formed "lean in circles," a harsh reality was revealed, notably by Michelle Obama, who critiqued the concept, saying, "That &#%! doesn't work." Laurel Wamsley, "Michelle Obama's Take on Lean In? 'That &#%! Doesn't Work,'" *National Public Radio*, December 3, 2018.

11 According to the World Economic Forum, as of 2018, there were 18 countries where husbands had the legal right to prevent their wives from working.

12 A special symposium issue of the *Michigan State Law Review* contains the scholarship generated by this event. Brenner and Knake, "Gender and the Legal Profession's Pipeline to Power."

13 Louis Uchitelle, "A Crowbar for Carla Hills," *New York Times*, June 10, 1990.

14 Ibid.

15 Rachel Denhollander, "The Price I Paid for Taking on Larry Nassar," *New York Times*, January 26, 2018.

16 Marcia Coyle, "How Many Women Lawyers Were Elected in the Midterms? Quite a Few," *National Law Journal*, November 8, 2018, www.law.com. ("The newly elected women attended 28 different law schools, including Ivy League Harvard and Yale as well as Cumberland, Santa Clara, George Washington, Cleveland-Marshall, University of Chicago, University of Virginia, Touro and others. Georgetown University Law Center can claim four graduates, and there are two each from law schools at the University of New Mexico, Cornell University, UCLA, University of Chicago and William and Mary."). After Coyle's article was published, another lawyer-legislator's win was confirmed, Krysten Sinema, a graduate of Arizona State Sandra Day O'Connor College of Law.

17 Carol J. Williams, "Cynthia Holcomb Hall Dies at 82; U.S. 9th Circuit Judge," *Los Angeles Times*, March 2, 2011.

18 Chuck Conconi, "Law and Ardor," *Washingtonian*, October 1994.

19 Hall, "Diversifying the Judiciary."

20 Ibid.
21 Ibid.
22 Lynn Lilliston and Marlene Cimons, "Women Front Runners for High Court," *Los Angeles Times*, September 30, 1971. ("A remark by Mrs. Nixon added a touch of mystery to the situation. Mrs. Nixon told reporters that she had been encouraging the President to name a woman.") The influence of presidents' wives, in particular, continued well beyond the women shortlisted pre-O'Connor. See, for example, Stephen Labaton, "Clinton Nears Choice for High Court Nominee," *New York Times*, May 19, 1993 (administration official noting that Hillary Clinton favored Judge Amalya Kearse for the Supreme Court nomination); Peter Baker, "Unraveling the Twists and Turns of the Path to a Nominee," *Washington Post*, July 25, 2005 ("Then first lady Laura Bush weighed in, telling an interviewer that she wanted her husband to replace O'Connor with another woman."). And the women on the Court have weighed in too. See Jeanne Cummings and Jess Bravin, "Bush Aides Consider Female Successor to O'Connor," *Wall Street Journal*, July 19, 2005 ("But some—including first lady Laura Bush and the court's two current women members, Justices O'Connor and Ruth Bader Ginsburg—have suggested the president should pick another woman.").
23 "Betty Ford Tells Interviewer Her Bedroom Views," *Los Angeles Times*, August 20, 1975.
24 Richard Nixon Presidential Oral History Program, Barbara Hackman Franklin Interview Transcription, March 7, 2007, 23.
25 Jean Rainey, "Oral History Interview with Julie Nixon Eisenhower," March 9, 1999, www.libraries.psu.edu.
26 Lillie, "Justice Mildred L. Lillie," 106–7.
27 Kay, "Herma Hill Kay," 48.
28 Allen, *To Do Justly*, 34.
29 Ibid., 28.
30 Hills, "Oral History of Carla A. Hills," interview by Janet McDavid, 4.
31 Klein, "Oral History of Joan Dempsey Klein," 16.
32 Ibid.
33 Ibid., 13.
34 Douglas Huron's Subject Files, Box 249, Folder Judicial Selection Strategy—Strategy Affirmative Action, Jimmy Carter Presidential Library.
35 *U.S. Congress, Senate, Confirmation Hearing on Amalya L. Kearse before the U.S. Senate Committee on the Judiciary*, 96th Congress, June 7, 1979, 127.
36 Ibid.
37 Ibid.
38 Remarks at a White House Reception for the National Association of Women Judges, October 3, 1980, Records of the Counsel's Office Lloyd Cutler's Files, Jordan, Hamilton 2/79–5/80 through Justice Department, 6/80–11/80, Box 93, Folder Judges, Jimmy Carter Presidential Library.

39 Alan Feuer, "A Judge Wants a Bigger Role for Female Lawyers. So He Made a Rule," *New York Times*, August 23, 2017.

40 Debra Cassens Weiss, "Supreme Court Law Clerks are Still Mostly White Men; Which Justices had the Most Diverse Clerks?," *American Bar Association Journal*, December 12, 2017.

41 Mabel C. McKinney-Browning, "'Don't Call Me Madam!': The Personal Side of the Law, From Women Who've Made it to the Top," *Update on Law Related Education* 5, no. 3 (1981), 53.

42 Ibid.

43 Ibid.

44 John Ingold, "EEOC Accuses DU Law School of Discriminating Against Women Professors," *Denver Post*, August 31, 2015.

45 Hall "Diversifying the Judiciary."

46 This term, first coined by Arlie Hochschild in her groundbreaking book of the same name published in 1989, *The Second Shift*, describes the enduring burden placed upon women when they enter the workforce and still find themselves doing the majority of housework. Hochschild and Machung, *The Second Shift*.

47 Louis Uchitelle, "A Crowbar for Carla Hills," *New York Times*, June 10, 1990.

48 Michelle K. Ryan and S. Alexander Haslam, "The Glass Cliff: Evidence that Women are Over-Represented in Precarious Leadership Positions," *British Journal of Management* 16 (February 9, 2005).

49 Culver, "The Rise of Self Sidelining."

50 Karen Higginbottom, "Two-Thirds of Women in the U.K. Suffer from Imposter Syndrome at Work," *Forbes*, July 29, 2018. A study of 3,000 adults living in the United Kingdom found that "while men were far from immune from experiencing imposter syndrome, they were 18% less likely to do so than their female counterparts." Ibid.

51 Hayes, *Without Precedent*, 25.

CONCLUSION

1 For a compelling documentation of this reality, see Kate Manne, *Down Girl: The Logic of Misogyny* (2018).

2 Sophie Tatum, "Grassley Suggests Lack of Women on Judiciary is Because 'It's a Lot of Work,' Then Says It's a Lot of Work for Men Too," *CNN*, October 5, 2018.

3 Joanna Walters, "Trump Calls Stormy Daniels 'Horseface' and Threatens More Legal Action," *Guardian*, October 16, 2018.

4 The iconic Norma Rae is based on the real-life experience of factory worker and union organizer Crystal Lee Sutton, who protested low wages and working conditions in 1973 and was subsequently fired for her activism. Sutton engaged in a legal battle and the court ordered she receive back pay and be rehired. An award-winning Hollywood film based on Sutton's life and legal battles, entitled *Norma Rae*, was produced in 1979 (Sally Fields played the role of Sutton). Dennis

Hevesi, "Crystal Lee Sutton, the Real-Life 'Norma Rae,' Is Dead at 68," *New York Times*, September 15, 2009.

5 Sasha Galbraith, "Justice Sonia Sotomayor's Advice for Women Today: Know When to Fight," *Forbes*, February 5, 2013.

6 Ibid.

APPENDIX 1. OUR METHODOLOGY FOR DETERMINING SUPREME COURT SHORTLISTS

1 Nemacheck, *Strategic Selection*, 55.

2 Ibid., 145–55.

3 Ibid. Other women may also have been excluded by Nemacheck.

4 Nemacheck, *Strategic Selection*, 13.

5 "Potential High Court Nominees," *New York Times*, October 14, 1971 (listing Sylvia Bacon, Robert C. Byrd, Charles Clark, Herschel H. Friday, Mildred Loree Lillie, and Paul H. Roney as "potential high court nominees"). John Dean has also written about Bacon's consideration by President Nixon. Dean, *The Rehnquist Choice*, 110.

6 Bacon's name was included for submission to "the ABA's evaluation committee" with "Mildred Lillie . . . Herschel Friday and whoever else they selected as camouflage. For the latter, Nixon suggested Federal Judge Charles Clark of Mississippi [and] Robert Byrd." Dean, *The Rehnquist Choice*, 153.

7 For example, in 1971, the National Women's Political Caucus named ten potential female nominees for President Nixon's consideration:

Three women judges were suggested by the caucus. They are Judge Shirley Hufstedler, 46 years old, of the United States Court of Appeals for the Ninth Circuit in Los Angeles; Judge Cornelia Kennedy, 48, of United States District Court in Detroit, and Judge Constance Baker Motley, 50, of United States District Court, Southern District of New York. The caucus suggested five professors of law. They are Soia Mentschikoff, 56, of the University of Chicago; Herma Hill Kay, 37, of the University of California at Berkeley; Ellen Peters, 41, of Yale; Dorothy Nelson, 45, dean of the University of Southern California School of Law, and Patricia Roberts Harris, 47, former dean of the Howard University School of Law and former Ambassador to Luxembourg. The caucus also suggested Representative Martha W. Griffiths, Republican of Michigan, 59, and Rita Hauser, 37, United States Representative to the United Nations Commission on Human Rights. ("10 Women Named as Caucus Choices for Court Seats," *New York Times*, September 28, 1971.)

8 Linda Greenhouse, "The Kind of Judge We Need," *New York Times*, January 17, 2019.

APPENDIX 2. A NOTE ON HISTORICAL RESEARCH

1 Walker, *Presidents and Civil Liberties from Wilson to Obama*. Katzenbach "did include Soia Mentschikoff of the University of Chicago Law School on an early list of possible Supreme Court nominees in 1962, probably the first such consideration in history." Ibid.

2 Nemacheck, *Strategic Selection*, 150 (listing Mentschikoff on Johnson's shortlist for the Fortas vacancy). Others credit President Ford as the first. "While Gerald Ford did not appoint a woman to the bench, instead naming John Paul Stevens, his administration was the first where women were seriously identified as candidates for a seat on the court." Martin, *The Presidency and Women*, 186.

3 Staci D. Kramer, "Enter O'Connor, Exit 'Mr. Justice,'" *New York Times*, November 16, 1990.

4 Epstein, "Beverly Blair Cook," 56.

5 For example, Susan B. Haire and Laura P. Moyer write in their book *Diversity Matters: Judicial Policy Making in the U.S. Courts of Appeals* that "Florence Allen was a graduate of the University of Chicago." Ibid., 36. But we confirmed through numerous other sources (including Allen's own biography) that Allen only attended law school at Chicago for one year before transferring to NYU Law School, where she graduated in 1913. Allen, *To Do Justly*, 25.

6 Richard Nixon Presidential Oral History Program, Barbara Hackman Franklin Interview Transcription, March 7, 2007, 23.

7 Verveer and Azzarelli, *Fast Forward*, 64.

SELECT BIBLIOGRAPHY

ARCHIVES AND LIBRARIES

"Cornelia Kennedy Papers: 1932–2012," Bentley Historical Library, University of Michigan. Ann Arbor, Michigan.

"Florence Ellinwood Allen Papers," Western Reserve Historical Society. Cleveland, Ohio.

Franklin D. Roosevelt Presidential Library. Hyde Park, New York.

George H. W. Bush Presidential Library Center. College Station, Texas.

Gerald L. Ford Presidential Library. Ann Arbor, Michigan.

Harry Truman Presidential Library. Independence, Missouri.

Herbert Hoover Presidential Library. West Branch, Iowa.

Jimmy Carter Presidential Library. Atlanta, Georgia.

LBJ Presidential Library. Austin, Texas.

Library of Congress. Washington, D.C.

Library of the U.S. Court of Appeals for the Sixth Circuit. Cincinnati, Ohio.

National Archives. College Park, Maryland.

Richard Nixon Presidential Library. Yorba Linda, California.

Ronald Reagan Presidential Library. Simi Valley, California.

"Soia Mentschikoff Papers 1913–1987," Special Collections Research Center, Joseph Regenstein Library, University of Chicago. Chicago, Illinois.

"Susie Sharp Papers," The Southern Historical Collection, Louis Round Wilson Special Collections Library, University of North Carolina at Chapel Hill. Chapel Hill, North Carolina.

CASE REFERENCES

Bradwell v. Illinois, 83 U.S. 130 (1873), affirming In re Bradwell, 55 Ill. 535 (1869).

Broadcast Music Inc. v. Columbia Broadcasting System, Inc., 441 U.S. 1 (1979).

Brown v. Board of Education of Topeka, 347 U.S. 483 (1954).

Craig v. Boren, 429 U.S. 190 (1976).

Davis v. Monroe County School Board, 526 U.S. 629 (1999).

Doe v. Dominion Bank of Washington N.A., 963 F.2d 1552, 1554 (D.C. Cir 1992).

Frontiero v. Richardson, 411 U.S. 677 (1973).

Gebser v. Lago Vista Independent School District, 524 U.S. 274 (1998).

Gonzales v. Carhart, 550 U.S. 124, 185 (2007).

Griswold v. Connecticut, 381 U.S. 479 (1965).

Hoyt v. Florida, 368 U.S. 57, 62 (1961).

Kaiser v. Stickney, 102 U.S. 176 (1880).

Korematsu v. United States, 323 U.S. 214 (1944).

Ledbetter v. Goodyear Tire and Rubber Co., 550 U.S. 618 (2007).

Lynum v. The State of Illinois, 368 U.S. 908 (1963).

Meritor Savings Bank v. Vinson, 477 U.S. 57 (1986).

Planned Parenthood v. American Coalition of Life Activists, 290 F.3d 1058 (9th Cir. 2002).

Planned Parenthood of Southeastern Pennsylvania v. Casey, 505 U.S. 833 (1992).

Roe v. Wade, 410 U.S. 113 (1973).

Safford Unified School District v. Redding, 557 U.S. 364 (2009).

Schuette v. Coalition to End Affirmative Action, 572 U.S. 291 (2014).

State v. Black, 60 N.C. 1 Win. 262 (1864).

Tennessee Valley Authority v. Tennessee Electric Power Company, 21 F. Supp. 947 (6th Cir. 1938).

United States v. Cherokee Nation, 202 U.S. 101 (1906).

NEWSPAPERS

American Lawyer

Arkansas Democrat Gazette

Boca Raton News

Charlotte Observer

The Express

Greensboro News and Record

Harvard Gazette

The Lincoln Journal Star

Miami Herald

National Law Journal

New York Post

New York Times

New York World Telegram

News and Record

Washington Post

BOOKS, ARTICLES, AND ORAL HISTORIES

Adichie, Chimamanda Ngozi. *We Should All Be Feminists*. New York: Anchor Books, 2012.

Allen, David W., and Diane E. Wall. "Role Orientations and Women State Supreme Court Justices." *Judicature* 77, no. 156 (1993).

Allen, Florence. *This Constitution of Ours*. New York: J.P. Putnam's Sons, 1940.

———. *To Do Justly*. Cleveland: The Press of the Western Reserve University, 1965.

Barondes, Royce de R. "Federal District Judge Gender and Reversals." Unpublished manuscript, July 2010. http://papers.ssrn.com.

Basile, Mary Elizabeth. "False Starts: Integrating Women into the Harvard Law School Faculty." *Harvard Journal of Law and Gender* 28, no. 1 (2005).

Batchelder, Alice. "In Memoriam of Judge Kennedy." *Ohio State Law Journal* 75, no. 5 (2014).

Beiner, Theresa M. "Is There Really a Diversity Conundrum?" *Wisconsin Law Review* 2017, no. 2 (2017).

Belknap, Michael R. *The Supreme Court Under Earl Warren, 1953–1969.* Columbia: South Carolina University Press, 2005.

Bell, Lauren Cohen. *Warring Factions: Interest Groups, Money, and the New Politics of Senate Confirmation.* Columbus: Ohio State University Press, 2002.

Boddie, Elise C. "Critical Mass and the Paradox of Colorblind Individualism in Equal Protection." *University of Pennsylvania Journal of Constitutional Law* 17, no. 3 (2015).

Boyd, Christina, et al. "Untangling the Causal Effects of Sex on Judging." *American Journal of Political Science* 54, no. 2 (April 2010).

Brenner, Hannah, and Renee Newman Knake. "Gender and the Legal Profession's Pipeline to Power." *Michigan State Law Review* 2012, no. 5 (2012).

———. "Rethinking Gender Equality in the Legal Profession's Pipeline to Power: A Study on Media Coverage of Supreme Court Nominees (Phase I, the Introduction Week)." *Temple Law Review* 84 (2012).

Califano Jr., Joseph A. *The Triumph & Tragedy of Lyndon Johnson: The White House Years.* New York: Touchstone, 2015.

Carmon, Irin, and Shana Knizhnik. *Notorious RBG: The Life and Times of Ruth Bader Ginsburg.* New York: Dey Street Books, 2015.

Carroll, Susan J. "Women in State Government: Historical Overview and Current Trends." In *The Book of the States 2007*, edited by Audrey Wall. Council of State Governments, 2007.

Carter, Stephen L. *The Confirmation Mess: Cleaning Up the Federal Appointments Process.* New York: Basic Books, 1995.

Chamallas, Martha. "Gaining Some Perspective in Tort Law: A New Take on Third-Party Criminal Attack Cases." *Lewis & Clark Law Review* 14, no. 4 (2010).

Chambliss, Elizabeth, and Christopher Uggen. "Men and Women of Elite Law Firms: Reevaluating Kanter's Legacy." *Law and Social Inquiry* 25, no. 1 (Winter 2000).

Choi, Stephen J., and Mitu G. Gulati. "Choosing the Next Supreme Court Justice: An Empirical Ranking of Judge Performance." *Southern California Law Review* 78, no. 1 (2004).

Choi, Stephen, et al. "Judging Women." *Journal of Empirical Legal Studies* 8, no. 3 (2011).

Clark, Mary L. "One Man's Token is Another Woman's Breakthrough—The Appointment of the First Women Federal Judges." *Villanova Law Review* 49, no. 3 (2004).

Collins, Gail. *When Everything Changed: The Amazing Journey of American Women from 1960 to the Present.* New York: Little, Brown, 2009.

Collins, Paul M., et al. "Gender, Critical Mass, and Judicial Decision Making." *Law & Policy* 32, no. 2 (2010).

Cook, Beverly B. "The First Woman Candidate for the Supreme Court." In *Yearbook 1981*. Washington, D.C.: Supreme Court Historical Society, 1981.

———. "Florence Ellinwood Allen." In *Notable American Women: The Modern Period—A Biographical Dictionary II*, edited by Barbara Sicherman and Carol Hurd Green. Cambridge, MA: The Belknap Press, 1980.

———. "Women as Supreme Court Candidates: From Florence Allen to Sandra O'Connor." *Judicature* 65, no. 6 (1982).

———. *Women in the Judicial Process*. Michigan: American Political Science Association, 1988.

———. "Women Judges: A Preface to Their History." *Golden Gate Law Review* 14, no. 3 (January 1984).

———. "Women Judges in the Opportunity Structure." In *Women, the Courts, and Equality*, edited by Laura Crite and Winifred L. Hepperle. Newbury Park, CA: Sage, 1987.

Cowan, Ruth B. "Do Women on South Africa's Courts Make a Difference?" In *Gender and Judging*, edited by Ulrike Schultz and Gisela Shaw. Oxford: Hart Publishing, 2013.

Crabb, Annabel. *The Wife Drought: Why Women Need Wives, and Men Need Lives*. North Sydney: Random House Australia, 2014.

Crenshaw, Kimberle. "Demarginalizing the Intersection of Race and Sex: A Black Feminist Critique of Antidiscrimination Doctrine, Feminist Theory and Antiracist Politics." *University of Chicago Legal Forum* 1989, no. 1 (1989).

———. "Mapping the Margins: Intersectionality, Identity Politics, and Violence against Women of Color." Stanford Law Review 43, no. 6 (1991).

Cruz, Jill L., and Melinda S. Molina. "Hispanic National Bar Association National Study on the Status of Latinas in the Legal Profession—Few and Far Between: The Reality of Latina Lawyers." *Pepperdine Law Review* 37, no. 3 (2010).

Culver, Leslie. "The Rise of Self Sidelining." *Women's Rights Law Reporter* 39, no. 3/4 (2018).

Dean, John W. *The Rehnquist Choice: The Untold Story of the Nixon Appointment that Redefined the Supreme Court*. New York: Free Press, 2001.

Dixon, Rosalind. "Female Justices, Feminism, and the Politics of Judicial Appointment." *Yale Journal of Law and Feminism* 21, no. 2 (November 2009).

Edwards, George C. *The Oxford Handbook of the American Presidency*. New York: Oxford University Press, 2009.

Edwards, India. "Oral History Interview with India Edwards." Interview by Jerry N. Hess, Harry S. Truman Library, January 16, 1969.

———. "Oral History Interview with India Edwards." Interview by Patricia Zellman, Harry S. Truman Library, November 10, 1975.

Ehrlichman, John. *Witness to Power: The Nixon Years*. New York: Simon & Schuster, 1982.

Eisgruber, Christopher L. *The Next Justice: Repairing the Supreme Court Appointments Process.* Princeton, NJ: Princeton University Press, 2007.

Epstein, Cynthia Fuchs. *Women in Law.* New Orleans: Quid Pro Quo Books, 2012.

Epstein, Lee. "Beverly Blair Cook." In *Women in Law: A Bio-Bibliographic Sourcebook,* edited by Rebecca Mae Salokar and Mary L. Volcansek. Westport, CT: Greenwood Press, 1996.

Epstein, Lee, and Jeffrey Segal. *Advice and Consent: The Politics of Judicial Appointments.* New York: Oxford University Press, 2005.

———. *Nominating Federal Judges and Justices.* New York: Oxford University Press, 2005.

Faderman, Lillian. *To Believe in Women: What Lesbians Have Done for America—A History.* Boston: Houghton Mifflin Company, 1999.

Farhand, Sean, and Gregory Wawro. "Institutional Dynamics on the U.S. Court of Appeals: Minority Representation under Panel Decision Making." *Journal of Law, Economics, and Organization* 20, no. 2 (2004).

Fink, Jessica. "Gender Sidelining and the Problem of Unactionable Discrimination." *Stanford Law and Policy Review* 29, no. 1 (2018).

Ford, Gerald R. *A Time to Heal: The Autobiography of Gerald R. Ford.* New York: Harper & Row, 1979.

Friedan, Betty. *The Feminine Mystique.* New York: Norton, 1963.

Frye, Marilyn. *The Politics of Reality: Essays in Feminist Theory.* Berkeley: Crossing Press, 1983.

Gilligan, Carol. *In a Different Voice: Psychological Theory and Women's Development.* Cambridge, MA: Harvard University Press, 1982.

Ginsburg, Ruth Bader. "The Supreme Court: A Place for Women." *Southwestern University Law Review* 32, no. 2 (2003).

Ginsburg, Ruth Bader, Mary Hartnett, and Wendy W. Williams. *My Own Words.* New York: Simon & Schuster, 2016.

Glynn, Adam M. and Maya Sen, "Identifying Judicial Empathy: Does Having Daughters Cause Judges to Rule for Women's Issues?" *American Journal of Political Science* 59, no. 1 (2014).

Goldman, Sheldon. *Picking Federal Judges: Lower Court Selection From Roosevelt through Reagan.* New Haven, CT: Yale University Press, 1997.

Goldman, Sheldon, et al. "Picking Judges in a Time of Turmoil: George W. Bush's Judiciary During the 109th Congress." *Judicature* 90, no. 6 (2007).

Gonzalez, Carmen G. "Women of Color in Legal Education: Challenging the Presumption of Incompetence." *The Federal Lawyer* 61 (July 2014).

Gonzalez, Carmen G., and Angela P. Harris. "Presumed Incompetent: Continuing the Conversation." *Berkeley Journal of Gender, Race, and Justice* 29, no. 2 (2014).

Greenburg, Jan Crawford. *Supreme Conflict: The Inside Story of the Struggle for Control of the United States Supreme Court.* New York: Penguin, 2007.

Greenhouse, Linda. *The U.S. Supreme Court: A Very Short Introduction.* New York: Oxford University Press, 2012.

Haire, Susan B., and Laura P. Moyer. *Diversity Matters: Judicial Policy Making in the U.S. Courts of Appeals*. Charlottesville: University of Virginia Press, 2015.

Hall, Cynthia Holcomb. "Diversifying the Judiciary: Interview with Cynthia H. Hall." Interview by Sarah Wilson, Federal Judicial History Office, Federal Judicial Center, March 10, 1995.

Hall, Joan M. "The Role of the ABA Standing Committee on the Federal Judiciary." *Northwestern University Law Review* 84, no. 3 & 4 (1990).

Hall, Kermit L. *The Supreme Court in American Society: The Path To and From the Supreme Court*. New York: Routledge, 2017.

Hayes, Anna R. *Without Precedent: The Life of Susie Marshall Sharp*. Chapel Hill, NC: UNC Press, 2008.

Hill, Anita F. "What Difference Will Women Judges Make? Looking Once More at the 'Woman Question.'" In *Women and Leadership: The State of Play and Strategies for Change*, edited by Barbara Kellerman and Deborah Rhode. San Francisco: Jossey-Bass, 2007.

Hills, Carla A. "Oral History of Carla A. Hills." Interview by Janet McDavid, ABA Senior Lawyers Division, Women Trailblazers in the Law, March 1, 2007.

———. "Oral History of Carla A. Hills." Interview by Richard Norton Smith, Gerald R. Ford Oral History Project, March 18, 2009.

Hirshman, Linda. *Sisters in Law: How Sandra Day O'Connor and Ruth Bader Ginsburg Went to the Supreme Court and Changed the World*. New York: HarperCollins, 2015.

Hochschild, Arlie, and Anne Machung. *The Second Shift: Working Families and the Revolution at Home*. New York: Penguin, 1989.

Hoff, Joan. *Law, Gender and Injustice: A Legal History of U.S. Women*. New York: NYU Press, 1991.

Horne, Jennifer. *Capitol Research: Women in State Government*. Council of State Governments, August 2015.

Hufstedler, Shirley. "Oral History of Shirley M. Hufstedler." Interview by Lee Edmon, ABA Senior Lawyers Division Women Trailblazers in the Law, November 22, 2005; April 15, 2006; January 13, 2007; February 3, 2007; May 28, 2007; October 13, 2007; September 13, 2008.

———. *Women and the Law*. Washington, D.C.: Aspen Institute for Humanistic Studies, 1977.

Jacobi, Tonja, and Dylan Schweers. "Justice, Interrupted: The Effect of Gender, Ideology, and Seniority at Supreme Court Oral Arguments." *Virginia Law Review* 103, no. 7 (2017).

Jamieson, Kathleen Hall. *Beyond the Double Bind: Women and Leadership*. New York: Oxford University Press, 1995.

Kalman, Laura. *The Long Reach of the Sixties: LBJ, Nixon, and the Making of the Contemporary Supreme Court*. New York: Oxford University Press, 2016.

Kamau, Winifred. "Women Judges and Magistrates in Kenya: Challenges, Opportunies, and Contributions." In *Gender and Judging*, edited by Ulrike Schultz and Gisela Shaw. Oxford: Hart Publishihg, 2013.

Kanter, Rosabeth Moss. *Men and Women of the Corporation*. New York: Basic Books, 1977.

Katzenbach, Nicholas. *Some of It was Fun: Working with RFK and LBJ*. New York: W.W. Norton & Co., 2008.

Kay, Herma Hill. "Herma Hill Kay: Professor, 1960–present, and Dean, 1992–2000, Boalt Hall School of Law, University of California, Berkeley." Interview by Germaine LaBerge, Regional Oral History Office, The Bancroft Library, University of California, Berkeley, 2005.

Kennedy, Cornelia Groefsema. "Oral History of Cornelia Groefsema Kennedy." Interview by Allyson A. Miller, ABA Senior Lawyers Division, Women Trailblazers in the Law, January 5, 2012; January 12, 2012; May 10, 2012; June 8, 2012; June 14, 2012; June 15, 2012; October 19, 2012.

Kenney, Sally J. "Choosing Judges: A Bumpy Road to Women's Equality and a Long Way to Go." *Michigan State Law Review* 2012, no. 5 (2012).

———. "Critical Perspectives on Gender and Judging." *Politics and Gender* 6, no. 3 (September 1, 2010).

———. *Gender and Justice: Why Women in the Judiciary Really Matter*. New York: Routledge, 2013.

———. "It Would Be Stupendous for Us Girls: Campaigning for Women Judges Without Waving." In *Breaking the Wave: Women, Their Organizations and Feminism, 1945–1985*, edited by Kathleen A. Laughlin and Jacqueline L. Castledine. New York: Routledge, 2011.

———. "Which Judicial Selection Systems Generate the Most Women Judges? Lessons from the United States." In *Gender and Judging*, edited by Ulrike Schultz and Gisela Shaw. Oxford: Hart Publishing, 2013.

Klein, Joan Dempsey. "Oral History of Joan Dempsey Klein." Interview by Andrea Sheridan Ordin, ABA Senior Lawyers Division, Women Trailblazers in the Law, November 20, 2006; February 7, 2007; November 6, 2007; March 3, 2011.

Klenke, Karen. *Women and Leadership: A Contextual Perspective*. New York: Springer, 1996.

Lillie, Mildred L. "Justice Mildred L. Lillie." Interview by Mary Louise Blackstone, Committee on the History of the California State Bar, November 20, 1989; July 26, 1990.

Lopez, Maria P., and Kevin R. Johnson. "Presumed Incompetent: Important Lessons for University Leaders on the Professional Lives of Women Faculty of Color." *Berkeley Journal of Gender, Law & Justice* 29, no. 2 (2014).

MacKinnon, Catharine. *Sexual Harassment of Working Women: A Case of Sex Discrimination*. New Haven, CT: Yale University Press, 1979.

Manne, Kate. *Down Girl: The Logic of Misogyny*. New York: Oxford University Press, 2018.

Marshall, Constance. "Judge Allen: Pioneer." *Woman Citizen*, June 1926.

Martin, Elaine, and Barry Pyle. "State High Courts and Divorce: The Impact of Judicial Gender." *University Toledo Law Review* 36, no. 4 (2004).

Martin, Janet M. *The Presidency and Women: Promise, Performance, and Illusion.* College Station: Texas A&M University Press, 2003.

Martin, Susan Ehrlich, and Nancy C. Jurik. *Doing Justice, Doing Gender.* Thousand Oaks, CA: Sage, 2006.

McCall, Madhavi, and Michael A. McCall. "How Far Does the Gender Gap Extend? Decision Making on State Supreme Courts in Fourth Amendment Cases, 1980–2000." *Social Science Journal* 44, no. 1 (2007).

Monopoli, Paula. "Gender Parity and the United States Supreme Court." *Georgetown Journal of Gender and the Law* VIII (2007).

Moraski, J., and Charles R. Shipan. "The Politics of Supreme Court Nominations: A Theory of Institutional Constraints and Choices." *American Journal of Political Science* 43, no. 4 (1999).

Nemacheck, Christine L. *Strategic Selection: Presidential Nomination of Supreme Court Justices from Herbert Hoover through George W. Bush.* Charlottesville: University of Virginia, 2007.

Norgren, Jill. *Stories From Trailblazing Women Lawyers: Lives in the Law.* New York: NYU Press, 2018.

O'Brien, David M. *Storm Center: The Supreme Court in American Politics.* New York: W.W. Norton & Co., 1986.

O'Connor, Sandra Day. "Madison Lecture: Portia's Progress." *New York University Law Review* 66, no. 6 (1991).

———. *The Majesty of the Law: Reflections of a Supreme Court Justice.* New York: Random House, 2003.

———. *Out of Order: Stories from the History of the Supreme Court.* New York: Random House Publishing, 2013.

O'Connor, Sandra Day, and Kim K. Azzarelli. "Sustainable Development, Rule of Law and the Impact of Women Judges." *Cornell International Law Journal* 44, no. 1 (2011).

Organ, Joan Ellen. "Sexuality as a Category of Historical Analysis: A Study of Judge Florence E. Allen, 1884–1966." PhD dissertation, Case Western Reserve University, 1998.

Padilla, Laura M. "A Gendered Update on Women Law Deans: Who, Where, Why, and Why Not?" *American University Journal of Gender, Society, Policy, and Law* 15, no. 3 (2007).

———. "Women Law Deans, Gender Sidelining and Presumptions of Incompetence." *Berkeley Journal of Gender, Law & Justice* 34 (forthcoming, 2020).

Perdue, Abigail. "Man Up or Go Home: Exploring Perceptions of Women in Leadership." *Marquette Law Review* 100, no. 4 (2017).

Perry, Barbara A. *A "Representative" Supreme Court? The Impact of Race, Religion, and Gender on Appointments.* Santa Barbara, CA: ABC-CLIO, 1991.

Quinn, Susan. *Eleanor and Hick: The Love Affair That Shaped a First Lady.* New York: Penguin, 2017.

Rhode, Deborah. *The Beauty Bias: The Injustice of Appearance in Life and Law*. New York: Oxford University Press, 2010.

———. "The Difference 'Difference' Makes." In *The Difference "Difference" Makes: Women and Leadership*, edited by Deborah L. Rhode. Stanford, CA: Stanford University Press, 2003.

Rhode, Deborah, and Barbara Kellerman, eds. *Women and Leadership: The State of Play and Strategies for Change*. San Francisco: Jossey-Bass, 2007.

Root, Veronica. "Combating Silence in the Profession." *Virginia Law Review* 105, no. 4 (2019).

Rove, Karl. *Courage and Consequence: My Life as a Conservative in the Fight*. New York: Threshold Editions, 2010.

Sandberg, Sheryl. *Lean In: Women, Work and the Will to Lead*. New York: Knopf, 2013.

Scherer, Nancy. *Scoring Points: Politicians, Activists, and the Lower Federal Court Appointment Process*. Stanford, CA: Stanford University Press, 2005.

Schultz, Ulrike, and Gisela Shaw, eds. *Gender and Judging*. Oxford: Hart Publishing, 2013.

Sherry, Susanna. "Civic Virtue and the Feminine Voice in Constitutional Adjudication." *Virginia Law Review* 72, no. 3 (1986).

Smith, Jr., Fred O. "Gendered Justice: Do Male and Female Judges Rule Differently on Questions of Gay Rights?" *Stanford Law Review* 57, no. 6 (2004).

Solberg, Rorie Spill. "Court Size and Diversity on the Bench: The Ninth Circuit and Its Sisters." *Arizona Law Review* 48, no. 2 (2006).

Songer, Donald R., and Kelley A. Crews-Meyer. "Does Judge Gender Matter? Decision Making in State Supreme Courts." *Social Science Quarterly* 81, no. 3 (September 2000).

Sotomayor, Sonia. *My Beloved World*. New York: Vintage Books, 2013.

Steffensmeier, Darrell, and Chris Hebert. "Women and Men Policymakers: Does the Judge's Gender Affect the Sentencing of Criminal Defendants?" *Social Forces* 77, no. 3 (1999).

Stephanopoulos, George. *All Too Human: A Political Education*. New York: Little, Brown, 2008.

Stevens, John Paul. "Fond Memory." *Ohio State Law Journal* 75, no. 5 (2014).

Stout, Lee. *A Matter of Simple Justice: The Untold Story of Barbara Hackman Franklin and a Few Good Women*. University Park: The Pennsylvania State University Libraries, 2013.

Stras, David R., and Ryan W. Scott. "Navigating the New Politics of Judicial Appointments." *Northwestern University Law Review* 102, no. 4 (2008).

Strebeigh, Fred. *Equal: Women Reshape American Law*. New York: W.W. Norton & Co., 2009.

Suk, Julie C. "Gender Quotas After the End of Men." *Boston University Law Review* 93, no. 3 (2013).

Tartt, Blake. "The Participation of the Organized Bar in Judicial Selection: What is Proper, and What is Improper." *South Texas Law Review* 43 (2001).

Thornton, Margaret. "'Otherness' on the Bench: How Merit is Gendered." *Sydney Law Review* 29, no. 3 (2007).

Totenberg, Nina. "Will Judges be Chosen Rationally?" *Judicature* 60 (1976).

Tuve, Jeannette E. *First Lady of the Law: Florence Ellinwood Allen.* Lanham, MD: University Press of America, 1984.

———. "Florence Allen, First Woman State Supreme Court Judge." *Gamut* 11 (Winter 1984).

Twining, William. "'Looking Back Will Still Keep Us Looking Forward': A Letter from Arthur Corbin to Soia Mentschikoff Upon the Death of Karl Llewellyn." *Yale Journal of Law & Humanities* 27, no. 1 (2015).

"2012–2013 Law Review Diversity Report." *New York Law School Law Review* and Ms. JD. 2013.

Verveer, Melanie, and Kim K. Azzarelli. *Fast Forward: How Women Can Achieve Power and Purpose.* New York: Houghton Mifflin Harcourt, 2016.

Wade, Christine L. "Burnita Shelton Matthews: The Biography of a Pioneering Woman, Lawyer and Feminist." Women's Legal History, Stanford Law, Course No. 579 (Spring 1996). http://whl-static.law.stanford.edu.

Walker, Samuel. *Presidents and Civil Liberties from Wilson to Obama: A Story of Poor Custodians.* New York: Cambridge University Press, 2012.

Whitman, Robert. "Soia Mentschikoff and Karl Llewellyn: Moving Together to the University of Chicago Law School." *Connecticut Law Review* 24 (1992).

Wilkins, David B., and G. Mitu Gulati. "Why Are There So Few Black Lawyers in Corporate Law Firms? An Institutional Analysis." *California Law Review* 84, no. 3 (1996).

Williams, Joan C. "Litigating the Glass Ceiling and the Maternal Wall: Using Stereotyping and Cognitive Bias Evidence to Prove Gender Discrimination." *Employee Rights and Employment Policy Journal* 7, no. 2 (2003).

———. *What Works for Women at Work: Four Patterns Working Women Need to Know.* New York: NYU Press, 2014.

Yalof, David Alistair. *Pursuit of Justices: Presidential Politics and the Selection of Supreme Court Nominees.* Chicago: University of Chicago Press, 1999.

Yelnosky, Michael. "Who Rates Prospective Federal Judges for the American Bar Association?" *Roger Williams University Law Review* 19, no. 1 (2014).

BOOKS ON FEMALE TRANSFORMATIVE LEADERS

This list of biographies and autobiographies represents but a fraction of the stories about transformative female leaders, but we hope it will serve as a starting place for inspiration.

Allred, Gloria, et al. *Fight Back and Win: My Thirty-Year Fight Against Injustice—and How You Can Win Your Own Battles.* New York: HarperCollins, 2006.

Anderson, Paul. *Janet Reno: Doing the Right Thing.* Hoboken, NJ: Wiley, 1994.

Babcock, Barbara. *Woman Lawyer: The Trials of Clara Foltz.* Stanford, CA: Stanford University Press, 2011.

Biskupic, Joan. *Sandra Day O'Connor: How the First Woman on the Supreme Court Became Its Most Influential Justice.* New York: HarperCollins, 2009.

Campbell, John. *The Iron Lady: Margaret Thatcher, From Grocer's Daughter to Prime Minister.* New York: Penguin, 2011.

Carmon, Irin, and Shana Knizhnik. *Notorious RBG: The Life and Times of Ruth Bader Ginsburg.* New York: HarperCollins, 2015.

Clark, Marcia. *Without a Doubt.* New York: West 26th Street Press, 2016.

Clinton, Hillary. *Hard Choices.* New York: Simon & Schuster, 2014.

———. *What Happened.* New York: Simon & Schuster, 2017.

Davis, Angela. *Angela Davis: An Autobiography.* New York: International Publishers, 1974.

Davis, Wendy. *Forgetting to be Afraid: A Memoir.* New York: Penguin, 2015.

Dehart, Jane Sherron. *Ruth Bader Ginsburg: A Life.* New York: Alfred A. Knopf, 2018.

Ebadi, Shirin. *Until We Are Free: My Fight for Human Rights in Iran.* New York: Penguin Random House, 2016.

Eyle, Claudia Pond, and Dan Salmon. *Helen Clark: Inside Stories.* New Zealand: Auckland University Press, 2015.

Friedan, Betty. *Life So Far.* New York: Simon & Schuster, 2001.

Fujino, Diane Carol. *Heartbeat of Struggle: The Revolutionary Life of Yuri Kochiyama.* Minneapolis: University of Minnesota Press, 2005.

Gabriel, Mary. *Notorious Victoria: The Uncensored Life of Victoria Woodhull, Visionary, Suffragist, and First Woman to Run for President.* Chapel Hill: Algonquin Books, 1998.

Ginsburg, Ruth Bader, and Mary Hartnett. *My Own Words.* New York: Simon & Schuster, 2016.

Harrington, Chief Penny. *Triumph of Spirit: An Autobiography.* Chicago: Brittany Publications, 1999.

Hayes, Anna. *Without Precedent: The Life of Susie Marshall Sharp.* Chapel Hill: North Carolina Press, 2008.

Hill, Anita. *Speaking Truth to Power.* New York: Anchor Books, 1997.

Hirshman, Linda. *Sisters in Law: How Sandra Day O' Connor and Ruth Bader Ginsburg Went to the Supreme Court and Changed the World.* New York: HarperCollins, 2016.

King, Coretta Scott. *My Life, My Love, My Legacy.* New York: Henry Holt and Company, 2017.

King, Gilbert. *Devil in the Grove: Thurgood Marshall, the Groveland Boys and the Dawn of a New America.* New York: HarperCollins, 2017.

Knapp, Sally. *Eleanor Roosevelt: A Biography.* Whitefish, MT: Kessinger Publishing, 2010.

Liliuokalani, Queen, and David Forbes. *Hawaii's Story.* Honolulu: University of Hawai'i Press, 2013.

Lloyd, Rachel. *Girls Like Us: Fighting for a World Where Girls Are Not for Sale, an Activist Finds Her Calling and Heals Herself.* New York: HarperCollins, 2011.

McKissack, Pat, and Frederick McKissack. *Sojourner Truth: Ain't I a Woman?* New York: Scholastic, 1994.

Mossman, Mary J. *The First Women Lawyers: A Comparative Study of Gender, Law, and the Legal Professions.* Oxford: Hart Publishing, 2006.

Nicks, Denver. *Private: Bradley Manning, Wikileaks, and the Biggest Exposure of Official Secrets in American History.* Chicago: Chicago Review Press, 2012.

Norgren, Jill. *Belva Lockwood: The Woman Who Would Be President.* New York: NYU Press, 2007.

Obama, Michelle. *Becoming.* New York: Penguin Random House, 2018.

Petersen, Ann H. *Too Fat, Too Slutty, Too Loud: The Rise and Reign of the Unruly Woman.* New York: Plume, 2017.

Rice, Connie. *Power Concedes Nothing: One Woman's Quest for Social Justice in America.* New York: Scribner, 2012.

Roberts, Betty. *With Grit and By Grace: Breaking Trails in Politics and Law, A Memoir.* Corvallis: Oregon State University Press, 2008.

Roberts, Liz. *First Lady: From Boyhood to Womanhood: The Incredible Story of New Zealand's Sex-Change Pioneer Liz Roberts.* Auckland, New Zealand: Upstart Press, 2015.

Rogers, Mary B. *Barbara Jordan, American Hero.* New York: Bantam Books, 1998.

Sheindlin, Judy. *Don't Pee on My Leg and Tell Me It's Raining: America's Toughest Family Court Judge Speaks Out.* New York: Harper Perennial, 1997.

Slevin, Peter. *Michelle Obama: A Life.* New York: Vintage Print, 2015.

Sotomayor, Sonia. *My Beloved World.* New York: Vintage Books, 2013.

Thomas, Evan. *First: Sandra Day O'Connor.* New York: Penguin Random House, 2019.

Toller, Lynn. *My Mother's Rules: A Practical Guide to Becoming an Emotional Genius.* Chicago: Agate, 2007.

Walton, Mary. *A Woman's Crusade: Alice Paul and the Battle for the Ballot.* New York: Palgrave Macmillan, 2010.

Williams, Evelyn. *Inadmissible Evidence: The Story of the African American Trial Lawyer Who Defended the Black Liberation Army.* New York: Universe, 2000.

Yousafzai, Malala. *I am Malala: How One Girl Stood Up for Education and Changed the World.* London: Weidenfeld & Nicolson, 2015.

INDEX

References to figures and tables are denoted by italics.

diversity, 178, 183; in shortlisting, 184–85;
United States Circuit Judge Nominating Commission on, 200–201
Diversity Lab, 5
Dixon, Rosalind, 255n23
Dole, Elizabeth, 99, 132
Dole, Robert, 63
domestic capabilities, of women nominated for Supreme Court, 116–17
double binds, 142–43; appearance/femi-
ninity/respectability, 150–52; feminin-
ity/competency, 143; feminism/racism,
144–50; motherhood/competing
careers, 158–64
Douglas, William O., 29, 47–48, 64, 67
Doyle, Sady, 164

early child care, as public good, 204–5
Edwards, India, 31–33
EEOC. *See* Equal Employment Opportu-
nity Commission
Ehrlichman, John, 58
Eisenhower, Dwight D., 17, 34–36, 43
Eisenhower, Julie Nixon, 195–96
England, 181
Equal Employment Opportunity Com-
mission (EEOC), 11–12, 203
equality, 131–32, 182, 199–203
Equal Protection Clause, of Fourteenth
Amendment, 50
Equal Rights Amendment (ERA), 9–11,
49–50, 86, 169; Allen against, 145; pro-
gressives opposing, 250n10; women
shortlisted for Supreme Court on,
145–46
Ethiopia, 182

FDR. *See* Roosevelt, Franklin Delano
Federalist Society, 187
female chief justices: or presidents, of
international high courts, 176, *177*,
178; of state Supreme Courts, 178,
178–80

femininity: Allen on, 142, 152; appearance,
respectability and, 150–52
femininity/competency double bind, 143
feminism, 9, 209; fourth-wave, 189–90;
gender and, 171; minority women and,
14; second-wave, 7–8, 11–12; third-wave,
12; white supremacy and, 231n31; women
shortlisted for Supreme Court and, 7–8,
144, 146; women's rights and, 185, 189–90
feminism/racism double bind, 144–50
feminists, 94, 255n23
Flowers, Mary E., 10
Ford, Betty, 51, 67
Ford, Christine Blasey, 11, 188
Ford, Gerald, 70, 169, 261n2; Hills, C.,
and, 64, 66, 205; on Kennedy, C., 92;
Supreme Court nominees of, 47–51;
women shortlisted for Supreme Court
by, 38, 47–51, 223
Fortas, Abe, 40–42
Fourteenth Amendment, 50
fourth-wave feminism, 189–90
France, 181
Frankfurter, Felix, 28–29, 39, 85
Franklin, Barbara Hackman, 46, 107, 164,
195, 223–24
Friday, Herschel, 43–44

Garland, Merrick, 124, 175, 187
gay rights, 171
*Gebser v. Lago Vista Independent School
District* (1998), 172–73
gender, 36, 253n7; in case outcomes,
169–70; disparity, in U.S., 182–83;
feminism and, 171; Ginsburg, R. B.,
and, 116–17; hiring and, statistics
on, 203; imbalance, tokenism and,
136–37; intersectionality and, 174; in
judicial performance, 170–71; Obama
nominees and, 122–23; O'Connor and,
97–98; parity, 181–82; quotas, 181–83;
segregation, 15; Supreme Court and, 4;
violence and, 136; voice and, 144–45

international high courts, female chief
justice or presidents of, 176, *177*, 178
intersectionality, 14, 76, 79, 174, 190
intimate relationships, 153–57, 193–95

Jackson, Kentanji Brown, 79
Jackson, Robert H., 29, 32, 34
Javits, Jacob, 77
"Jewish seat," 40
Johnson, Lady Bird, 40–41
Johnson, Lyndon B., 38, 40–41, 220, 223
Jones, Edith: Bush, G. H. W., on, 111–12;
on ERA, 146; maternity leave, 204;
Reagan and, 111; shortlisted for Su-
preme Court, 102, 104, 110–13, *111*
Joslin, Ted, 16
Judd, Ashley, 13
judges, minority, 102–3, 113, 174–75, 190
judges, women. *See* women judges
judicial performance, gender in, 170–71
Judicial Procedures Reform Bill of 1937,
26
justice, women in administration of, 176,
177, 178, *179–80*, 180–83

Kagan, Elena, 4, 39; *New York Times*
on, 123–24; nomination for Supreme
Court, 121–24; Obama and, 121–22,
211; outfit of, 227n3 (preface); Sotomayor and, *115*, 121–24
Kanter, Rosabeth Moss, 129–30
Katsav, Moshe, 257n9
Katzenbach, Nicholas, 39–40, 261n1
Kavanaugh, Brett, 187–89
Kay, Herma Hill, 181, 197
Kearse, Amalya Lyle, 90, 112, 130, 150;
as black woman, 133; discrimination
against, 137; Leahy and, 201; Reagan
and, 78; shortlisted for Supreme
Court, 75–80, *76*, 104, 117, 196;
before Supreme Court, 77; tokenism
and, 133; on United States Circuit

Judge Nominating Commission,
200
Kelly, Mary, 45–46
Kennard, Joyce Luther, 174
Kennedy, Anthony, 124–25, 172, 187
Kennedy, Cornelia, 38, 49, 196; ABA on,
71; age of, 165–66; on children and
marriage, 160; discrimination against,
137–38; Ford, G., on, 92; on honorifics,
199; in NCFTJ, 197; O'Connor and, 91–
99; racist views of, 148; Reagan and,
93, 165–66; shortlisted for Supreme
Court, 68–72, *69*, 74; on tokenism, 129;
on women judges, 130–31; on women
on Supreme Court, 71; women's rights
and, 147
Kennedy, John F., 38–40, 85
Kennedy, Ted, 102–3
Kenya, 182
Kenyon, E. L., 17–19
Kesler, John, 86, 156
Kidd, Alexander, 56
Klein, Joan Dempsey, 98, 135; on appearance, 151–52; children and marriage,
158–59, 193–94; on disclosure of hiring
statistics, 203; on discrimination,
138–40, 199–200; Coffman and, 153; in
law school, 198–99; mentorship and
support for women lawyers, 196–97;
on O'Connor nomination, 90–91, 135;
shortlisted for Supreme Court, *87*,
87–91; on women on Supreme Court,
91, 135
Klenke, Karin, 248n8
Klobuchar, Amy, 188–89
Korematsu v. United States (1944), 27
Kottinger, John W., 87
Kozinski, Alex, 139

Lafontant, Jewel, 41
Lat, David, 227n3 (Preface)
Latina, 134, 175–76

minority women, 76, 174–75; feminism and, 14; judges, 190
Minton, Sherman, 33–34
misogyny, 12–13, 209
Mitchell, John, 42–43, 58, 63–64
Mitchell, William, 16–17
motherhood, 122, 124, 160, 162
motherhood/competing careers double bind, 158–64
Motley, Constance Baker, 41, 174
Murphy, Frank, 28–29, 33
Mussey, Ellen Spencer, 18
My Day column, by Roosevelt, E., 29–30

NAACP. *See* National Association for the Advancement of Colored People
Nassar, Larry, 192
National Association for the Advancement of Colored People (NAACP), 148
National Association of Women Judges (NAWJ), 90–91, 138, 140, 197, 201, 223
National Association of Women Lawyers, 4, 32, 60–61
National Conference of Federal Trial Judges (NCFTJ), 197
National Law Journal, 202
National Women's Conference of 1977, 11
National Women's Political Caucus, 45, 50, 260n7
NAWJ. *See* National Association of Women Judges
NCFTJ. *See* National Conference of Federal Trial Judges
Nemacheck, Christine, 219–20
Neunenfelt, Lila, 68
New Deal, 26–27
Newman, Jon O., 78, 80
New York Post, 54, 135–36, 150
New York Times, 13–14, 36, 44, 58, 82, 117; on Ginsburg, R. B., 116; on Kagan, 123–24; on Lillie, 1–2, 135; on Miers,

120; O'Connor and, 101, 160, 223; on Sotomayor, 123; on suffrage movement and white supremacy, 144; on women in talent pool, 140–41
New York University (NYU) Law School, 20
Nineteenth Amendment, 10, 21
Nixon, Pat, 195–96
Nixon, Richard, 47–48; Bacon and, 59–63, 165, 220; Hall, C. H., and, 106, 194–95; Kennedy, C., and, 70; Lillie and, 1, 3, 58–59, 93, 132, 146, 224; National Women's Political Caucus to, 260n7; Nixon, P., and, 195–96; O'Connor to, 95; on Powell, 120; Supreme Court nominees of, 1, 3, 41–46; against women on Supreme Court, 42, 44–45, 195–96; women shortlisted for Supreme Court by, 38, 41–46, 58–63, 102
non-mothers, 162
Norma Rae (1979), 259n4 (Conclusion)
North Carolina, 81–86
NYU. *See* New York University Law School

Obama, Barack, 39, 79, 247n60; Garland nomination by, 124, 175, 187; Ginsburg, R. B., and, 211; Kagan and, 121–22, 211; Lilly Ledbetter Fair Pay Act signed by, 174; Sotomayor and, 121–22, 176; women as Supreme Court nominees of, 121–23; women shortlisted and selected by, 121–22
O'Connor, Sandra Day, 3–4, 6–7, 26, 28, 38, 115, 167–68; age of, 166; on *Bush v. Gore*, 98–99; career before Supreme Court, 96–97; "different voice" theory and, 170; gendered critiques of, 97–98; Hall, C. H., and, 106–7; on honorifics, 223; Kennedy, C., and, 91–99; Klein on nomination of, 90–91, 135;

ABOUT THE AUTHORS

Renee Knake Jefferson and Hannah Brenner Johnson have been colleagues and friends for more than a decade. Renee is a Professor of Law and holds the Joanne and Larry Doherty Chair in Legal Ethics at the University of Houston Law Center. She received her JD from the University of Chicago Law School. Hannah is the Vice Dean for Academic and Student Affairs and an Associate Professor of Law at California Western School of Law in San Diego. She received her JD from the University of Iowa College of Law.

Hannah Brenner Johnson and Renee Knake Jefferson